REAL ESTATE LAW REVIEW MANUAL

John Dunn, Attorney
Dunn, Abplanalp & Christensen, P.C.
Vail, Colorado

Karen Dunn, CLAS
Dunn, Abplanalp & Christensen, P.C.
Vail, Colorado

Virginia Koerselman, J.D.
Metropolitan Community College
Omaha, Nebraska

In cooperation with
The National Association of Legal Assistants, Inc.
Tulsa, Oklahoma

West Publishing Company
Minneapolis/St. Paul   New York   Los Angeles   San Francisco

Diagrams in Figures 8–3, 8–4, 8–5, and 8–6 were taken from Krendl, *Colorado Methods of Practice, Revised Third Edition* Volume 2. Copyright 1991 West Publishing Company.

WEST'S COMMITMENT TO THE ENVIRONMENT

In 1906, West Publishing Company began recycling materials left over from the production of books. This began a tradition of efficient and responsible use of resources. Today, 100% of our legal bound volumes are printed on acid-free, recycled paper consisting of 50% new fibers. West recycles nearly 27,700,000 pounds of scrap paper annually—the equivalent of 229,300 trees. Since the 1960s, West has devised ways to capture and recycle waste inks, solvents, oils, and vapors created in the printing process. We also recycle plastics of all kinds, wood, glass, corrugated cardboard, and batteries, and have eliminated the use of polystyrene book packaging. We at West are proud of the longevity and the scope of our commitment to the environment.

West pocket parts and advance sheets are printed on recyclable paper and can be collected and recycled with newspapers. Staples do not have to be removed. Bound volumes can be recycled after removing the cover.

Production, Prepress, Printing and Binding by West Publishing Company.

 TEXT IS PRINTED ON 10% POST CONSUMER RECYCLED PAPER

DEDICATION

To Kay Kasic, who started it all.

CONTENTS

INTRODUCTION   1
 Feudalism   1
 The Court System   3
 Free Tenure   4

Chapter 1 - FREEHOLD ESTATES   5
 The Fee Simple Absolute   6
  Defeasible Fee Simple   6
  Fee Simple Subject to Condition Subsequent   7
  The Fee Tail   8
 The Life Estate   9
  Chapter 1 Quiz   10

Chapter 2 - FUTURE INTERESTS   15
 Types of Future Interests   15
  Vested Remainders   17
  Contingent Remainders   17
  Executory Interests   17
 The Statute of Uses   18
 Restraints on Alienation   21
 Chapter 2 Quiz   25

Chapter 3 - CONCURRENT OWNERSHIP   31
 The Unities of Ownership   31
 Figure 3-1 Unities of Concurrent Ownership   31
  Unity of Time   32
  Unity of Title   32
  Unity of Interest   32
  Unity of Possession   32
 Tenancy in Common   33
  Joint Tenancy   34
  Tenancy by the Entireties   35
 Marital Rights   36
 Chapter 3 Quiz   37

Chapter 4 - COMMON INTEREST OWNERSHIP   41
 Cooperatives   42

Condominiums   42
    Figure 4-1 Condominium Plat   45
    Figure 4-2 Condominium Map   46
Planned Communities   47
    Figure 4-3 Subdivision Map 47
    Figure 4-4 Party Wall Diagram   48
Time Share Estates   49
    Figure 4-5 Condominium Declaration   *50*
    Figure 4-6 Party Wall Agreement   64
Chapter 4 Quiz   67

Chapter 5 - LANDLORD AND TENANT   73
Nonfreehold Estates 73
    Tenancy for Years   73
    Periodic Tenancy   73
    Tenancy at Will   74
    Tenancy at Sufferance   74
    Figure 5-1 Comparison of Leasehold Characteristics   75
Rights, Duties, and Liabilities of the Tenant   75
Rights, Duties, and Liabilities of the Landlord   77
    Uniform Residential Landlord and Tenant Act   81
    Landlord's Remedies   81
    Figure 5-2 Notice to Quit   82
Assignment and Subletting 84
    Figure 5-3 Assignment of Lease   85
    Figure 5-4 Sublease 86
Drafting a Lease   87
    Identity of the Parties   87
    Description of the Premises 87
    Term 87
    Rent 87
    Maintenance of the Premises   87
    Use of the Premises 88
    Alterations and Additions   88
    Insurance   88
    Destruction of the Premises and Eminent Domain 88
    Assignment and Subletting   88
    Sale or Foreclosure 88
    Figure 5-5 Estoppel Certificate   89
    Default   90
    Figure 5-6 Form of Lease   91
Chapter 5 Quiz   95

Chapter 6 - SERVITUDES AND OTHER LAND USE LIMITATIONS 99
    Common Law Profits   99
    Easements   100
        Figure 6-1 Appurtenant Easement   *102*
        Figure 6-2 Easement in Gross   *103*
        Figure 6-3 Light Easement *105*
    Licenses   110
        Figure 6-4   License to Use Real Estate   110
    Drafting Nonpossessory Rights   111
        Grant of Appurtenant Easement   111
        Reservation of Appurtenant Easement   111
        Grant of Easement in Gross 111
        Grant of License   111
        Grant of Profit   112
    Real Covenants   112
        Figure 6-5 Protective Covenants   116
    Nuisance   117
    Lateral and Subjacent Support   118
    Airspace   118
        Figure 6-6 Airspace Easement   120
    Chapter 6 Quiz   121

Chapter 7 - PLANNING AND ZONING 125
    The Master Plan   125
    Euclidean Zoning   126
        Figure 7-1 Selected Zoning Ordinances & Map   *127*
        Figure 7-2 Ordinances for Nonconforming Uses and Variances 134
        Amendment of Zoning Ordinances 136
    Planned Unit or Cluster Zoning   137
    Constitutional Limitations on Zoning   137
    Subdivision Regulation   140
        Figure 7-3 Subdivision Improvements Agreement & Map 141
    Design Review   145
    Building Codes and Boards of Building Appeals   145
    Chapter 7 Quiz   147

Chapter 8 - SOURCES AND CONVEYANCE OF TITLE   151
    Land Patents 151
        Figure 8-1 Tax Deed   152
    Adverse Possession 153
        Figure 8-2 Fence Line   154
    Statute of Frauds   157

Recording Acts   157
        Pure Race Statute   160
        Pure Notice Statute   160
        Race Notice Statute   160
Property Description 161
        Subdivision Maps   161
        United States Government Survey   162
            Figure 8-3 Township Map and Numbering Diagram 163
            Figure 8-4 Section Layout in each Township 164
            Figure 8-5 Description of Parcels within a Section 165
        Metes and Bounds   165
            Figure 8-6 Diagram of Metes-and-Bounds Description 167
The Deed   169
        Covenant of Seisin   173
        Covenant of the Right to Convey   173
        Covenant Against Encumbrances   173
        Covenant of Warranty   173
        Covenant of Quiet Enjoyment   173
        Covenant of Further Assurances   173
        Breach of Covenants 174
            Figure 8-7 General Warranty Deed   177
            Figure 8-8 Special Warranty Deed   178
            Figure 8-9 Quitclaim Deed 179
            Figure 8-10 Sheriff's Deed   180
Chapter 8 Quiz   181

Chapter 9 - SALE AND FINANCING OF REAL ESTATE   187
Contract for Sale of Land   187
        Figure 9-1 Contract for Sale of Residential Real Estate 193
The Title Search   197
        Figure 9-2 Title Insurance Commitment   199
Land Financing   204
        Mortgage   205
            Figure 9-3 Mortgage   206
        Deed of Trust   209
            Figure 9-4 Deed of Trust   210
        Default   214
            Figure 9-5 Promissory Note   217
        RESPA   219
Environmental Issues   219
Delivery of the Deed — The Closing   220
        FIRPTA   225
        Like-Kind Exchange 225

Installment Sale Contract   226
Chapter 9 Quiz   228

Chapter 10 - NATURAL RESOURCES   231
Water Rights 231
Mineral Rights   238
Figure 10-1 Lode Claim Map   238
Chapter 10 Quiz   239

Chapter 11 - REAL ESTATE LITIGATION   245
Jurisdiction   245
In Rem Jurisdiction   245
Service by Publication   246
Quiet Title Suit   247
Figure 11-1 Quiet Title Complaint 250
Eminent Domain   251
Methods of Appraisal   252
Partition   254
Figure 11-2 Complaint in Partition 256
Judicial Foreclosure 257
Figure 11-3 Mortgage Foreclosure Complaint 259
Notice of Lis Pendens   261
Figure 11-4 Notice of Lis Pendens 262
Chapter 11 Quiz   263

Answers to Chapter Quizzes   267

Bibliography 273

Index 275

PREFACE

What in the world did William the Conqueror and Henry VIII have to do with real estate law? When were wills invented and what did people do before they were? What are springing and shifting uses. The answers to those questions are in this book along with more practical guides to understanding and preparing leases, deed, closing documents, and a vast array of other real estate documents. The reader will cover such diverse subjects as how to prepare a chain of title and what to know about real estate litigation. S/he even will gain an understanding of mining and water law.

We believe this book will provide legal assistants with all they need to know to be knowledgeable and to work in a real estate environment. Although it is intended to be a study source for the NALA real estate specialty exam, it is not designed to "teach the test." It is always a good idea for test candidates to consult more than one source.

This book is also suitable for use as a textbook for course study and in the classroom. Self-study quizzes are provided at the end of each chapter. An instructor's manual will be available. The instructor's manual includes a test bank of true-false, multiple choice, and essay questions for each chapter. In addition, it suggests practical projects to be used for individual assignments or group study and suggests discussion questions.

We do offer one disclaimer. The forms included in this book never should be copied for actual use. They are intended as examples only.

ACKNOWLEDGMENTS

Writing a book and having it scrutinized by reviewers is, shall we say, a learning experience. In fact, the people who reviewed the book provided direction and help which was invaluable. I am indebted to them, as I am indebted to our editor, Virginia Koerselman. But I am most indebted to my co-author, Karen, who read and commented on my part of the book. Truth be told, Karen knows more law than many lawyers. She also has an ability which often surpasses my own to explain what she knows. Without her help and encouragement, this book could not have been written.

John Dunn
Vail, Colorado   May 25, 1995

I gratefully acknowledge the contributions of our editor, Virginia Koerselman, without whom this book would not have been possible, and the following people who provided support and encouragement:

Pamela J. Bailey, CLAS
Pittsburgh, Pennsylvania

Vicki Kunz, CLAS
Bismarck, North Dakota

Marge Dover, CAE
Tulsa, Oklahoma

Carole D. Olson
El Centro College, Texas

Marie Greninger
Tulsa, Oklahoma

Susan P. Plumlee, CLAS
Walla Walla, Washington

Carol D. Holler, CLAS
Ft. Lauderdale, Florida

Karen Sanders-West, CLAS
Wichita, Kansas

Pamela Hostetter, CLAS
Lancaster, Pennsylvania

Jane Terhune, CLAS
Tulsa, Oklahoma

Karen Judd, CLAS
Champaign, Illinois

Vicki Voisin, CLAS
Charlevoix, Michigan

Kay Kasic, CLA
Napa, California

Pamela Poole Weber
Seminole Community College, Florida

Connie Kretchmer, CLA
Omaha, Nebraska

I would also like to thank Diane L. Herman, Esq. and R. C. Stephenson, Esq. of Vail, Colorado, for their resources and help; the firm of Dunn, Abplanalp & Christensen, P.C.; and the many lawyers, paralegal educators, and legal assistants who supplied insight into the subject matter.

Most of all, I acknowledge my co-author, who did the lion's share of the work, met all his deadlines with time to spare, shared his considerable knowledge, and gave me encouragement and support. Absent his contributions, this book never would have seen the light of day.

Karen Dunn
Vail, Colorado   May 25, 1996

ABOUT THE AUTHORS

John W. Dunn was admitted to the practice of law in Colorado in 1964. Mr. Dunn was born in Peoria, Illinois, and was educated at the University of Edinburgh, Scotland, and Wabash College, where he was elected a member of Phi Beta Kappa. He attended New York University School of Law as a Toot-Tilden Scholar, was editor-in-chief of the Annual Survey of American Law, and thereafter clerked for the United States Court of Appeals for the First Circuit. He served as County Attorney of Lake County, Colorado, from 1971 to 1994 and is a past president of the Colorado Bar Association and of the Continental Divide Bar Association, and he was the 1972 recipient of the Fellow and Trustee of the Colorado Bar Foundation and a Fellow of the American Bar Association. Mr. Dunn is a member of the firm of Dunn, Abplanalp & Christensen, P.C., in Vail, Colorado. His practice emphasizes real estate and land use issues. He is the general editor of <u>Colorado Contract Forms</u> and <u>Colorado Real Estate Forms</u> (Lawyers' Cooperative Publishing Co.).

Karen M. Dunn, CLA Specialist, is a legal assistant with Dunn, Abplanalp & Christensen, P.C., Vail, Colorado. She attended Central Illinois Community College and Millikin University. Karen attained her Certified Legal Assistant designation in 1983, certification as a Civil Litigation Specialist in 1987, and certification as a Real Estate Specialist in 1988. She is an associate member of the American Bar Association and of the Colorado Bar Association. From 1987-1991, Karen was a member of the faculty of Colorado Mountain College, teaching introductory courses for legal assistants. She is a member of NALA's CLA Short Court faculty. Karen has served NALA as a member of the Manual Revision Committee, as Chairman of NALA's Certifying Board, and as NALA's President (1992-94). She now serves as NALA's State Specialty Certification Task Force Chairman.

INTRODUCTION

As every legal scholar knows, any worthwhile review of American real property law should begin with an overview of its history. Many of the terms we use today evolved through the English feudal system, but they originated even earlier. Many of the historical concepts continue as well, although we now identify them by different terms. For example, the concept of the "use" was developed early in the common law as a device to avoid obligations that otherwise were owed to one's lord or to the crown. Similarly, we have developed the trust in modern times as an estate planning device to avoid tax obligations to the government.

Feudalism

The modern law of real property began on the European continent during the Dark Ages. The fall of Rome in the Fifth Century marked the beginning of the Dark Ages, which lasted until around the year 1000. This period was marked by a complete disintegration of society. Each individual had only himself or herself to look to for the essentials of life.

The need for personal security gave rise to the practice of *commendation*, by which one person became the tenant of another person (a lord) through a ceremony of homage. Through *homage*, the tenant and the lord promised mutual duties of support and protection to each other. The tenant sought protection for himself and his property, which consisted almost exclusively of land, while the lord sought the personal services of the tenant, as a knight or otherwise. This arrangement was known as *feudalism*.

1

From its start, the feudalism of the Dark Ages was a system of government as well as a method of property ownership. In fact, the term "fee," as used in "fee simple," (which is how we describe property ownership today) derives from the same root word as the term "feudal." Having conveyed title to his land to the lord, the tenant thereafter held only a right to possess the land as a *tenant in demesne*. The interest that he possessed was his *fief*.

The process known as *subinfeudation* created a chain of ownership descending from overlord to tenant in chief or *tenant in capite* to various mesne lords and then to the tenant in demesne, who actually possessed the land. As organized society returned, the king or queen stood at the top of this chain. Ultimately, in 1066, at the Battle of Hastings, William the Conqueror invaded England and carried this method of ownership with him. By right of conquest, he literally became the owner of England although he initially owned England as a tenant of the King of France. From that date, English lords held their land as tenants of William.

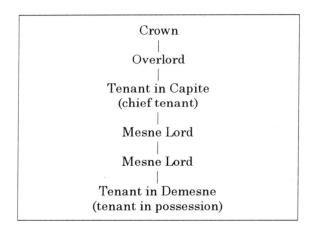

Within a generation, the Anglo-Saxon law of England absorbed the Norman scheme of feudal land ownership. William stood atop the land-owning pyramid, and all of England was "held of him." During William's reign (1066-87), the *Domesday Book*, a complete register of landholders, was compiled for tax purposes. The Book became, in a sense, the first and most extensive abstract of title ever compiled to show land ownership.

Each tenant owed certain obligations to his lord, which were called "incidents of tenure." These incidents fell into two classes. First were *homage, fealty, and aids*, which existed during the lifetime of the parties and involved the personal relationship between the lord and the tenant. Second were *escheat, relief, wardship, and marriage*, which arose upon death of the tenant. Much of English real property law was developed to avoid these obligations in some fashion.

   Homage was the ceremony by which the tenant became the lord's man. The ceremony consisted of the tenant's kneeling before the lord and promising loyalty. *Fealty* was the oath given by the tenant. The lord thereby became the owner of the land, with the tenant retaining the right of possession. *Aids* was a duty of financial support owed on certain occasions, such as ransoming the lord. In exchange for his right of possession, the tenant also owed certain services to the lord, whether as a knight, as a courtier, or by raising crops on the lord's land. As the central government grew, these obligations became primarily financial, similar to modern-day taxes.

   Escheat occurred when the tenant died without an heir or when he was convicted of a felony, causing title to revert to the lord or to the crown. Relief took place when the tenant died, leaving an adult heir. Wills did not exist at early common law, and the land was permitted to pass to the oldest son only upon payment of a sum of money called *relief*. The inheritance and estate taxes of today have some similarity to this practice.

   When the heir was a minor (21 for males and 14 for females) and, therefore, was not legally competent to provide services, the lord was allowed the profitable rights of wardship and marriage. *Wardship* allowed the lord to remain in possession and to retain the profits of the land during the heir's minority. Upon obtaining majority, the heir had an enforceable right to obtain possession but only upon payment of a half year's profits. The *right of marriage* allowed the lord to select the female heir's husband, which he did in exchange for a handsome amount of money.

The Court System

The local courts of the lord handled most of the problems of the manor. However, the king also had a court; and it was to that court which the tenants in chief resorted concerning property disputes. Pleading practice in the king's court permitted a limited number of claims or *writs*. One of the writs was a *praecipe in capite* for the recovery of land. However, it included trial by battle, a custom introduced by William from Normandy. The theory was that God saw to it that the one in the right was victorious. A writ of entry and the action of ejectment ultimately evolved; and by the time of Henry II (1154-89), the *royal courts* had taken over most of the controversies concerning land ownership.

During the same period, the *courts of chancery* developed, in which principles of equity, rather than of law, were applied. The origin of these courts is obscure, although the dichotomy of law and equity is common to all the major legal systems. It seems reasonable to assume that it became the practice of the king to refer petitions for relief to the chancellor of the exchequer, his highest officer. Ultimately, the chancellor instituted his own court, the court of chancery. The foremost creature of equity in the jurisprudence of real property was the *use*, a device designed to avoid the incidents of tenure, among other things.

Free Tenure

By the thirteenth century, feudalistic tenure was firmly rooted, and modern property law began its evolution. In 1290, the Statute of Westminster (18 Edw. I, chap 1), Quia Emptores, abolished subinfeudation (the creation of new manors) and required that future alienation of land be by substitution, i.e., by modern means of transfer. Before Quia Emptores, ownership of the land could not be transferred; either it descended to an heir, or it escheated to the lord. By the Statute, when possession of the land was sold, the new tenant was substituted for the old instead of becoming a subtenant of the old. A fee simple absolute thereby could be conveyed, causing the grantee to become the tenant of the grantor's lord.

The effect of Quia Emptores was to permit the tenant to sell his lands without the consent of his overlord. The new tenant held of the chief lord and not of any mesne lord. The feudal chain was severed, and land thereafter could be conveyed without restraint. However, it was not until 1540 and the Statute of Wills (32 Henry VIII) that land could be devised by will, bringing to an end the rule of escheat in the absence of heirs.

This historical background need not be memorized to take and pass the CLA® real estate specialty examination. However, some of the more tedious aspects of real property may be a bit more interesting and definitely are easier to grasp if this piece of English history is kept in mind.

Chapter 1
FREEHOLD ESTATES

Estates in land are divided into two categories: freehold estates and nonfreehold estates. Freehold estates are those typically thought of as the ownership of land. They can be sold, devised by will, or inherited by heirs. Freehold estates were so called because the owner "held free" of the right of reversion to the king or to a lord. Nonfreehold estates are tenancies, which involve possessory rights only.

Freehold estates sometimes are said to join ownership (*seisin*) and possession. **Seisin** (pronounced "season") described the tenant's possessory rights in the land, as opposed to the ownership of the land, which was vested in the king or in a lord. The person *in seisin* was the person to whom the lord looked for feudal services. It was said that "seisin can never be in abeyance" because if the lord did not know who was *in seisin*, the feudal system could not work. It was only by the formal ceremony of *livery of seisin* that ownership and possession of property were transferred. By that ceremony, the parties went upon the land, and the seller delivered a handful of dirt to the buyer. Today, *seisin* is analogous to ownership; and when we say that "seisin can never be in abeyance," we mean that real property always must be owned by someone.

The freehold estates are the *fee simple absolute*, the *fee tail*, and the *life estate*. The fee tail no longer is used, but its historical impact helps us to understand the fee simple absolute more clearly. The life estate still is used; however, it is often replaced by the trust, which accomplishes much the same purpose, i.e., ownership of the property until death, followed by automatic transfer. The fee simple absolute continues in the modern method of ownership of real property.

The Fee Simple Absolute

The fee simple absolute, sometimes called the fee simple, is full ownership of land. Fee simple ownership descends to heirs. It can be *alienated* (sold or given away), it can be leased, it can be devised by will, or it can pass to one's heirs when no will exists (intestate succession). It contains all the rights that possibly could relate to land. For this reason, real property is sometimes described as a "bundle of sticks," analogizing the collection of sticks in the bundle to the collection of rights involved in the ownership of property. The fee simple absolute is the full bundle.

The Statute <u>Quia Emptores</u> dealt with *emptores* (purchasers) and permitted the free alienation of property. At common law, the fee simple absolute was created by a conveyance phrased "to Alan and his heirs." The words "to Alan" were *words of purchase*. Those words caused the land to be "purchased" by Alan. The words "and his heirs" were *words of limitation*. A conveyance "to Alan" created a life estate only; the conveyance had to be made "to Alan and his heirs" to create a fee simple absolute. In effect, the qualifying words "and his heirs" indicated there was no limitation on the conveyance; it was the intent of the transferor that the interest conveyed be fully inheritable: a fee simple absolute.

There is no requirement for words of limitation when conveying land today. Virtually all land is held in fee simple ownership. Unless an intent appears otherwise in the deed, the law assumes that a fee simple estate is conveyed.

The fee simple estate, however, may be limited in terms of the use to which the real property is or may be put. There are two types of such estates: the *defeasible* or *determinable fee simple* and the *fee simple subject to a condition subsequent*. Either one is a fee simple estate and may be sold, inherited, or devised by will. However, the grant or creation of the estate contains language of limitation that limits continuation of the fee simple estate to a particular use of the property.

<u>Defeasible Fee Simple</u>   A defeasible fee simple, sometimes called a *fee simple determinable*, is one in which ownership automatically terminates if the condition contained in the conveyance is violated.

> Oscar sells Broadway Estates "to Alice and her heirs as long as the premises are not used for the sale of alcoholic beverages and no longer."

The words "and no longer" often are used to emphasize that the estate terminates when the prohibited use occurs but are not necessary to create a defeasible fee.

A few sticks are withheld from the bundle of rights conveyed in the example. As long as Broadway Estates is not used for the sale of alcoholic beverages, Alice is the owner of a fee simple estate. However, if Alice opens a restaurant and bar on the premises, a *defeasance* occurs. That is, Broadway Estates automatically reverts to Oscar or to Oscar's heirs if he has died. The fee simple thereby is given an additional dimension. Alice is seized of a defeasible estate (a fee simple determinable), while Oscar has the *possibility of reverter*. In the event of a defeasance, the sticks come back together; and Oscar is again seized of an unlimited fee simple absolute.

> Example A: Oscar sells Broadway Estates "to Alice and her heirs as long as the premises are not used for the sale of alcoholic beverages and no longer." Alice sells Broadway Estates to Luis, who opens a cocktail lounge.

When Luis opens the cocktail lounge on the premises, ownership automatically reverts to Oscar or his heirs.

Fee Simple Subject to Condition Subsequent A fee simple subject to condition subsequent is similar to a defeasible fee simple, but it does not terminate automatically when the condition is violated.

> Olivia sells Park Estates "to Abe and his heirs; but if the premises shall be used for the sale of alcoholic beverages, then Olivia may enter and repossess the same."

Similar to the defeasible fee simple, Abe is seized of a fee simple estate; but that estate will not terminate automatically if a restaurant and bar are opened on the premises. Rather, Olivia has a right of entry for condition broken or, as it is sometimes known, a power of termination. If Olivia exercises the right of entry or power of termination, she regains the entire bundle of sticks comprising the fee simple estate; and Abe has no interest.

> Example B: Olivia sells Park Estates "to Abe and his heirs; but if the premises shall be used for the sale of alcoholic beverages, then Olivia may enter and repossess the same." Olivia does nothing.
>
> Example C: Olivia sells Park Estates "to Abe and his heirs; but if the premises shall be used for the sale of alcoholic beverages, then Olivia may enter and repossess the same." Olivia exercises her right of entry.

In Example B, Abe retains title to the premises, subject to Olivia's right of entry. In Example C, title reverts to Olivia; and Abe has nothing.

The distinction between conveyance of a fee simple determinable (defeasible fee simple) and conveyance of a fee simple subject to condition subsequent is an important one. Under Example A, when a bar and restaurant are opened for business, a title examiner would express the opinion that title had re-vested in Oscar under the fee simple determinable conveyance. Under Example B, when a bar and restaurant are opened for business, a title examiner would express the opinion that title remains vested in Abe, subject to Olivia's right of entry.

The Fee Tail

The estate in fee tail has fallen into disuse, but it was an important property interest in England, where it was used to preserve the blood line. The word *tail* is derived from the French *tailler,* which means "to carve." That estate was "carved out," for example, by a conveyance by Oliver "to Alexander and the heirs of his body." If Alexander died without *issue* (lineal descendants, such as children, grandchildren, and so on), the fee reverted to Oliver. If Alexander died with issue, the fee descended to the eldest male by *primogeniture* (ancient common law of descent that gave exclusive right of inheritance to the eldest son). The property's descent continued through generations, until some descendant of Alexander died without issue. At that point, the fee reverted to Oliver or, if he was deceased, to Oliver's heirs. The interest of Oliver and his heirs was known as a possibility of reverter.

There were variations on the fee tail general that is described above. For example, a conveyance "to Albert and the heirs of his body and of the body of his wife, Yolanda" created a *fee tail special.* For Albert's issue to inherit, it was necessary that Albert remain married to Yolanda. A conveyance "to Arthur and the male heirs of his body" created a *fee tail male.* If Arthur died without a male heir, a reversion occurred. Finally, a conveyance "to Arthur and the female heirs of his body" created a *fee tail female.*

In order fully to understand the fee tail, it is important to distinguish between issue (lineal descendants) and heirs. For example, one's spouse is an heir but is not an issue (lineal descendant). Only children, grandchildren, and so on down the blood line comprise one's issue. Blood relatives, including one's spouse, comprise one's heirs.

Examples of Issue	Examples of Heirs
Children	Spouse
Grandchildren	Children
Great-grandchildren	Grandchildren
(continue down blood line)	Parents
	Siblings
	Nieces and Nephews

The absence of issue was a common occurrence in the early, plague-ridden days of England. This made the fee tail estate more significant than it typically would be in modern real estate law.

The Life Estate

The life estate remains in use today, although its use is fairly rare. More often, a trust device is used in its place. The following examples include language to create a life estate.

Ophelia conveys Madison Estates "to Abigail for life."

Ophelia conveys Madison Estates "to Abigail for life, remainder to Bob."

Upon the death of Abigail, the life estate terminates. A life estate is a freehold estate and may be sold during Abigail's lifetime, although it is unlikely anyone would want to buy one. It is not an estate of inheritance, because the interest terminates upon the death of the life tenant. In each of the above examples, Abigail is a *life tenant*. In the first example, Ophelia holds a *reversion*. In the second example, Bob holds a *remainder*. Both the remainder and the reversion may be sold, devised by will, or inherited by intestate succession.

A life estate also may be created for the life of another. This is called a *life estate pur autre vie*, which means "for another life."

Oren conveys Riverside Estates "to Agatha for the life of Bridget."

Bridget is the *cestui que vie* or, in English, "the one whose life [is the measure]." Once again, the interest of Agatha is not an estate of inheritance, because it terminates upon the death of Bridget. However, it is a freehold estate and may be sold or devised, subject to the death of Bridget as the measuring life.

A life tenant has the right to use the estate during her life by growing crops, by renting it to another and keeping the rent, or by subjecting it to any other reasonable use. However, the life tenant may not commit *waste* upon the land. In other words, the life tenant may not use the land in such a way as to alter its value unreasonably and permanently. A life tenant cannot reduce the land's value by strip mining it, for example. This is called *voluntary waste* or active waste. Neither can she reduce the land's value by permitting it to fall into disrepair. This is known as *permissive waste* or passive waste. A tenant may commit waste that increases the value of the property, for example, by removing a dilapidated building. This is *ameliorative waste*. If the life tenant commits waste or threatens to commit waste, the holder of the reversion may bring an action for an injunction or for damages.

Today, trusts often are used to accomplish the same result that life estates were used to accomplish in the past. Thus, Thomas may establish or "settle" a trust, to which he conveys certain assets to be held by the trustee, upon the death of Thomas, for the benefit of Wilma for her life. Upon the death of Wilma (or upon the death of Thomas if Wilma predeceases him), the trust property is distributed to the children of Thomas and Wilma. The effect is the same as the life estate, permitting Wilma's use of the asset for her lifetime. The trust device is more often used when there are a variety of assets to be treated together in one document, giving full consideration to tax planning.

Chapter 1 Quiz

Fill in each blank with the most correct word or phrase.

1. That seisin never can be held in abeyance means:

   _____.

2. Fee simple absolute, fee tail, and life estate are types of:
   _____.

3. The modern method of ownership of real property is _____.

4.   The limiting words, "to A and her heirs, but if Blackacre shall be used for the sale of alcoholic beverages, then X may re-enter and repossess the premises," creates a(n) _____.

5.   If a life tenant commits waste or threatens to commit waste, the holder of the reversion may bring an action for _____ or _____.

6.   Freehold estates join _____ and _____.

7.   One who leases real property has a(n) _____ estate.

Circle the correct answer.

8.   True or False. Modern conveyances must contain words of limitation (such as "and his or her heirs") to establish fee simple title.

9.   True or False. A fee simple estate may be limited as to the use to which real property may be put.

10.   True or False. A fee simple determinable or a fee simple subject to condition subsequent is extinguished by a subsequent conveyance.

11.   True or False. A life estate is a freehold estate and may be conveyed.

12.   True or False. Quia Emptores limited the alienation of property.

13.   True or False. Life estates are less common today; instead, options more typically are used.

14.   True or False. A fee tail contained the possibility of reverter.

15.   In his will, Big Daddy expressed a wish to provide support for Shannon in the event she did not marry. He devised Redacre to Shannon "so long as she remains single and unmarried," but if Shannon married, "such property to be divided among Ken, Loretta, and Shannon in equal shares." Ken and Loretta predeceased Shannon. Upon advice of her attorney, Shannon, then age 99, instituted a quiet title action against Jordan, Erin and Mariah, the heirs of Ken and Loretta, to quiet her title to the real property, alleging that the prohibition against her marriage was contrary to public policy and thus was void. Shannon further alleged that she was given a determinable fee in the real property to be reduced only upon her

marriage. Erin, Jordan, and Mariah contended that it was clear that Big Daddy intended Shannon to have only a life estate and that Ken, Loretta, and Shannon or their heirs, *per stirpes*, each should have a one-third interest upon the marriage or death of Shannon. Will Shannon succeed in her claim?

1. Yes. Since the will is silent about what happens upon the death of Shannon, the argument that she was given only a life estate fails.
2. Yes. A provision in general restraint of marriage is contrary to public policy.
3. No. The intent of the testator that Shannon be provided for in the event that she did not marry carves out an exception to the argument that a restraint against marriage is against public policy.
4. No. The provision that the property would be divided equally among Shannon, Ken, and Loretta should Shannon marry conveys a life estate in Shannon.
5. Yes. While the intent of the testator that Shannon be provided for in the event she did not marry carves out an exception to the argument that a general restraint of marriage is contrary to public policy, the absence of clear and decisive words of limitation reasonably may be construed to mean Shannon took a fee simple determinable.

16. Ishmail conveys Greenacre to Abbie for life. Abbie leases Greenacre to Acme Investment Co. for 35 years. Abbie dies 25 years later. What happens?

1. Acme's leasehold interest continues until the lease terminates by its terms, and then Greenacre reverts to Ishmail.
2. Acme's leasehold is terminated, and title to Greenacre reverts to Ishmail.
3. Acme's leasehold interest continues until the lease terminates by its terms, and then Greenacre reverts to Abbie's heirs.
4. Acme's leasehold interest continues until the lease terminates by its terms, and then Greenacre passes to Ishmail's heirs.

Briefly answer each of the following questions.

17. In 1957, John Doe sold part of his farm to Richard Roe for $50,000. The deed contained the following language:

> John Doe . . . by these presents does grant, bargain, sell and convey, unto the Grantee, Richard Roe and his heirs, the following described real property . . . but if said real property shall be used for an airport, then John Doe may re-enter and repossess the premises . . ..

At the time of the sale, the real property had an appraised value of $1,000.00. John Doe died in 1961 from injuries sustained when he fell from a tractor, leaving his son David as his only heir. Richard Roe sold the real estate to Acme Investments in 1990 for $100,000. In 1992, Acme Investments opened an airport on the property. What type of estate was transferred?

1. Fee simple absolute.
2. Fee tail.
3. Fee simple determinable.
4. Fee simple subject to condition subsequent.

18. In the fact pattern above, may Acme Investments retain ownership of the real property?_____ Why or why not? _____
_____

19. In the fact pattern above, may someone other than Acme Investments claim an interest in the real property? _____ If so, who? _____ State the nature of the claim, if any._____ How would such claim be asserted?_____

20. Upon the death of her father, Luis, Tita received a life estate in a farm, with the remainder to her oldest son Juan, who always had shown an interest in the farm. Stating a desire that all Tita's children share equally in his estate, Luis bequeathed a sum equal to the value of the farm to each of Tita's only other children, Carlos and Jose. Tita never lived on the farm after the death of her father, leasing it instead to a family friend. Before Tita's death, the farm land increased in value, making the value of Jose's interest far greater than the sums Carlos and Jose had received. Remembering her father's desire that her children share equally in his estate, Tita devised one-half of the property to her son, Juan, and one half of the property to Carlos and Jose in equal shares in her will. Upon Tita's death, Jose entered into a contract for sale of his one-fourth interest to Marvin. Marvin's attorney advised not to complete the purchase. Why not?_____
_____

Chapter 2
FUTURE INTERESTS

Real property is a multi-dimensional concept. We think of real property as a bundle of sticks, or bundle of rights; but the bundle of rights is also infinite in time. If a particular estate is of less than infinite duration, such as a fee tail or a life estate, a future interest must follow it. A future interest is a freehold, nonpossessory interest. In other words, it is a present interest in the real estate; but the nature of that interest defers the right of possession to a future time.

A future interest is fully transferable. It may be retained by the grantor, or it may be either conveyed (sold) or devised by will to a third party. It is, however, subject to certain limitations.

Types of Future Interests

Historically, future interests in English common law were either legal or equitable. Only legal interests were recognized by the law courts (the courts administered under the authority of the crown). Equitable interests were recognized only by the courts of chancery (the courts administered under the authority of the Chancellor of the Exchequer). The legal future interests consisted of the *reversion*, the *remainder*, the *possibility of reverter*, and the *right of reentry*, each of which was discussed in Chapter 1. The equitable future interests consisted of the shifting use and the springing use. "Uses" became legal interests in the sixteenth century and thereafter were called *executory interests* (discussed *infra*).

The following examples review and reinforce concepts related to future interests that were presented initially in Chapter 1.

> Alfred conveys Greenacre to Kensington and his issue.

> Alfred conveys Redacre to Willis for life.

A *reversion* is vested in Alfred and his heirs when he conveys either a fee tail or a life estate. A reversion also would vest in Alfred if he were to convey an estate for years or some other, periodic tenancy. In other words, the fee automatically will revert to Alfred, or to the heirs of Alfred if Alfred is deceased, at the end of the intervening interest.

> In 1976, Anna Marie sold Freehold Estates to Lionel "for so long as the property is used as a park and no longer." Lionel built a condominium on the property in 1989.

A *possibility of reverter* vested in Anna Marie and her heirs when she conveyed a fee simple determinable to Freehold Estates. This possibility of reverter was vested in Anna Marie as a future interest from 1976 until 1989. When Lionel built a condominium on the property, the fee (the title) reverted automatically to Anna Marie, causing her to become the owner of the condominium.

> As the developer of Four Seisins Estates, Adam created a park in 1976 on Lot 1, Four Seisins Estates. He sold it to Karen, adding the provision "but if the premises cease to be used as a park, Adam may enter and repossess the estate." Karen opened a bar on Lot 1 in 1989.

A *right of entry* vested in Adam when he conveyed a fee simple subject to a condition subsequent in the above example. From 1976 to 1989, he was vested with a right of entry for condition broken. In 1989, the right ceased to be conditional; and from that date forward, an absolute right of entry was vested in Adam and his heirs.

Unlike the possibility of reverter, a right of entry is not automatic. In the example, Adam (or his heirs if he is deceased) must take some affirmative step to exercise the right, either by physical entry of the premises or by commencement of a lawsuit to recover possession. This right of entry is also described as a power of termination. It can exist only in favor of a grantor and never can be reserved in favor of a stranger.

By contrast, a *remainder* is a reversion existing in a third party. The remainder may be either vested or contingent.

<u>Vested Remainders</u>   A *vested remainder* is a future interest in which possession will occur automatically at the natural termination of the preceding estate (interest) in the land.

> Terence devised Friendly Farms by will "to Allison for life, remainder to Bruce."

Upon the death of Terence, Allison is vested with a life estate; and Bruce is vested as the remainderman. Bruce's interest is vested, since nothing remains except the death of Allison for Bruce to become seized in ownership and possession (the fee simple owner).

During Allison's lifetime, Bruce has a present, freehold, nonpossessory future interest. Bruce's interest is transferable and inheritable. If Bruce dies before Allison dies, his future interest as the vested remainderman will descend to his heirs.

<u>Contingent Remainders</u>   A *contingent remainder* is a future interest which may or may not vest, depending on the occurrence of some other condition.

> Teresa devised Arid Acres by will "to Ben for life, remainder to the eldest son of Ben."

If Ben has no sons at the time of the conveyance, there is no person in whom the future interest presently can vest. A future interest must exist, however, because the interest of Ben (a life estate) is not infinite in time. The future interest, therefore, is contingent on the occurrence of a condition (that Ben has a son).

Once a son is born to Ben, the remainder vests in that son and his heirs. If Ben dies without a son having been born, the remainder is destroyed; and the fee reverts to Teresa or her heirs at Ben's death.

Contingent remainders are *destructible* and, therefore, a possibility of reverter remains in addition to the remainder. In the example, a possibility of reverter remained in Teresa and her heirs until the birth of a son to Ben.

<u>Executory Interests</u>   The early common law took the concept of remainders one step further by creating the shifting use and the springing use, which came to be known as executory interests in modern real estate law. An *executory* *interest* is a future interest that cuts off the preceding estate in land before it otherwise would have ended.

> Thaddeus devised Happy Canyon Estates by will "to Beatrice and her heirs (a fee simple); but if Beatrice dies without heirs, then for the use of Candace and her heirs."

By this conveyance, Thaddeus has created a fee simple determinable in Beatrice, with a shifting use or interest in Candace and her heirs. A springing use is slightly different.

> Upon the birth of Bart, his Aunt Dolores signed and delivered to Bart's father a deed to Air Acres "for the use of Bart and his heirs, Bart's interest to commence upon Bart's attaining the age of 25 years."

Dolores has created a springing use or interest in Bart. The fee remains vested in Dolores, but it is subject to Bart's springing use until Bart reaches age 25. If Bart dies before reaching age 25, his springing use terminates; and the fee remains vested in Dolores.

Note carefully the difference between executory interests and contingent remainders. Although an executory interest is contingent in the sense that it may never vest (Bart may die before he attains the age of 25), it is not a remainder. A remainder takes effect only upon the natural termination of the prior estate, such as a life estate or an estate for years.

In the example of the springing use, the prior estate is held by Dolores, the donor or grantor of the springing use. If the contingency occurs (if Bart attains the age of 25), the interest of Bart cuts off or destroys Dolores's interest. As such, it is a springing interest (executory interest) and not a remainder. A remainder never cuts off the prior estate. It was that aspect of the use that the law courts could not accept, forcing its development in equity.

The Statute of Uses

The Statute of Uses was enacted by the English Parliament in 1536, during the reign of Henry VIII. The reasons for its enactment were, for Henry, the recovery of lost revenue and, for Parliament, the recovery of common law jurisdiction over the conveyancing of real property. In effect, the Statute converted equitable interests into legal interests, with this operative language:

> *If any person be seised of any lands to the use of any
> other person, such person that have such use shall
> henceforth be deemed in lawful seisin and possession of
> the same lands in such like estate as he had in use.*

By the year 1536, the concept of the use had become widespread and had extended well beyond the concepts of shifting and springing uses. The Courts of Chancery, under the equity jurisdiction of the Chancellor of the Exchequer, had become popular as an alternative to the inflexible law courts, which were under the jurisdiction of the crown.

To understand the growth of the use as an alternative to legal ownership, one must understand the formality of conveyancing in early England. One must also understand that, prior to the Statute of Wills (1540), real property could not be devised by will. Real estate was conveyed by a formal ceremony of going upon the land and handing over some of its dirt to the purchaser, which ceremony was known as *livery of seisin*. The ceremony was memorialized in writing by a *charter of enfeoffment*. Only by this method could the legal interests discussed above be created, enforceable in the courts of law. Moreover, prior to the Statute of Wills, the fee simple thereby conveyed came to an end when the family line ran out, that is, when some purchaser or some descendant of the purchaser died without heirs. When that happened, escheat occurred, whereby the monarch once again became the owner.

Uses were created in three ways. First was the device called the *feoffment to uses*, created as follows:

> Frank, by a charter of enfeoffment conveying Lazy Acres "enfeoff
> Angela and her heirs to the use of Becky and her heirs."

A legal fee simple estate was thereby vested in Angela; but an equitable fee simple estate for the benefit of Becky and her heirs was also created, enforceable only in the Courts of Chancery. Becky was entitled to the profits of the estate and, upon demand, to its conveyance.

Second was the *bargain and sale deed*:

> Sally might "bargain and sell Elegant Estates to Aldo and his
> heirs."

A bargain and sale deed was a document of conveyance executed without livery of seisin. In other words, the parties did not physically go upon the land and did not hand over the soil as the common law required. Because there was no livery of seisin, legal title did not vest in Aldo, much as legal title would not vest in Aldo today under an installment sale contract in which Aldo is the purchaser. However, the Courts of Chancery treated Aldo as the beneficial owner and would require Sally to convey to Aldo upon demand (by *specific performance*, which is discussed in a later chapter).

Finally, persons related by blood or marriage might enter into a *covenant to stand seized*:

> "I, Charles, covenant to stand seized to the use of my wife, Cecilia, and her heirs."

Upon the death of Charles, title passed to Cecilia and her heirs. This created, within the family relationship, what we describe today as a family trust. Again, only the Courts of Chancery provided enforcement.

The bargain and sale deed and the covenant to stand seized also reflect the development of the use of the seal in conveyancing. The use of the seal continues today, although only as a formality. The use of a seal originated at a time when people were unable to write. The seal was used in lieu of a signature and imparted formality and ease of proof to a document of conveyance.

Uses were popular for a number of reasons. They permitted the creation of shifting and springing interests. The bargain and sale deed permitted conveyance of land at a distance from the location of the property being conveyed. Probably most important, employment of the use allowed ownership of real property to survive the end of the family line before the enactment of the Statute of Wills permitted land to be devised by will. Also, feudal incidents owed to the lord were avoided in much the same way that trusts are employed today to avoid or limit tax liability. Uses also were employed to avoid (or defraud) creditors as well as to eliminate rights of dower, i.e., the rights of the wife in the estate of the husband. Forfeiture of ownership of real estate for treason or conviction of a felony also was avoided through the use. Uses permitted citizens of other nations to own land, and secrecy was provided by employment of the use.

With the adoption of the Statute of Uses, the right of use became the right of possession. Centuries later, the concept of the use was reincarnated in the trust.

Restraints on Alienation

The Statute of Uses, together with the Statute <u>Quia Emptores</u> (1290) that earlier had provided for the free alienation of real property, gave to the common law the system of real property ownership which has survived to this day. In general, while restraints on the use of property will be permitted, restraints on alienation were and are not permitted. Any attempt to restrain totally the alienability of a fee simple estate is void.

> Octavia conveyed High Country Estates "to Amy and her heirs; but if Amy attempts to convey High Country Estates to Betty, this conveyance to Amy shall be null and void."

This conveyance will not be given effect. Because courts will not recognize such a restraint on alienation, Amy may convey High Country Estates to Betty with impunity.

Certain partial restraints on alienation are permitted, however. Thus, a provision in a cooperative apartment agreement that restrains sale of stock to a third party without the consent of the cooperative's board of directors will be upheld. Since cooperative owners are liable for the entire mortgage on the building and, therefore, are in the position of having to indemnify any default by another owner, such a restriction will be upheld as serving a valid purpose.

Similarly, condominium declarations often contain a right of first refusal, whereby any owner in the condominium is given a first right to match any offer to purchase by a third party. Such rights of first refusal are upheld on the basis of protecting the interests of existing owners. They may not, however, be employed to prevent sale of a condominium unit to a member of a minority or other protected class or otherwise to practice discrimination.

Agreements not to seek partition, which are entered into by joint tenants or tenants in common, are also valid if they are limited in time and if they serve a reasonable purpose. Thus, the right of *partition* (the right of one tenant in common or joint tenant to separately convey his or her interest) may be waived for a specified time and for a valid consideration. For example, condominium declarations routinely provide that the interest of the owners in the common elements, held as tenants in common, may not be partitioned.

Certain restrictions on conveyancing were developed by the courts of law, in particular the Rule in Shelley's Case, the Doctrine of Worthier Title, and the

Rule Against Perpetuities, which limited the general rule that total restraints on alienation will not be permitted.

(The Rule in) Shelley's Case, 1 Co.Rep. 93b (1581) represented a line of authority which originated in the fourteenth century. The rule was a simple one. If Omer conveyed to Anita, with a remainder in the heirs of Anita (or the heirs of Anita's body), a fee simple (or fee tail) was created in Anita, rather than a life estate. In other words, according to the Rule in Shelley's Case, the fee simple bundle of sticks may not be divided up between Anita during her life and Anita's heirs thereafter. The life estate and the remainder merge in Anita. The original reason for the rule was to prevent the avoidance of feudal obligations that otherwise would occur upon the death of Anita. More recently, the rule has been either abolished or described as a rule of construction. Using the example above, the courts would construe the grant to be a grant of the entire fee simple estate to Anita, absent a clear intent on the part of the grantor to divide the fee simple estate between Anita during her life and Anita's heirs thereafter.

The Doctrine of Worthier Title similarly was designed to protect the lord's interest in the incidents of feudal tenure. The doctrine was two-fold: 1) that descent takes precedence over devise and 2) that a remainder in a grantor is a reversion.

The first aspect of the doctrine is that, for example, if William devised his estate by will to his eldest son, the devise was treated as an inheritance since the oldest son would have inherited under the concept of primogeniture in any event. Thus, the feudal incidents, which did not exist with respect to a devise by will, were preserved. That aspect of the doctrine did not survive the end of feudalism.

The second aspect of the doctrine is the rule that a person may not "make his or her heir a purchaser." In other words, one could not convey a remainder to one's heir. Thus, a conveyance by Emily "to Adriana for life, remainder to the heirs of Emily" will create a reversion in Emily, to the exclusion of her heirs. Emily's heirs will take their interest only if Emily dies before Adriana. If, instead, Adriana dies during the lifetime of Emily, title will revert to Emily rather than go to her heirs. That aspect of the doctrine has been abolished in some states and has been reduced to a rule of construction in others, at least where it has been considered.

Unlike the Rule in Shelley's Case and the Doctrine of Worthier Title, the *Rule Against Perpetuities* did not serve the purpose of preventing the avoidance of feudal incidents. Rather, it represented the culmination of a struggle between the royal courts and the landowners, who wished to keep their land within their families forever.

The Rule Against Perpetuities originated in the Duke of Norfolk's Case, 3 Ch. Cas. 1, 22 Eng. Rep. 931 (1681), as a compromise between the landed class and the common law judges. In that case, the Earl of Arundel had created trust indentures to protect his family from the insanity of his oldest son. The Chancellor recognized the concern as a legitimate one and, accordingly, in that case and other cases, an appropriate period was developed during which the father's judgment could prevail.

The theory that developed was that the father realistically and wisely could assess the capabilities of living members of the family, and the father's judgment was given effect with respect to family members. The father, as testator, was permitted to extend his control to unborn persons only if one of the persons in that next generation was still a minor. After about 150 years, the judges fixed the period as " a life in being plus 21 years" thereafter:

> *No interest is good unless it must vest, if at all, not later than twenty-one years after some life in being at the creation of the interest.*

The Rule Against Perpetuities was necessary because the adoption of the Statute of Uses permitted contingent interests to vest at a remote time. For example, without the Rule, a springing use could become effective multiple generations in the future.

It is important to keep in mind that the Rule applies only to contingent remainders and to executory interests. It does not apply to a reversion, possibility of reverter, right of entry, or vested remainders.

The Rule Against Perpetuities is not violated by the fact that the contingent interest may never vest. That fact is true of all future interests.

> Arnold conveys "to Angela and her heirs, but if Angela dies without heirs, then to Bertha and her heirs" (a shifting interest).

This conveyance does not violate the Rule by virtue of the fact that Angela may die with heirs; and, therefore, Bertha's interest may never vest. Of course, if Bertha's interest does vest, it can vest only at Angela's death (without heirs), which is technically during Angela's lifetime. Therefore, it does not violate the Rule.

The "what might happen" test is generally used to determine whether an interest violates the Rule Against Perpetuities. If anything could happen that would prevent the interest from vesting within the time of the measuring life plus 21 years, the Rule is violated; and the conveyance is void from the outset. The creation of an interest that violates the Rule is not saved by the fact that, at some later time, the interest does vest. The Rule and the "what might happen test" must be applied as of the time of the creation of the interest.

> In 1995, Tamara conveys Grand Manor in trust for "the first child of Andrew who marries." Andrew is alive at the time the trust is created.

Potential measuring lives are those lives in existence (including gestation) in 1995 that can affect vesting. Only Andrew can affect vesting in this example (by fathering children); and Andrew's life is, therefore, the measuring life. The interest, however, is void.

Andrew's first child to marry may not have been born or in gestation in 1995 and may not marry within 21 years after Andrew's death. Additionally, it may be that Andrew might never have children or that his children might never marry, in which case the interest never would vest. The point is that it is possible that the interest could vest more than 21 years after Andrew's death. As such, the conveyance violates the Rule and is void, regardless of what actually happens.

> In 1995, Timothy conveys Faraway Vistas in trust for "the first child of Arlene to attain the age of 21." Arlene is alive when the conveyance is made.

Arlene's life is the measuring life, because only her life can affect the vesting of the interest. The conveyance is valid.

Arlene's first child to attain the age of 21 will do so, if at all, within 21 years of Arlene's death. The worst that could happen is that Arlene may die without children or that she may give birth to a child who dies before reaching age 21. In either case, the interest would fail within 21 years of Arlene's death; and the Rule Against Perpetuities would not be violated.

An easier example of a violation of the Rule Against Perpetuities is a right-of-first refusal that is unrestricted as to time. Rights-of-first refusal are frequently contained in condominium declarations and provide that a condominium unit may not be sold to an outsider unless other owners in the same condominium complex have a "first right" to purchase the unit on the same terms. Such rights are a type of future interest, contingent upon the receipt of an offer for purchase of the particular condominium unit. Therefore, such rights must be limited in time or to some life in being (usually the surviving developer) plus 21 years. If the right is not so limited, it violates the Rule because an offer may be received, causing the contingent interest to vest more than 21 years after the death of the current owner of the unit (or any other life currently in being).

As a practical matter, the problem of the Rule Against Perpetuities is avoided by including a clause in any instrument creating a contingent future interest that the interest "must vest, if at all, within 21 years after the death of . . ." (the surviving child of the Prince of Wales, for example).

Approximately half of the jurisdictions, by statute or by court decision, have abandoned the common law version (the "what might happen" test) of the Rule. The prevailing substitute for the common law rule is the "wait and see" test. Using that substitute test, the question is not whether the future interest might vest in violation of the Rule Against Perpetuities but, rather, is whether it actually does. The future interest is invalidated only if it actually does vest outside the period of the Rule (life in being plus 21 years).

Chapter 2 Quiz

Fill in each blank with the most correct word.

1. A future interest in real property may be described as a(n) _____ interest in real estate, but the nature of that interest defers the right of _____ to a future time.

2. When A conveys a life estate, a(n) _____ exists.

3. A remainder may be _____ or _____.

4. When A conveys a periodic tenancy, a(n) _____ exists.

5. When A conveys a fee simple subject to condition subsequent, a right _____ exists.

6. When A conveys a fee simple determinable, a(n) _____ exists.

7. When Jones conveys Blackacre "to Smith for life, remainder to Chow and the heirs of Chow," Chow is a(n) _____.

8. _____ is more formally known as "the right of entry for condition broken" and may also be described as a "power of termination."

9. A(n) _____ never cuts off a prior estate, while a springing interest destroys the grantor's prior interest.

10. The concept of the equitable "use" is seen today in the form of _____.

Circle the correct answer.

11. True of False. Rights of real property are infinite in time.

12. True or False. A future interest is a freehold, nonpossessory interest and is fully transferable except that limitations may be placed on the use of the property.

13. True or False. In England, future interests were either legal or illegal.

14. True or False. A right of entry is not automatic.

15. True or False. A remainder is a reversion existing in a third party.

16. True or False. A reversion automatically occurs at the end of the intervening interest.

17. True or False. Prior to the Statute of Wills, real property in England could not be devised by will.

18. True or False. The Statute of Uses effectively converted equitable interests into legal interests.

19. True or False. The Statute Quia Emptores and the Statute of Uses provided to the common law the system of real property ownership which survives to this day.

20. True or False. Restraints on alienation generally are not permitted.

21. True or False. Restraints on the use of property are not permitted.

22. True or False. The Rule in Shelley's Case concerned the division of a fee simple estate between the grantee and his heirs.

23. True or False. The Doctrine of Worthier Title holds that descent takes precedence over devise and that a remainder in a grantor is a reversion.

24. True or False. The Rule Against Perpetuities provides: No interest is good unless it must vest, if at all, not later than twenty-five years after some life in being at the creation of the interest.

25. True or False. A right of first refusal that is unlimited as to time may violate the Rule Against Perpetuities.

Choose the best answer.

26. In 1957, John Doe sold part of his farm to Richard Roe for $50,000. The deed contained the following language:

> John Doe . . . by these presents does grant, bargain, sell and convey, unto the Grantee, Richard Roe and his heirs, the following described real property . . . but if said real property shall be used for an airport, then John Doe may re-enter and repossess the premises . . . .

At the time of the sale, the real property had an appraised value of $1,000.00. John Doe died in 1961 as a result of injuries sustained when he fell from a tractor, leaving his son, David, as his only heir. Richard Roe sold the real estate to Acme Investments in 1990 for $100,000. In 1992, Acme Investments opened an airport on the property. What rights does Richard Roe have?

a. None because the right of re-entry can never be reserved in favor of a stranger.

b. None because the subsequent conveyances extinguish the power of termination.

c. Fee simple automatically reverts to Richard Roe.

d. Richard Roe has a right of re-entry, which he must take steps to exercise.

27. In 1965, Williemae, owner of both Greenacre and Blueacre, executed and delivered two deeds conveying two separate tracts of land by the following language. Greenacre was conveyed "to Troy and his heirs as long as it is used exclusively for residential purposes, but if it is used for other than residential purposes, to the March of Dimes." Blueacre was conveyed "to Missy and her heirs as long as it is used exclusively for residential purposes, but if it is used for other than residential purposes before 1985, then to the Society for the Prevention of Cruelty to Animals." In December 1970, Williemae died, leaving a valid will by which she devised all her real estate to her brother, Bill. The will had no residuary clause. Williemae was survived by Bill and by Williemae's son, Sam, who was her sole heir. *For purposes of this question, you may assume that the common law rule against perpetuities applies in the state where the land is located and that the state has a statute providing that all future estates and interests are alienable, descendible, and devisable in the same manner as possessory estates and interests.*

i. In 1975, Troy and Sam entered into a contract with John, agreeing to sell Greenacre to John in fee simple. Upon advice of his attorney, who examined the title, John refused to perform on the ground that Troy and Sam could not give good title. Troy and Sam brought an action against John for relief. Relief performance will be:

1. granted because Troy and Sam together own a fee simple absolute in Greenacre.

2. granted because Troy alone owns the entire fee simple in Greenacre.

3. denied because Bill has a valid interest in Greenacre.

4. denied because the March of Dimes has a valid interest in Greenacre.

ii. In 1966, the interest of the March of Dimes in Greenacre best could be described as a:

a. valid contingent remainder.

b. void executory interest.

c. valid executory interest.

d. void contingent remainder.

iii. In 1971, Bill's interest in Greenacre best could be described as:

a. a possibility of reverter.

b. an executory interest in a possibility of reverter.

c. an executory interest.

d. none of the above.

iv. In 1968, Missy and the SPCA contracted to sell Blueacre to Crammond, promising title in fee simple. After a title examination, Crammond refused to perform, asserting that Missy and the SPCA could not convey marketable title. Missy and the SPCA brought suit for relief. Relief will be:

a. granted because the attempted restrictions on use are a restraint against alienation.

b. granted because the deed violates the Rule Against Perpetuities.

c. granted because Missy and the SPCA together own a fee simple absolute.

d. denied because Williemae must join in the deed to convey marketable title.

Chapter 3
CONCURRENT OWNERSHIP

Real property may be conveyed or devised by will to more than one person, typically called co-owners or cotenants. A conveyance or devise to more than one person creates one of the forms of concurrent ownership: tenancy in common, joint tenancy, or tenancy by the entireties.

The Unities of Ownership

Figure 3-1
Unities of Concurrent Ownership

Type of Tenancy	Unity Required	Right of Survivorship	Relationship Required	May Convey Separately
Tenancy in common	Possession	No	None	Yes
Joint tenancy	Possession Time Title Interest	Yes	None	Yes
Tenancy by the entireties	Possession Time Title Interest	Yes	Husband and Wife	No

Concurrent tenancies possess one or more of the unities of ownership, that is, characteristics of ownership that the owners have in common. These unities of ownership are unity of time, unity of title, unity of interest, and unity of possession. All four unities of ownership are required to create a joint tenancy or a tenancy by the entireties.

Unity of Time   The unity of time exists only if the interests of the cotenants were created at the same time. For example, the unity of time exists if Andrew conveys one-half interests to Barbara and to Charles by the same deed. It does not exist, however, if Andrew conveys a one-half interest to Barbara in 1994 and a one-half interest to Charles in 1995. In the latter case, Barbara and Charles could be tenants in common only, since unity of time is not necessary for this type of tenancy (ownership).

Unity of Title   The unity of title exists only if the interests of the owners were conveyed from the same grantor. For example, the unity of title exists if Alice conveys one-half interest to each of Bob and Cathryn by the same deed. It does not exist if Alice and Arnold each own a one-half interest, Alice conveys her one-half interest to Bob, and Arnold conveys his one-half interest to Cathryn. On these facts, Bob and Cathryn could be tenants in common only.

Unity of Interest   The unity of interest exists only if each owner has a proportionately equal interest. For example, unity of interest exists if Alan and Bridget each owns a one-half interest. It does not exist if Alan owns a one-third interest and Bridget owns a two-thirds interest. In the latter case, Alan and Bridget could be tenants in common only.

Unity of Possession   The unity of possession exists only if each owner has an undivided share of the property. For example, unity of possession exists if Alicia and Bruce each owns "an undivided one-half interest." It does not exist if Alicia owns "the north half of Lot 1, Grand Estates," and Bruce owns the south half. On these facts, there is no concurrent ownership of any kind.

Co-owners or cotenants are presumed to be tenants in common unless the creating document expresses a clear intent that some other tenancy is being established. In any form of concurrent ownership, each co-owner has a simultaneous, proportionate share of the entire property. No co-owner owns any specifically identifiable portion of the property to the exclusion of the others. If three people own the same parcel of property, each is presumed to own an undivided one-third interest. However, each has an equal right to possess and to enjoy any portion or all of the property subject to the rights of the others. This unity of possession is characteristic of all forms of co-ownership.

Tenancy in Common

Under common law, joint tenancy was preferred over tenancy in common. Therefore, a document creating a property interest was construed to create a joint interest unless it clearly provided otherwise. Today, the contrary is true. Concurrent ownership is presumed to be a tenancy in common unless the creating document clearly provides for some other form of co-ownership. The only unity required for a tenancy in common is the unity of possession. For example, if two people own Green Acres, one owning the north half and the other owning the south half, they are not tenants in common. They can be tenants in common only if each owns an undivided interest in the whole.

The other three unities are not required to create a tenancy in common. There is no requirement of the unities of time or of title; the ownership interest may be acquired from different sources and at different times. There is no requirement of the unity of interest; the undivided interests need not be the same. Thus, one tenant in common may have a one-tenth share, while the other has a nine-tenths share.

Unity of possession means that each tenant in common is entitled to exercise all the rights of ownership as though he or she were the sole owner. If one tenant in common derives profit from the land, he or she has a duty to account to the remaining tenants in common but may be entitled to offset expenses incurred in deriving that profit. Even when no profit has been realized, one tenant in common may have a right against the other tenants in common for contribution for expenses incurred in the upkeep of the property.

Each tenant in common has a duty to the other tenants not to commit *waste*. *Active waste* occurs when one tenant in common intentionally causes damage to the property or diminishes the property in some way (cutting timber, for example). *Passive waste* or *permissive waste* occurs when the property is permitted to fall into disrepair. *Ameliorative waste* occurs when the value of the property is enhanced. Ameliorative waste may be permitted in some circumstances (removing improvements having no value, for example).

No right of survivorship exists between tenants in common. When one tenant in common dies, the heirs or devisees of that tenant succeed to the interest of the deceased tenant.

Each tenant in common has a *right of partition*, whereby he or she may request a court to divide the property into separate parcels according to the percentage interest of each tenant. If the land cannot be divided reasonably or equally (if it has a home on it, for example), the court may order the property sold and the proceeds divided among the cotenants according to their respective percentage interests.

Joint Tenancy

The principal difference between joint tenancy and tenancy in common is that each joint tenant has a right of survivorship. When one joint tenant dies, the remaining joint tenant or joint tenants automatically succeed to the interest of the deceased joint tenant without the need for probate. For example, if Alexandra, Brian, and Carl are joint tenants of Mountain Estates and if Alexandra dies, Brian and Carl are the surviving joint tenants, with each now owning a one-half interest in the real estate. Alexandra's interest as a joint tenant does not pass to her estate or to her descendants.

Joint tenancy is created today only when the governing instrument expressly provides for it. Joint tenancy is not presumed. Thus, a deed which conveys Madison Manor "to Albert and Beverly as joint tenants and not as tenants in common" creates a joint tenancy in Albert and Beverly. As a general rule, when the instrument contains the magic words *joint tenancy*, it is not necessary to include either the words *and not as tenants in common* or the words *with right of survivorship* unless a particular state statute so requires.

Joint tenancy includes all four unities of ownership and continues only so long as those unities remain intact. The interests must be created at the same time and must be obtained from the same source. Each joint tenant's interest must be equal to all other joint tenants' interests, and each joint tenant must have an undivided interest in the whole. The joint tenancy terminates if any one of the four unities is severed.

> Amos, Boris, and Catarina were joint tenants of Ajax Estates. In
> 1995, Amos conveyed his one-third interest to Luisa.

In this example, Boris and Catarina still are joint tenants of an undivided two-thirds interest (each owns an undivided one-third interest); but Luisa is a tenant in common of her undivided one-third interest. If either Boris or Catarina dies, the survivor will succeed to the interest of both and will own an undivided two-thirds interest. Luisa will continue to own only her one-third interest. If Luisa dies, her heirs will succeed to her interest. This is because the unities of time and of title are no longer intact for her one-third interest.

The simplest form of estate planning involves placing title in joint tenancy to save the expense of probate. When sophisticated, tax-motivated estate planning is used, property ordinarily is not placed in joint tenancy because the automatic survivorship can skew the estate plan. An exception to that rule exists when a single piece of property (for example, a vacation residence) is owned in a state other than the principal residence of the person whose estate is being planned. In that situation, it may be more prudent to place the property in joint tenancy to avoid the necessity of an ancillary probate proceeding in the other state.

The rights and duties of joint tenants between or among themselves are the same as those of tenants in common. In legal theory, each joint tenant owns the whole, subject to the rights of the others. Like tenancy in common, joint tenancy may be terminated by partition.

Tenancy by the Entireties

Tenancy by the entireties has all the characteristics of joint tenancy; in addition, however, the joint tenants must be married to each other.

At common law, a conveyance to husband and wife was deemed to create an estate by the entireties. For that matter, the wife was not capable of the independent ownership of real property during the marriage relationship under common law rules. It was only with the adoption of the Married Women's Property Acts throughout the United States in the latter part of the nineteenth century that separate ownership of property by a wife became possible.

In more than half the states, adoption of that Act brought an end to the use of tenancy by the entireties. In the other states, it has continued because of the protection against creditors that this form of tenancy gives. In those states in which tenancy by the entireties still exists, if the marriage relationship is ended, tenancy in common usually results. However, in some states, joint tenancy results if the marriage relationship is ended.

During the marriage, one spouse may not convey his or her interest separately. Any attempt by one spouse to do so is void. Because of this rule, the creditor of one spouse may not levy on that spouse's interest in some states.

Marital Rights

The common law marital rights were *dower* and *curtesy*. **Curtesy** was for the benefit of the surviving husband and gave him a life estate in all freehold interests of the wife, both legal and equitable, to the exclusion of the children. However, curtesy did not attach unless issue of the marriage had been born. Upon the birth of issue, the right of the husband was known as *curtesy initiate*. Upon death of the wife, it became *curtesy consummate*. **Dower** was for the benefit of the surviving wife. At common law, the wife was entitled to a life estate equal to a one-third interest in her husband's estate, whether or not there were issue of the marriage. Dower attached at the time of marriage as to land that was owned then or thereafter when the land was acquired. It was *inchoate*. In other words, it did not attach until the husband died. If the wife predeceased her husband, her *inchoate dower* was extinguished.

Modern statutes treat surviving spouses equally, generally giving the surviving spouse the right to elect against the will to receive a **marital share** or **forced share** of the estate. There is no requirement that there be children; and the surviving spouse receives a fee simple estate, not a life estate. The amount of the spouse's share usually represents what he or she would have received in intestacy (that is, with no will) or some percentage of that. Thus, if the marital share is one-third of the husband's estate and if the husband's will leaves only one-quarter of his estate to his wife, the wife may elect against the will to receive the statutory one-third share. The will otherwise is left intact insofar as that is possible. The trend is to make the marital interest a percentage based upon the length of the marriage.

During the marriage partners' lives, other rights exist. In community property states (generally in the Southwest and along the Pacific Coast), married persons are deemed to be co-owners of property acquired during the marriage but not of property given or devised by will to one spouse alone. Noncommunity property states take a different approach. During marriage, property remains owned as it is titled; no co-ownership is deemed to be created. However, when the marriage is dissolved, all property generally is treated as marital property and is divided equally between the parties.

Because the marital property right may exist even in a noncommunity property state, many states require a spouse to join in the conveyance of property owned by the other spouse alone. Thus, a conveyance may be from Andrew and Beatrice "as husband and wife" or from Andrew "joined by his spouse, Beatrice." If Andrew is single, the conveyance might be from Andrew "as a single person."

Chapter 3 Quiz

Fill in each blank with the most correct word or phrase.

1. Identify the unities with these characteristics of ownership:

Characteristic	Unity
1. Creation of concurrent ownership at the same time	_____
2. Each owner having an equal interest	_____
3. Each owner having an undivided share	_____
4. Ownership obtained from the same source	_____

2. A and B own Blackacre as tenants in common. B removes a dilapidated shed from the property. He has committed _____ waste.

3. A and B own Blackacre as joint tenants. A, who lives on the property, fails to repair fences and unused outbuildings. A has committed _____ waste.

4. A tenancy which requires that the joint tenants be married to each other is _____.

5. Common law marital rights were _____ and _____.

Circle the correct answer.

6. True or False. Co-owners are presumed to have equal, undivided interests in the real property.

7. True or False. Only the unity of possession is required for tenancy in common.

8. True or False. All tenants in common must join in any conveyance from one cotenant to a third party.

9.   True or False. Tenants in common may identify specifically what portion of the real property each owns (such as the west half or the south half) and may reserve that portion for his or her own use.

10.   True or False. Joint tenants may identify specifically what portion of the real property each owns (such as the west half or the south half) and may reserve that portion for his or her own use.

11.   True or False. Only unimproved real property may be partitioned because of the impracticality of dividing a dwelling.

12.   True or False. Joint tenancy once was used extensively as an estate planning tool, but the Tax Code of 1988 rendered it ineffective.

13.   True or False. Tenants in common each owe a duty to the other tenants not to commit waste.

14.   True or False. Joint tenancy must be created and will not be presumed.

15.   True or False. All unities of ownership must be present to create joint tenancy, but joint tenancy will survive so long as three of the unities continue.

16.   True or False. Specific legislation allowed separate ownership of property by a wife.

17.   True or False. A type of co-ownership exists which prohibits a spouse from separately conveying his or her interest in real property.

18.   True or False. A surviving spouse may elect against the will to receive a marital share of a deceased spouse's estate, but such an election gives the surviving spouse only a life estate.

19.   True or False. In community property states, married persons are deemed to be co-owners of all property regardless of when or how the property was acquired.

20.   True or False. In noncommunity property states, co-ownership with the spouse is deemed to be created when property is conveyed to a married person.

21.   True or False. All states now require that a spouse join in a conveyance of real property owned by the other.

22.   Unless otherwise stated in the conveying instrument, concurrent ownership is:

    1.   Tenancy by the entireties in the majority of states.
    2.   Joint tenancy with right of survivorship in the majority of states.
    3.   Tenancy in common in the majority of states unless the grantees are husband and wife.
    4.   Tenancy in common in the majority of states.
    5.   None is correct.

23.   Modern forms of concurrent ownership are:

    1.   Tenancy in common and joint tenancy.
    2.   Tenancy in common, joint tenancy, and tenancy by the entireties.
    3.   Tenancy in common, joint tenancy, tenancy by the entireties, and tenancy by dower and curtesy.
    4.   Joint tenancy, tenancy in common, tenancy by the entireties, and tenancy in community property.
    5.   None is correct.

24.   Andrew, William, and Thomas purchased a soybean farm from Paul. Title was conveyed to them as joint tenants. They hired a tenant farmer, and the farming operation continued for 18 years. As part of his estate planning, Andrew conveyed his interest to himself and his wife, Diane, as joint tenants. William and Thomas were not grantees on the deed. Six months later, Diane died. Diane left all her interest in real property to her children of a former marriage. What type of tenancy does Andrew have?

    1.   Andrew, William, and Thomas hold the property as tenants in common with each other because a conveyance by one joint tenant destroys the joint tenancy as to all.
    2.   Tenancy in common as to William and Thomas and joint tenancy as to Diane's children.
    3.   Andrew remains a joint tenant with William and Thomas because as joint tenants, they did not join in the conveyance to Andrew and Diane, rendering the conveyance invalid.
    4.   Tenancy in common with William and Thomas, who are joint tenants with each other.

Essay Question

25.   In 1980, Chris, Grace, and Helen purchased a house on the beach and took title as tenants in common. The three agreed that Chris, who was an author, would use the house during November, December, January, and February (occupying the apartment over the garage); Grace would have the main house during March, April, May, and June; and Helen would live in it from July through October. This arrangement continued for 15 years. During that time Helen never occupied the premises during October. On October 25, 1995, Helen arrived at the beach house and declared her intention to live there permanently. Much to her surprise, she discovered that Chris had leased the premises to Charles for the months of October, November, December, and January. As an owner, Helen declared that Chris could not lease the house without her consent and demanded that Charles vacate the premises. Chris asserted that he could lease the premises for the months allotted to him. He further argued that since Helen never had exercized her right to use the premises in October, she had abandoned that right. At the most, he argued, Helen must abide by the terms of their agreement and was entitled to use the premises only during the months allocated to her. Grace agreed that Chris could lease his share of the premises (his apartment) for the months during which he was to have use of the property, but could not lease the entire premises in any event. Charles maintained that he was entitled to remain until the end of January. Briefly discuss the rights of the parties.

Chapter 4
COMMON INTEREST OWNERSHIP

This chapter discusses cooperatives, condominiums, and other forms of common interest ownership for multi-family and commercial properties. Cooperatives and condominiums are distinct forms of common interest property ownership. Other forms of common interest ownership have a variety of characteristics and may share the characteristics of each other. Thus, a duplex may be part of a planned unit development, it may be a condominium form of ownership, or it may be one building containing two dwelling units separated by a party wall. A common element of all these forms of ownership is ownership in common of some part of the real estate, whether the common areas or just a party wall.

The concepts of condominium and cooperative ownership did not exist at common law, just as corporations did not exist at early common law. However, there is nothing in the concept of the party wall which could not have existed at common law. It is likely that it did exist in the form of a common wall that was subject to easements in favor of both properties.

Condominium ownership depends entirely upon statute, and all jurisdictions have such statutes in effect. The cooperative form of ownership does not require any special statute apart from those statutes dealing with corporations.

Traditionally, no statutory treatment has been given to the other forms of community and multi-family ownership. As a consequence, the Commissioners on Uniform State Laws, the entity responsible for the promulgation of uniform laws such as the Uniform Commercial Code, have promulgated a Uniform Common Interest Ownership Act. This act has been adopted in only a few states.

41

Much of the discussion contained in this chapter is based upon its provisions in anticipation of its wider adoption.

Cooperatives

Cooperatives are multi-unit dwellings (apartment buildings) owned by a corporation. Instead of purchasing an individual apartment, one purchases stock in the corporation. Each shareholder of the corporation leases an apartment in the building from the corporation and has a right to use the common areas of the building. A shareholder agreement provides for the joint payment of costs of acquisition and maintenance of the building in monthly installments and governs use of the common areas. Common areas include the lobby, meeting rooms, swimming pool, and so forth. Cooperative ownership has not proven popular nationwide, probably because of the reluctance of lenders to rely on the security of stock and an apartment lease. When a lender does provide a mortgage on a unit, the result is that the shareholders become jointly and severally liable for the loan as guarantors.

The Uniform Common Interest Ownership Act includes the cooperative as a form of common interest community.

Condominiums

One tends to think of a condominium as a high-rise building. In fact, condominium ownership is far more flexible. A condominium may be a high-rise, but it also may be two, free-standing, single-family homes on one lot or on one parcel of land. Parking spaces and boat slips even have been "condominiumized." Condominiums may be either residential or commercial.

The key to the condominium form of ownership is *airspace*. Each owner of a condominium unit is the owner in fee simple of a defined airspace within a structure *(see Figure 4-2)* together with an undivided interest as a tenant in common in the common elements of the condominium. The *common elements* generally are the land and the condominium building, including all walls, floors and ceilings, common areas available to all owners, and any appurtenant easements and rights of way. Each owner, accordingly, owns only the airspace of his or her unit, the furniture and fixtures within the unit, and any interior partitions. Although a unit owner may obtain a loan to finance the purchase of her unit, other owners have no liability on that loan.

Certain of the common elements are limited common elements. In general, the *limited common elements* are the common elements limited to the exclusive use of one or more—but not all—unit owners. Limited common elements are balconies, utilities serving a particular unit, interior walls, and so forth. Common areas serving less than all owners, such as hallways, may be either limited or general common elements. The condominium declaration and map *(see Figures 4-1, 4-2, and 4-5)* identify which common elements are limited and which are general. It also may provide for the conversion of general common elements into limited common elements by the board of directors of the condominium association.

Specific documents, including a condominium declaration and a condominium map, are necessary to create a condominium. By the *condominium declaration*, the developer of the condominium project subjects the real estate to condominium ownership under statutory authorization. The condominium declaration creates the airspace that comprises each condominium unit and identifies each unit by letter or number. Each unit then may be conveyed by reference to its identifying letter or number, together with an appropriate reference to the declaration. For example, the following conveyance might be made:

> Unit B, Columbine Condominium, according to the Declaration therefor, recorded in book 549 at page 50, Carbon County records.

To provide an owners association for the management of the condominium regime, a nonprofit corporation is created, which may or may not be tax exempt under § 501(c)(7) of the Internal Revenue Code. Therefore, additional documents are necessary to complete the condominium regime, such as articles of incorporation and bylaws. Each unit owner is a member of the owners association. As with any corporation, the articles of incorporation provide for a board of directors (or board of managers) and the usual officers, who are responsible for management of the condominium association. The initial board of directors is appointed by the developer and thereafter is elected by the members of the association after the condominium units are sold. In multi-unit associations, the declaration typically provides for the appointment of a general manager, who assumes day-to-day responsibility for management.

In addition to creating the condominium form of ownership, the condominium declaration is the basic governing document of the condominium regime. It provides the rules that regulate ownership of a condominium unit and use of the common elements. A *right of first refusal* or *preemptive right*, which grants each owner a first right to purchase other units sold to third parties, may be included. The declaration also provides procedures for maintenance of the common elements, for construction of improvements, for repair or reconstruction of the building after damage or destruction, and for sale or reconstruction of the building when it becomes obsolete.

The condominium declaration gives each owner complete control of his or her unit and makes each owner responsible for the maintenance and repair of that unit. The declaration further establishes a condominium association whose board of directors has responsibility for management of the common elements. Other provisions of the declaration govern condominium ownership. For example, provisions may be included to require that condominium units cannot be modified without the consent of the condominium association or to place restrictions on pets, restrictions on the parking of automobiles, or other such "house rules." The declaration may also provide the developer with certain rights for future development or expansion of the complex and, if the Common Interest Ownership Act applies, may provide for termination of the developer's initial control of the board of directors of the condominium association.

In addition, the condominium declaration provides for assessment of charges for the management and maintenance of the condominium building and premises. These common expenses include such things as premiums for insurance on the building and the common elements, water and other utility charges, operation of recreational or other common facilities, maintenance of the common elements, and employment of a manager and other employees.

The board of directors (or board of managers) of the condominium association annually adopts a budget for common expenses and for the accrual of a reserve account for major maintenance items and emergencies. The declaration establishes the precise percentage of ownership of the common elements appurtenant to each unit, and the total assessment is divided according to those percentages. Thus, if the condominium contains four units of equal size, each unit will have a one-quarter interest in the common elements and a one-quarter responsibility for common expenses.

Each unit owner is billed either monthly or quarterly, and the amount of the assessment becomes a lien against the unit if it is not paid. This type of lien may be foreclosed in the same manner as any other lien. The condominium declaration also provides for the levy of special assessments and, frequently, for the fines as to unit owners who violate the rules contained in the declaration. The assessment lien usually is a first lien, except only for the lien of real estate taxes and a first mortgage or deed of trust.

Figure 4-1
Condominium Plat

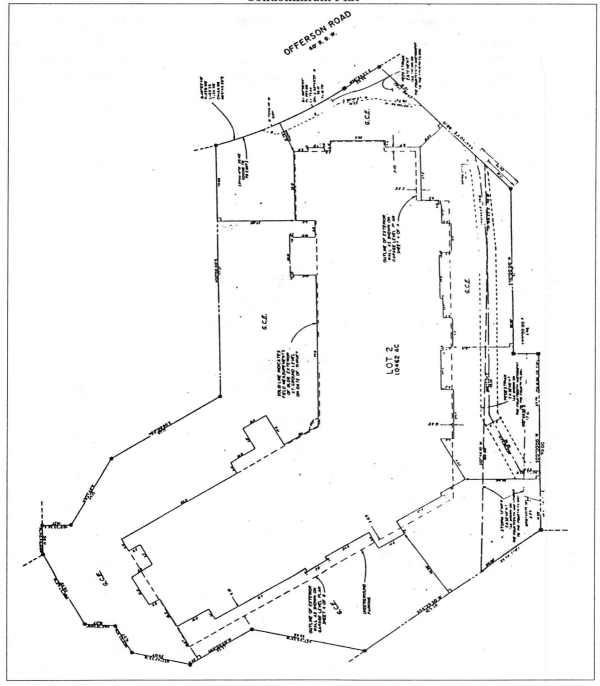

Associated with the condominium declaration (actually a part of the declaration under the Uniform Common Interest Ownership Act) is the condominium plat or map. The *as-built* plat or map, prepared by a registered engineer or land surveyor, describes the precise dimensions of each condominium unit (including vertical and horizontal dimensions in the case of a map but including only vertical dimensions in the case of a plat). The plat or map must be signed by the declarant (the condominium developer) and recorded in the county records along with the declaration.

Figure 4-2
Condominium Map

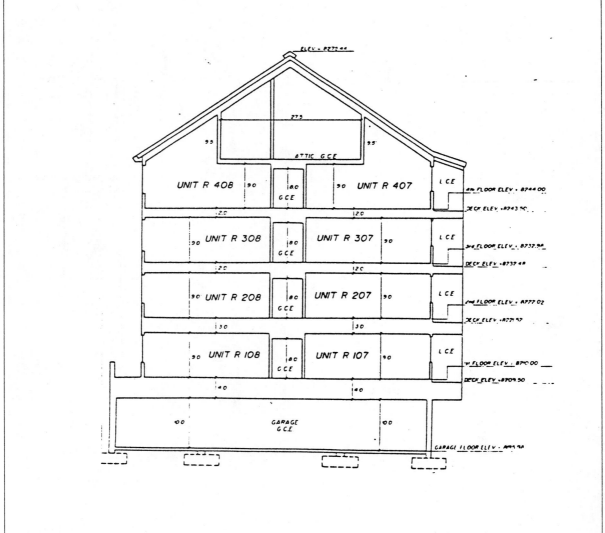

Planned Communities

The Uniform Common Interest Ownership Act also provides for a form of property ownership described as a planned community. The Act defines a *planned community* as "a common interest community that is not a condominium or cooperative." As such, the planned community covers the type of ownership traditionally associated with planned unit (clustered) developments and multiplex ownership (duplex, triplex, and the like). However, residential planned communities which contain no more than ten units and which have annual common expenses of no more than $300 a unit are exempt from the Act.

The planned unit development, or *pud*, is discussed in detail in Chapter 7. For present purposes, it may be described as a major residential real estate development, characterized by single-family homes (sometimes multi-family homes) located in clusters. Condominium ownership may be a part of the overall pud development. The remaining portion of the development is common area, which is owned by a nonprofit corporation such as an owners association.

Figure 4-3
Subdivision Map

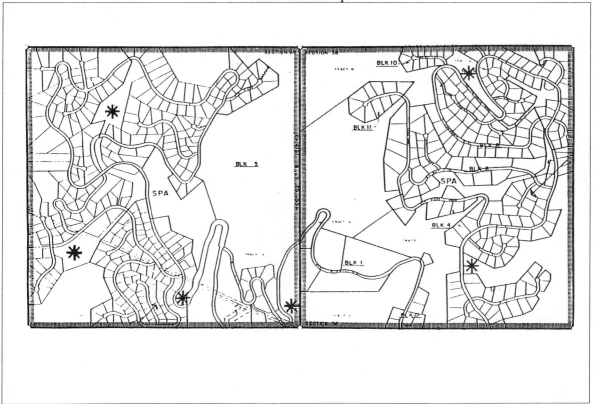

The documents necessary to create a planned unit development are a subdivision map, articles of incorporation and bylaws in connection with the owners association, and protective covenants. The declaration of *protective covenants*, like the condominium declaration, establishes the rules governing ownership within the development. Typically, protective covenants establish design guidelines for buildings within the development, including such things as minimum building size and height limitations. They also establish parking regulations and regulate such mundane matters as clothes lines, mail boxes, and trash dumpsters. The Uniform Common Interest Ownership Act includes protective covenants within the definition of a *declaration*. In other words, the Act makes no distinction between condominiums and planned communities in that regard. In each case, the declaration establishes the rules governing ownership.

A planned community also may take the form of a *multiplex*. Larger multiplexes may take the form of a *townhome development*. Smaller multiplexes generally consist of one building constructed on two or three separate, subdivided lots. Each lot and each contiguous portion of the building is a separate dwelling unit. The point at which the lots and contiguous portions of the buildings join is a *party wall*. A subdivision plat is prepared and recorded to show the location of each lot.

Figure 4-4
Party Wall Diagram

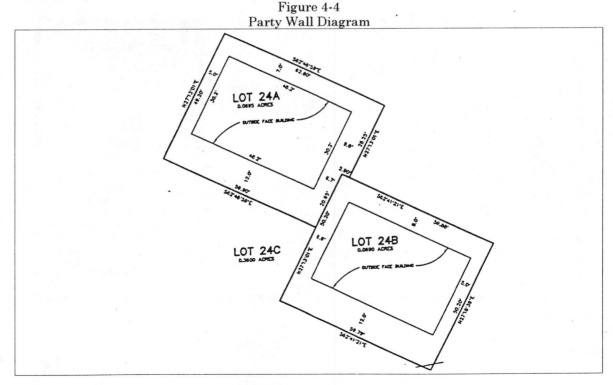

The relationship of adjacent owners with respect to the party wall is governed by a *party wall agreement* or *party wall declaration.* At a minimum, the document provides for maintenance and repair of the party wall. In the usual situation, it provides for maintenance, repair, and insurance of the entire building. It also may provide for the types of matters covered by the other forms of declarations already discussed. It likely provides for construction of improvements or additions to the building by one owner, requiring the consent of the other owner to do so.

No corporation or owners association is necessary, since each owner owns both the building and the adjacent portion of the lot, including yard and driveway. It is not unusual for the driveway to be a common one, use of which is governed by the declaration. The party wall agreement or declaration is signed and recorded by the developer of the multiplex; the owners of the various units of the multiplex become bound to it by accepting a deed that is subject to it *(see Figure 4-6).*

To summarize, the owner of a condominium owns only the airspace within the condominium building, together with an undivided interest in the common elements that she owns along with the owners of the other units. In a planned community, the property owner owns the land and the building (or portion of the building) constructed on the land. In a planned unit development (clustered housing), the residences generally are free-standing. The green areas are common elements, managed by an owners association. In a multiplex, the residences are joined by a party wall, and the rights of the owners are governed by a party wall agreement. Each owner separately owns his or her part of the green areas. What is called a duplex or multiplex may be a condominium in legal form. When this is so, it properly should be categorized as a condominium and not as a multiplex.

Time Share Estates

Time share estates are not governed by the Uniform Common Interest Ownership Act. In some states, time share estates can exist under legislation authorizing condominium ownership. Most states, however, have enacted legislation that deals specifically with this form of ownership.

The most common form of time share ownership is a leasehold. Each owner of a time share interest is granted an estate for years, usually fifty years, recurring annually in one week or longer time periods. The owner also has an interest in the remainder as a tenant in common with other lessees of the particular unit. During the time period assigned to a particular owner, she has an exclusive right to possess the unit.

In addition to the cost of the time share estate itself, a time share owner typically is required to pay a proportionate share of the common expenses. This type of ownership is used most often in connection with popular vacation sites around the country.

Figure 4-5
Condominium Declaration

Condominium Declaration for THE LEDGES

THIS CONDOMINIUM DECLARATION is made as of the 15th day of December, 1995, by THOMAS KAMASUKA and ACME CONSTRUCTION COMPANY, a Colorado corporation, together a Colorado general partnership, which declares hereby that "The Ledges" (as hereinafter defined) is and shall be held, transferred, sold, conveyed and occupied subject to the covenants, restrictions, easements, charges and liens hereinafter set forth and as a "common interest community" pursuant to the terms and provisions of the Act (as hereinafter defined).

1. **DEFINITIONS** The following words when used in this Declaration (unless the context shall prohibit) shall have the following meanings:

1.1 "Act" shall mean and refer to the Colorado Common Interest Ownership Act.

1.2 "Allocated Interests" or "Sharing Ratio" shall mean the percentage of the total undivided interests in the Common Elements allocated to a Condominium Unit pursuant to Section 4.1(b) hereof; and the percentage of the total liability for assessments for Common Expenses allocated to a Condominium Unit pursuant to Section 5.2(b) hereof. The formula utilized to determine the Sharing Ratio of each Condominium Unit is the ratio of the gross floor area of each Unit to the gross floor area of all Units.

1.3 "Association" shall mean and refer to **THE LEDGES CONDOMINIUM ASSOCIATION, INC.**, a Colorado corporation not for profit.

1.4 "Board of Directors" shall refer to the members of the Board of Directors of the Association.

1.5 "Common Elements" shall mean and refer to each portion of the Common Interest Community other than a Unit. Some of the Common Elements are identified on the Map as such or as "C.E." "Common Elements" shall also include the appurtenant easements and licenses described in Section 2.3 hereof.

1.6 "Condominium Unit" shall refer to a Unit together with the undivided interest in the Common Elements and the right to the exclusive use of the Limited Common Elements allocated thereto (which exclusive use may be shares with one or more other Condominium Units). An individual Condominium Unit may be referred to in the Declaration by reference to such Condominium Unit's "identifying number" (as such term is defined in the Act).

1.7 "Declarant" shall mean and refer to Thomas Kamasuka and Acme Construction Company, a Colorado corporation, together a Colorado general partnership, its successors and such of its assigns as to which the rights of Declarant hereunder are specifically assigned. Declarant may assign all or a portion of its rights hereunder, or all or a portion of such rights in connection with appropriate portions of The Ledges. In the event of such a partial assignment hereunder, the assignee shall not be deemed the Declarant, but may exercise such rights of Declarant specifically assigned to it. Any such assignment must be executed by Declarant and recorded in the public records of the County, and may be made on a non-exclusive basis.

1.8 "Limited Common Elements" shall mean any portion of the Common Elements which is now or hereafter designated in writing by the Declarant as such and assigned to a Unit or Units to be used (but not owned) by the Owner(s) or Member's Permittee(s) of such Unit(s) to the exclusion of Owner(s) of other Units (but not to the exclusion of the Declarant, the Association or applicable governmental bodies and authorities or utility companies). Some of the Limited Common Elements are identified on the Map as such or as "L.C.E." In the event that any Limited Common Elements are assigned to a Unit(s), the right to use (but not ownership of) such Limited Common Elements shall become an appurtenance to such Unit and shall pass with the title thereto, regardless of whether or not same is mentioned or provided in the deed or other instrument of conveyance of the Unit.

1.9 "Unit" shall mean a physical portion of The Ledges designated for separate ownership by individuals or entities the boundaries of which are determined from the Map together with (a) all fixtures and improvements contained within such boundaries; (b) the inner decorated finished surfaces of all walls, floors and ceilings which constitute such boundaries; (c) all doors and windows which constitute such boundaries; and (d) all space and interior, nonsupporting walls contained within such boundaries.

1.10 "Member" shall mean all Owners who are Members of the Association as provided in Section 3.1.

1.11 "Members' Permittee" shall mean a person described in Section 7.2 hereof.

1.12 "Owner" shall mean and refer to the record owner, whether one or more persons or entities, of the fee simple title to any Unit within The Ledges.

1.13　　　"Owner Control Date" shall mean and refer to a date which is no later than: (i) sixty (60) days after conveyance of twelve (12) Units to Owners other than the Declarant, or (ii) two (2) years after the last conveyance of a Unit by Declarant in the ordinary course of business, or (iii) two (2) years after any right to add new Units was last exercised.

1.14　　　"Plat" or "Map" shall mean and refer to the plat and map for The Ledges, recorded in the records of the Clerk and Recorder for Carbon County, Colorado, contemporaneously with the recording of this document.

1.16　　　"Special Declarant Rights" means the Special Declarant Rights as set forth in the Act and all rights reserved for the benefit of the Declarant as permitted by the Act, including, without limitation, the right: to complete improvements indicated on the Plat; to exercise any development right; to maintain sales offices, management offices, signs advertising The Ledges, and models; to use easements through the Common Elements for the purpose of making improvements within The Ledges or within real estate which may be added to The Ledges; or to appoint or remove any officer of the Association or any executive board member at all times during the Declarant Control Period.

1.17　　　"The Ledges" shall mean and refer to all such existing properties as set forth in Section 2.1 below, and additions thereto as are now or hereafter made subject to this Declaration.

2.　　　PROPERTY SUBJECT TO THIS DECLARATION; RIGHT TO ADD UNITS

2.1　　　_Legal Description_. The real property which is and shall be held, transferred, sold, conveyed and occupied subject to this Declaration is located in the Town of Oro, Carbon County, Colorado, and is more particularly described in Exhibit "A" attached hereto, all of which real property (and all additions and improvements thereto and less any withdrawals therefrom) is herein referred to collectively as "The Ledges" ("the Property").

2.2　_Right to Create Additional Units_. Declarant reserves the right to create, from time to time within ten (10) years following the recording of this Declaration, within the area described in Exhibit "B" attached hereto, a maximum of twelve (12) additional Units by recorded supplemental declarations, which shall not require the consent of then existing Owners, the Association or any Owner's mortgagee. Nothing herein, however, shall obligate the Declarant to create such additional Units. All Owners, by acceptance of a deed to, or other conveyance of, their Units, thereby automatically consent to any such creation of additional Units and shall evidence such consent in writing if requested to do so by the Declarant at any time (provided, however, that the refusal to give such written consent shall not avoid the general effect of this provision).

2.3　_Appurtenant Easement, Agreement and Licenses_. There shall be appurtenant to and a part of the Common Elements the rights and obligations of the following easement and agreement:

(a) Easement recorded January 30, 1987, in Book 456 at Page 749, Carbon County records and to be assigned to the Association upon completion of the additional units provided for in Section 2.2 hereof, or no later than ten years from the recording hereof if the rights provided for in Section 2.2 hereof are not exercised, for pedestrian and vehicular access to and egress from, and to provide utilities to, the Common Elements.

(b) Easements shown on the Plat or otherwise of record and appurtenant to the subject property.

Declarant hereby specifically limits use of the common areas adjacent to and underlying Gore Creek to fishing by the use of fly rods and flies only; all fish caught while fishing on common areas shall be released and returned to Gore Creek; all persons while fishing shall comply with all laws, rules and regulations of the Colorado Department of Wildlife. This covenant may be enforced by Declarant, the Members of the Association or any member of the public.

3.　　　MEMBERSHIP AND VOTING RIGHTS IN THE ASSOCIATION

3.1　　　_Membership_. Every person or entity who is a record Owner of a fee or undivided fee interest in any Unit shall be a Member of the Association. Notwithstanding anything else to the contrary set forth in this Section 3.1, any such person or entity who holds such interest merely as security for the performance of an obligation shall not be a Member of the Association.

3.2　　　_Voting Rights_. Each Member shall be entitled to one (1) vote for each Unit in which they hold the interests required for membership by Section 3.1. When more than one person holds such interest or interests in any Unit, all such persons shall be Members, and the vote for such Unit shall be exercised as they among themselves determine, but, in no event shall more than one (1) vote be cast with respect to any such Unit.

3.3　　　_The Board of Directors_. The affairs of the Association shall be managed by the Board, which may by resolution delegate any portion of its authority to an executive committee, a director or a managing agent. There shall be not less than three (3) nor more than (5) members of the Board, as set forth from time to time in the Bylaws, all of whom shall be Owners (or designees of the Declarant) and be elected by the Owners as specifically provided in, and subject to the limitations as set forth in, the Bylaws. Notwithstanding anything to the contrary herein, until the Owner Control Date, the officers and members of the board shall be appointed and removed as follows:

(a)　　　From the date that The Ledges is created to a date sixty (60) days after conveyance of four (4) Units to Owners other than Declarant, or persons designated by it, Declarant may appoint and remove the officers and members of the Board;

(b)　　　Thereafter to a date sixty (60) days after conveyance of eight (8) Units to Owners other than the Declarant, at least one member and not less than twenty-five percent (25%) of the members of the Board must be elected by owners other than Declarant;

(c)　　　Thereafter, and until the Owner Control Date, not less than thirty-three and one-third percent (33 1/3%) of the members of the Board must be elected by Owners other than Declarant;

(d)　　　Not later than the Owner Control Date, the Owners shall elect the Board, at least a majority of whom must be Owners other than Declarant;

(e)　　　The Owners, by a two-thirds (2/3) vote of all persons present and entitled to vote at any meeting of the Owners at which a quorum is present, may remove any member of the Board other than a member appointed by Declarant.

Notwithstanding the foregoing, the Declarant may voluntarily surrender the right to appoint and remove officers and members of the Board before the Owner Control Date, but, in that event, the Declarant shall have the right, until the Owner Control Date, to require certain actions of the Association or the board to be first approved in writing by Declarant before such actions become effective, provided said right is reserved in a recorded instrument executed by Declarant.

3.4　　　<u>General Matters</u>. When reference is made herein, or in the Articles, Bylaws, rules and regulations of the Association, management contracts or otherwise, to a majority or specific percentage of Members, such reference shall be deemed to be a reference to a majority or specific percentage of the votes of Members present at a duly constituted meeting thereof (i.e., one for which proper notice has been given and at which a quorum exists) and not of the Members themselves.

4.　　　<u>PROPERTY RIGHTS IN THE COMMON ELEMENTS; OTHER EASEMENTS</u>

4.1 <u>Condominium Units.</u> (a) The Property is hereby divided into four (4) Condominium Units designated as Condominium Units C11, C12, D25 and D26. Each Condominium Unit consists of the Unit identified by such Condominium Unit's identifying number on the Map, the undivided interest in the Common Elements allocated to such Condominium Unit pursuant to Section 4.1(b) hereof and the exclusive right to the Limited Common Elements allocated to such Condominium Unit pursuant to Section 4.1(c) hereof.

(b)　　　The total undivided interests in the Common Elements are hereby allocated to the Condominium Units in the following percentages:

Unit C11	39.26%
Unit C12	39.26%
Unit D25	10.74%
Unit D26	10.74%

(c)　　　Those portions of the Common Elements are Limited Common Elements which are assigned to the specific Condominium Units comprising each individual residence.

4.2　　　<u>Legal Description</u>. Any contract of sale, deed, lease, deed of trust, mortgage, will or other instrument affecting a Condominium Unit shall legally describe it substantially as follows:

"Condominium Unit _____, The Ledges, Town of Oro, Carbon County, Colorado, according to the Condominium Declaration for The Ledges Condominiums recorded on _____, 1994, in Book _____ at Page_____ of the real estate records of Carbon County, Colorado (collectively such declaration and map are hereinafter called the "Declaration");

Every such description shall be good and sufficient for all purposes to sell, convey, transfer, encumber, lease or otherwise affect not only the Condominium Unit, but also the interest in the Easements made appurtenant to such Condominium Unit by this Declaration. The interest in the Easements made appurtenant to any Condominium Unit shall be deemed conveyed or encumbered with that Condominium Unit, even though the legal description in the instrument conveying or encumbering such Condominium Unit may only refer to that Condominium Unit. The reference to the Declaration in any instrument shall be deemed to include any supplements or amendments to the Declaration, without specific reference thereto.

4.3　　　<u>Member Easements</u>. Each Member, and each Member's Permittee, shall have a non-exclusive permanent and perpetual easement over and upon the Common Elements (except, however, for the Limited Common Elements) for the intended use and enjoyment thereof in common with all other such Members and their Member's Permittees in such manner as may be regulated by the Association. Without limiting the generality of the foregoing, such rights of use and enjoyment are hereby made subject to the following:

(a)　　　The right and duty of the Association to levy assessments against each Unit for the purpose of maintaining the Common Elements in compliance with the provisions of this Declaration and with the restrictions on The Ledges (or portions thereof) from time to time recorded.

(b)　　　The Special Declarant Rights, which are hereby expressly reserved unto Declarant to the maximum extent permitted by the Act.

(c) The use restrictions set forth herein and the right of the Association to adopt at any time and from time to time, and to enforce rules and regulations governing, among other things, the use of the Common Elements and all facilities at any time situated thereon, including the right to fine Members as hereinafter provided. Any rule and/or regulation so adopted by the Association shall apply until rescinded or modified as if originally set forth at length in this Declaration.

(d)　　　The right to the use and enjoyment of the Common Elements and facilities thereon shall extend to all Members' Permittees, subject to regulation from time to time by the Association in its lawfully adopted rules and regulations.

(e)　　　The right of the Association to grant permits, licenses and both general ("blanket") and specific easements over, under and through the Common Elements.

(f)   The right of Declarant to withdraw certain property from The Ledges as is otherwise permitted herein.

(g)   The right of the Association to enter onto, under and into all Units, pursuant to Section 4.4 hereof, to make emergency repairs and to do other work necessary for the proper maintenance and operation of the Units and other portions of The Ledges.

4.4   <u>Easements Appurtenant.</u> The easements provided in Section 4.1 shall be appurtenant to and shall pass with the title to each Unit, but shall not be deemed to grant or convey any ownership interest in the Common Elements subject thereto.

4.5   <u>Common Elements Maintenance</u>. The Association shall at all times maintain in good repair and manage, operate and insure, and shall replace as often as necessary, the Common Elements and, to the extent not otherwise provided for, the paving, drainage structures, landscaping, street lighting fixtures and appurtenances, improvements and other structures (except public utilities) situated on the Common Elements, if any; all such work to be done as ordered by the Board of Directors of the Association.

The obligation of the Association to maintain the Common Elements shall include the obligation to pay the reasonable and necessary pro-rata cost of the maintenance of the improvements associated with the easements and licenses described in Section 2.3 hereof.

4.6   <u>Right of Entry</u>. There is hereby created an easement in favor of the Association and its applicable successors, assigns, employees, contractors and assignees over each Unit for the purpose of entering onto such Unit in the performance of the work herein described, provided that the notice requirements of this Declaration, if applicable, are complied with and any such entry is during reasonable hours, except in the case of an emergency.

4.7   <u>Utility and Access Easements - Common Elements and Units.</u> The use of the Common Elements for utilities and for access, as well as the use of the other utility and access easements as shown on the Plat or described in Section 2.3 hereof, shall be in accordance with the applicable provisions of this Declaration and the Plat. The Declarant shall have a perpetual easement over, upon and under the Common Elements for access and for installation, operation, maintenance, repair, replacement, alteration and expansion of utilities and/or cable television and security and other communication lines, equipment and materials and other similar underground installations for service to the Units and other portions of The Ledges.

In the event that any utility lines, equipment, meters or fixtures ("Utilities") are now or hereafter installed, a non-exclusive easement therefor, and for the initial installation (if applicable), maintenance, repair and replacement thereof, shall exist in favor of whichever of the applicable governmental authority, utility company, or the Association has the responsibility for the installation, maintenance, repair or replacement of the Utilities. The Owner(s) and the Member's Permittees of such Owner(s) shall not do anything in, on or about the Unit which interferes with the operation of any Utilities or the installation, maintenance, repair or replacement thereof. Any user of the easement herein created shall, promptly after the completion of any applicable work thereon, restore the property to the condition in which it existed immediately prior to the commencement of such use.

Easements are hereby reserved over the Common Elements in order to permit drainage and run-off from one Unit (and its improvements) to another or to the Elements or from the Common Elements to any Unit or Units.

4.8 <u>Ownership</u>. Beginning from the date this Declaration is recorded, the association shall be responsible for the maintenance, insurance and administration of the Common Elements, all of which is to be performed in a continuous and satisfactory manner without cost to the general taxpayers of the County or the Town. It is intended that all taxes (real, personal or otherwise) assessed against the Common Elements shall be (or have been, because the purchase prices of the Units have already taken into account their proportionate shares of the values of the Common Elements) proportionally assessed against and payable as part of the taxes of the applicable Units within The Ledges. However, in the event that, notwithstanding the foregoing, any such taxes are assessed directly against the Common Elements, the Association shall be responsible for the payment (subject to protest or appeal before or after payment) of same, including taxes on any improvements and any personal property located thereon, which taxes accrue from and after the date this Declaration is recorded, and such taxes shall be prorated between Declarant and the Association as of the date of such recordation. At all times prior to the date when all of the Units within The Ledges have been conveyed to a purchaser, Declarant and its affiliates shall have the right from time to time to enter upon the Common Elements and other portions of The Ledges for the purpose of the installation, construction, reconstruction, repair, replacement, operation, expansion and/or alteration of any improvements or facilities on the Common Elements that Declarant and its affiliates or designees elect to effect, and to use, without charge, the Common Elements and other portions of The Ledges owned by Declarant for sales, displays and signs or for any other purpose during the period of construction and sale of any portion of The Ledges. Without limiting the generality of the foregoing, the Declarant and its affiliates shall, at all times prior to the date when all of the Units are conveyed to a purchaser, have the specific right to maintain upon the Common Elements and any other portion of The Ledges owned by Declarant, sales, administrative, construction or other offices without charge, and appropriate easements of access and use are expressly reserved unto the Declarant and its affiliates, and its and their successors, assigns, employees and contractors, for this purpose. Any obligation (which shall not be deemed to be created hereby) to complete portions of the Common Elements shall, at all times, be subject and subordinate to these rights and easements and to the above-referenced activities.

5.   **COVENANT FOR MAINTENANCE ASSESSMENTS**

    5.1   <u>Creation of the Lien and Personal Obligation of the Assessments</u>. Except as provided elsewhere herein, the Declarant (and each party joining in any supplemental declaration), for all Units within The Ledges, hereby covenants and agrees, and each Owner of any Unit by acceptance of a deed therefor or other conveyance thereof, whether or not it shall be so expressed in such deed or other conveyance, shall be deemed to covenant and agree to pay to the Association assessments and charges for the operation of the Association and the maintenance, management, operation and insurance of the Common Elements as provided elsewhere herein, including such reasonable reserves as and only to the extent deemed necessary or desirable by the Association (there being no obligation for the maintenance of any such reserves), capital improvement assessments as provided elsewhere herein, assessments for maintenance and all other charges and assessments hereinafter referred to or lawfully imposed by the Association, all such assessments to be fixed, established and collected from time to time as herein provided. In addition, special assessments may be levied against particular Owners and Units for fines, expenses incurred against particular Units and/or Owners to the exclusion of others and other charges against specific Units or Owners as contemplated in this Declaration. The annual, special and other assessments, together with interest thereon and costs of collection thereof as are hereinafter provided, shall be a charge on the land and shall be a continuing lien upon the Unit against which each such assessment is made. Each such assessment, together with such interest thereon and costs of collection thereof as are hereinafter provided, shall also be the personal obligation of the person who is the Owner of such property at the time when the assessment fell due and all subsequent Owners until paid, except as provided in Section 5.9 below. Reference herein to assessments shall be understood to include reference to any and all of said charges whether or not specifically mentioned. Except as provided herein with respect to special assessments which may be imposed on one or more Units and Owners to the exclusion of others and in Section 5.10 below, all assessments imposed by the Association shall be imposed against all Units subject to its jurisdiction by application of the formula set forth in Section 5.2 below.

    5.2   <u>Rates of Assessments</u>. Subject to the provisions below and of Section 5.10, each Unit shall be assessed a proportionate amount of the total estimated operating expenses of the Association, such rates being as follows:

    (a) Until the Association establishes an annual assessment for Common Expenses for the initial fiscal year of the Association, Declarant shall pay all Common Expenses. The Association shall establish prior to the conveyance of any Unit by Declarant, an annual assessment with respect to the initial fiscal year of the Association for the purpose of paying or creating a reserve for Common Expenses.

    (b) Each Unit shall be responsible for, and assessed, a percentage of the estimated operating expenses of the Association, said percentage being set forth below and based generally upon the maximum available gross residential floor area ("GRFA") attributable to each Unit as it relates to the total maximum GRFA of all the Units:

Unit	Max. GRFA	Percentage
C11	2300	39.26
C12	2300	39.26
D25	629	10.74
D26	629	10.74

    (c) If additional Units are created pursuant to Section 2.2 hereof, the percentage of the estimated operating expenses for which each Unit shall be responsible shall be reallocated among all Units based upon the same formula.

    5.3   <u>Purpose of Assessments</u>. The regular assessments levied by the Association shall be used exclusively for the purposes expressed in Section 5.1.

    5.4   <u>Special Assessments</u>. In addition to the regular and capital improvement assessments which are or may be levied hereunder, the Association (through the Board of Directors) shall have the right to levy special assessments against an Owner(s) to the exclusion of other Owners for: (i) the repair or replacement of damage to any portion of the Common Elements (including, without limitation, improvements and landscaping thereon) caused by the misuse, negligence or other action or inaction of a particular Owner or Owners or such Owner's Member's Permittee(s); or (ii) the costs of work performed by the Association in accordance with Section 4.3 of this Declaration. Any such special assessment shall be subject to all of the applicable provisions of this Section 5 including, without limitation, lien filing and foreclosure procedures and late charges and interest. Any special assessment levied hereunder shall be due within the time specified by the Board of Directors in the action imposing such assessment.

    5.5   <u>Capital Improvements</u>. Funds which, in the aggregate, exceed ten percent (10%) of the total amount of the current operating budget of the Association in any one fiscal year which are necessary for the addition of capital improvements (as distinguished from repairs and maintenance) relating to the Common Elements and which have not previously been collected as reserves or are not otherwise available to the Association (other than by borrowing), shall be levied by the Association as special assessments only upon approval of a majority of the Board of Directors of the Association and upon approval by two-thirds (2/3) favorable vote of the Members of the Association voting at a meeting or by ballot as may be provided in the Bylaws of the Association. Any funds which do not exceed ten percent (10%) of the total amount of the current operating budget of the Association and which are necessary for the addition of capital improvements (as distinguished from repairs and maintenance) relating to the

Common Elements, shall be levied by the Association as special assessments, without requiring any consent by the Owners. The ability of the Association to levy such a Capital Improvement Assessment may be restricted by, and may only be implemented in accordance with, the Act.

    5.6   <u>Date of Commencement of Annual Assessments; Due Dates</u>. Each annual assessment shall be imposed for the year beginning January 1 and ending December 31. The annual assessments shall be payable in advance, in quarterly installments, or in annual, semi-annual or monthly installments if so determined by the Board of Directors of the Association (absent which determination they shall be payable quarterly). Except as fixed in Section 5.2 above, the assessment amount (and applicable installments) may be changed at any time by said Board from that originally stipulated or from any other assessment that is in the future adopted and the original assessment for any year shall be levied for the calendar year (to be reconsidered and amended, if necessary, every six (6) months), but the amount of any revised assessment to be levied during any period shorter than a full calendar year shall be in proportion to the number of months (or other appropriate installments) remaining in such calendar year. The due date of any special assessment or capital improvement assessment shall be fixed in the Board resolution authorizing such assessment.

    5.7   <u>Duties of the Board of Directors</u>. The Board of Directors shall adopt an annual budget for the Association prior to the ensuing fiscal year of the Association and fix the date of commencement and the amount of the assessment against each Unit subject to the Association's jurisdiction for each assessment period, to the extent practicable, at least thirty (30) days in advance of such date or period, and shall, at that time, prepare a roster of the Units and assessments applicable thereto which shall be kept in the office of the Association and shall be open to inspection by any Owner. Written notice of the assessment shall thereupon be sent to every Owner subject thereto thirty (30) days prior to payment of the first installment thereof, except as to the special assessments. In the event no such notice of a change in the assessments for a new assessment period is given, the amount payable shall continue to be the same as the amount payable for the previous period, until changed in the manner provided for herein. Subject to other provisions hereof, the Association shall upon demand at any time furnish to any owner liable for an assessment a certificate in writing signed by an officer of the Association, setting forth whether such assessment has been paid as to any particular Unit. Such certificate shall be conclusive evidence of payment of any assessment to the Association therein stated to have been paid. The Association, through the action of its Board of Directors, shall have the power, but not the obligation, to enter into an agreement or agreements from time to time with one or more persons, firms or corporations for management services. The Association shall have all other powers provided in its Articles of Incorporation and Bylaws. Notwithstanding the provisions of Section 5.6 above and this Section 5.7, the establishment of the annual assessments shall comply with the requirements of CRS 38-33.3-315 and 38-33.3-303(4).

    5.8   <u>Effect of Non-Payment of Assessment; the Personal Obligation; the Lien; Remedies of the Association</u>. If the assessments (or installments provided for herein) are not paid on the date(s) when due (being the date(s) specified herein), then such assessments (or installments) shall become delinquent and shall, together with late charges, interest and the cost of collection thereof as hereinafter provided, thereupon become a continuing lien on the Unit which shall bind such property in the hands of the then Owner, his heirs, personal representatives, successors and assigns. Except as provided in Section 5.9 below to the contrary, the personal obligation of the then owner to pay such assessment shall pass to his successors in title and recourse may be had against either or both.

    If any installment of an assessment is not paid within fifteen (15) days after the due date, at the option of the Association, a late charge not greater than the amount of such unpaid installment (the exact amount to be determined by the Board) may be imposed (provided that only one late charge may be imposed on any one unpaid installment and if such installment is not paid thereafter, it and the late charge shall accrue interest as provided herein but shall not be subject to additional late charges, provided further, however, that each other installment thereafter coming due shall be subject to one late charge each as aforesaid) and all such sums shall earn interest from the dates when due until paid at eighteen percent (18%) per annum and the Association may bring an action at law against the Owner(s) personally obligated to pay the same, may record a claim of lien (as evidence of its lien rights as hereinabove provided for) against the Unit on which the assessments and late charges are unpaid, may foreclose the lien against the Unit on which the assessments and late charges are unpaid, or may pursue one or more of such remedies at the same time or successively, and attorneys' and paralegals' fees and costs actually incurred preparing and filing the claim of lien and the complaint, if any, and prosecuting same, in such action (and any appeals therefrom) shall be added to the amount of such assessments, late charges and interest, and in the event a judgment is obtained, such judgment shall include all such sums as above provided and attorneys' and paralegals' fees actually incurred together with the costs of the action, through all applicable appellate levels.

    In addition to the rights of collection of assessments stated in this Section, any and all persons acquiring title to or an interest in a Unit as to which the assessment is delinquent, including without limitation persons acquiring title by operation of law and by judicial sales, shall not be entitled to the occupancy of such Unit or the enjoyment of the Common Elements until such time as all unpaid and delinquent assessments due and owing from the selling Owner have been fully paid; provided, however, that the provisions of this sentence shall not be applicable to the mortgagees and purchasers as provided in Section 5.9.

    It shall be the legal duty and responsibility of the Association to enforce payment of the assessments hereunder. Failure of the Association to send or deliver bills shall not, however, relieve Owners from their obligations hereunder.

All assessments, late charges, interest, penalties, fines, attorney's fees and other sums provided for herein shall accrue to the benefit of the Association.

Owners shall be obligated to deliver the documents originally received from the Declarant, containing this and other declarations and documents, and any amendments thereto hereafter adopted to any grantee of such Owner.

5.9   Priority of the Lien to Mortgages. The lien of the assessments provided for in this Section 5 shall be prior to the lien of any first mortgage to the extent of: (i) an amount equal to the common expense assessments based on a periodic budget adopted by the Association under Section 38-33.3-315(1), C.R.S., which would have become due, in the absence of any acceleration, during the six (6) months immediately preceding institution of an action to enforce the lien, but in no event shall the priority referenced above to such lien exceed one hundred fifty percent (150%) of the average monthly assessment during the immediately preceding fiscal year multiplied by six (6); and (ii) attorneys' fees and costs incurred in an action to enforce the lien.

5.10 Association Funds. The portion of all regular assessments collected by the Association for reserves for future expenses, and the entire amount of all special assessments and capital improvement assessments, shall be held by the Association and may be invested in interest bearing accounts or in certificates of deposit or other like instruments or accounts available at banks or savings and loan institutions the deposits of which are insured by an agency of the United States.

6.   CERTAIN RULES AND REGULATIONS
6.1   Applicability. The provisions of this Article 6 shall be applicable to all of The Ledges.
6.2   Land Use and Building Type. No Unit shall be used except for single-family residential purposes, unless otherwise approved by the Board. In no event shall any portion of The Ledges be used for any unlawful purposes or in a manner which is or becomes noxious, offensive, unhealthy or harmful as a result of generating fumes, dust, smoke, noise, vibration, extraordinary waste or toxic or hazardous waste.
6.3   Nuisances. Nothing shall be done in any Unit which may be or become an annoyance or nuisance to others within The Ledges. Any activity in a Unit which interferes with television, cable or radio reception on another Unit shall be deemed a nuisance and a prohibited activity. In the event of a dispute or question as to what may be or become a nuisance, such dispute or question shall be submitted to the Board of Directors, which shall render a decision in writing, and such decision shall be dispositive of such dispute or question.
6.4   Pets. Owners may have pets in their Units, provided that the pets do not become a nuisance or annoyance to any neighbor by reason of barking or otherwise and provided further that no such pets are raised, bred or kept for any commercial purpose. No pets shall be permitted to have excretions on any Common Elements, except areas designated by the Association, if any, and Owners shall be responsible to clean up any such excretions. ALL PETS SHALL BE KEPT ON A LEASH WHEN NOT IN THE APPLICABLE UNIT, IF ANY. Pets shall also be subject to all applicable rules and regulations.
6.5   Commercial Trucks, Trailers, Campers and Boats. No vehicle having a shell, camper, trailer or other attachment, or commercial vehicles, campers, mobile homes, motorhomes, house trailers or trailers of every other description, recreational vehicles, boats, boat trailers, horse trailers or vans, shall be permitted to be parked or to be stored at any place within The Ledges, nor in dedicated areas, except in a garage. For purposes of this Section, "commercial vehicles" shall mean those which are not designed and used for customary, personal/family purposes. The absence of commercial-type lettering or graphics on a vehicle shall not be dispositive as to whether it is a commercial vehicle. The prohibitions on parking contained in this Section shall not apply to temporary parking of trucks and commercial vehicles, such as for providing pick-up and delivery, nor to passenger-type vans or utility vehicles with windows for personal use which are in acceptable condition in the sole opinion of the Board (which favorable opinion may be changed at any time), nor to any construction vehicles or trailers during periods of construction within The Ledges.

In all cases, vehicles kept within The Ledges shall be roadworthy, including, without limitation, not having flat tires, being in operating condition and having a current license plate/registration. No owner of any Unit and no permittee of any owner of any Unit shall park more than two vehicles per Unit at any time. Vehicles shall be parked only in designated parking areas.

Subject to applicable laws and ordinances, any vehicle parked in violation of these or other restrictions contained herein or in the rules and regulations now or hereafter adopted, including, without limitation, leaking oil or other fluids, may be towed by the Association at the sole expense of the owner of such vehicle if such vehicle remains in violation for a period of 24 hours from the time a notice of violation is placed on the vehicle. The Association shall not be liable to the owner of such vehicle for trespass, conversion or otherwise, nor guilty of any criminal act, by reason of such towing and once the notice is posted, neither its removal, nor failure of the owner to receive it for any other reason, shall be grounds for relief of any kind. An affidavit of the person posting the aforesaid notice stating that it was properly posted shall be conclusive evidence of proper posting.

6.6   Garbage and Trash Disposal. No garbage, refuse, trash or rubbish (including materials for recycling) shall be deposited except as permitted by the Association. The requirements from time to time of the applicable governmental authority (or other company or association) for disposal or collection of waste shall be complied with. All trash must be bagged in sturdy plastic bags of not more than 30 gallons and shall be kept in a clean and sanitary condition. Such containers may not be placed out for collection sooner than 6 hours prior to scheduled collection. In the event that the Association, in its sole discretion, provides depositories for recyclable materials, the same shall be the only ones used in The Ledges and shall be collected by a private entity hired by the Association or public authority, if available.

    6.7   Prohibited Activities.

      (a) No clothing, laundry or wash shall be aired or dried on any portion of The Ledges.

      (b) Storage of items of personal property shall not be permitted on decks or outside of Units. Nor shall items of personal property be hung from decks or be enclosed under decks.

      (c) There shall be no permanent installation of items of personal property outside of Units such as swings or yard games.

    6.8   Leases. All leases shall be in writing, shall be approved as to form by the Association and shall provide (and if they fail to so provide, shall be automatically deemed to provide as if expressly included therein) that the Association shall have the right to terminate the lease in the name of and as agent for the lessor upon default by tenant in observing any of the provisions of this Declaration, the Articles of Incorporation and Bylaws of the Association, applicable rules and regulations, or other applicable provisions of any agreement, document or instrument governing The Ledges or administered by the Association. No lease shall be terminated pursuant to this section except by action of the Board of Directors taken at a meeting after at least seven (7) days notice to the Owner.

    6.9   Architectural Control. No building, wall, fence or other structure or improvement of any nature to the limited common elements (including, but not limited to, the screen enclosures, patios (or patio expansions), hedges or landscaping, exterior paint or finish, play structures, awnings, shutters, basketball hoops, decorative plaques or accessories, birdhouses, other pet houses, lighting fixtures, antennae, satellite dishes, signage, asphalting, or other improvements or changes of any kind, even if not permanently affixed to the land or to other improvements) shall be erected, placed or altered on, or removed until the construction plans and specifications and a plan showing the location of the structure (and landscaping, if any) and of the materials proposed to be used, all as may be required by the Board of Directors, have been approved in writing by the Board of Directors and all necessary governmental permits are obtained. Each building, wall, fence or other structure or improvements of any nature, together with landscaping, shall be erected, placed or altered upon the limited common elements only in accordance with the plans and specifications so approved and applicable governmental permits and requirements. Refusal of approval of plans, specifications and materials, or any of them, may be based on any ground, including purely aesthetic grounds, in the sole and uncontrolled discretion of the Board of Directors. Any change in the exterior appearance of any building, wall, fence or other structure or improvements, and any change in the appearance of the landscaping, shall be deemed an alteration requiring approval. The Board of Directors shall have the power to promulgate such rules and regulations as it deems necessary to carry out the provisions and intent of this Section.

    In the event that any new improvement or landscaping is added, or any existing improvement is altered, in violation of this Section, the Association shall have the right (and an easement and license) to enter upon the applicable limited common elements and remove or otherwise remedy the applicable violation after giving the Owner of the Unit at least ten (10) days prior written notice of, and opportunity to cure, the violation in question. The costs of such remedial work and a surcharge equal to twenty-five percent (25%) of the costs shall be a special assessment against the Unit, which assessment shall be payable upon demand and secured by the lien for assessments provided for in this Declaration.

    The approval of any proposed improvements or alterations by the Board of Directors shall not constitute a warranty or approval as to, and the Association or the Board of Directors shall not be liable for, the safety, soundness, workmanship, materials or usefulness for any purpose of any such improvement or alteration nor as to its compliance with governmental or industry codes or standards. By submitting a request for the approval of any improvement or alteration, the requesting Owner shall be deemed to have automatically agreed to hold harmless and indemnify the Board of Directors and the Association generally, from and for any loss, claim or damages connected with the aforesaid aspects of the improvements or alterations.

    The foregoing provisions shall not be applicable to the Declarant or its affiliates or to construction activities conducted by the Declarant or such affiliates.

    6.10   Variances; Exceptions. The Board of Directors of the Association shall have the right and power to grant variances from the provisions of this Section 6 for good cause shown, as determined in the reasonable discretion of the board. No variance granted as aforesaid shall alter, waive or impair the operation or effect of the provisions of this Section 6 in any instance in which such variance is not granted. Notwithstanding anything to the contrary, the provisions of this Section 6 shall not be applicable to the Declarant (or any of its designees) or Units or other property owned by the Declarant (or such designees).

7.   RESALE OF UNITS; OCCUPANCY RESTRICTIONS

    7.1   Estoppel Certificate. Upon fourteen (14) days prior written notice from any Owner or any mortgagee or prospective mortgagee of a Unit, the Association shall issue a written statement setting forth the amount of the unpaid assessment, if any, with respect to the subject Unit, the amount of the current assessment installment, the date such assessment installment becomes due, the amount of the balance of such Owner's reserve on deposit with the Association and any credit for advanced payments for prepaid items, including, without limitation, insurance premiums, which statement shall be conclusive upon the Association in favor of all persons who rely thereon in good faith. Unless a request for such a statement shall be fulfilled in writing in accordance with the foregoing, all unpaid assessment installments which become due prior to the making of such a request shall be subordinate to the interest of the person requesting such statement.

    7.2   Members' Permittees. No Unit shall be occupied by any person other than the Owner(s) thereof or the applicable Members' Permittees and in no event other than as a residence. For purposes of this Declaration, Members' Permittees shall be the following persons and such persons' families and/or guests: (i) an individual Owner, (ii) an officer, director, stockholder or employee of a corporate owner, (iii) a partner in or an employee of a partnership owner, (iv) a fiduciary or beneficiary of an ownership in trust, (v) occupants named or described in a lease or sublease, or (vi) short-term tenants. In no event shall occupancy (except for temporary occupancy by guests) exceed two (2) adult persons per bedroom. The Board of Directors shall have the power to authorize occupancy of a Unit by persons in addition to those set forth above.

    As used herein, "family" or words of similar import shall be deemed to include a spouse, children, parents, brothers, sisters, grandchildren, domestic employees of the Owner and other persons permanently cohabiting in the Unit as or together with the Owner or permitted occupant thereof. As used herein "guest" or words of similar import shall include only those persons who have a principal residence other than the Unit. Unless otherwise determined by the Board of Directors of the Association, a person(s) occupying a Unit for more than one (1) month shall not be deemed a guest but, rather, shall be deemed a lessee for purposes of this Declaration (regardless of whether a lease exists or rent is paid) and shall be subject to the provisions of this Declaration which apply to leases and lessees.

8.   ENFORCEMENT

    8.1   Compliance by Owners. Every Owner and Member's Permittee shall comply with the restrictions and covenants set forth herein and any and all rules and regulations which from time to time may be adopted by the Board of Directors of the Association.

    8.2   Enforcement. Failure of an Owner or his Member's Permittee to comply with such restrictions, covenants or rules and regulations shall be grounds for immediate action which may include, without limitation, an action to recover sums due for damages, injunctive relief, or any combination thereof. The offending Owner shall be responsible for all costs of enforcement including attorneys' and paralegals' fees actually incurred and court costs, including those relating to appeals.

9.   INSURANCE AND MAINTENANCE

    9.1   Common Areas. The Association shall keep all improvements, facilities and fixtures located within the Common Elements insured against loss or damage by fire or other casualty for the full insurable replacement value thereof (with reasonable deductibles and normal exclusions for land, foundations, excavation costs and similar matters), and may obtain insurance against such other hazards and casualties as the Association may deem desirable. The Association may also insure any other property, whether real or personal, owned by the Association, against loss or damage by fire and such other hazards as the Association may deem desirable, with the Association as the owner and beneficiary of such insurance for and on behalf of itself and all Members. The insurance coverage with respect to the Common Elements and the Limited Common Elements shall be written in the name of, and the proceeds thereof shall be payable to, the Association. Insurance proceeds shall be used by the Association for the repair or replacement of the property for which the insurance was carried. The costs of obtaining and maintaining all insurance which is carried by the Association pursuant to the provisions hereof shall be a Common Expense to be prorated among all Owners as set forth in the Declaration, notwithstanding the fact that the Owners may have disproportionate liability.

    9.2   Waiver of Subrogation. As to each policy of insurance maintained by the Association which will not be voided or impaired thereby, the Association hereby waives and releases all claims against the Board, the officers of the Association, the Members, Declarant and the agents and employees of each of the foregoing, with respect to any loss covered by such insurance, whether or not caused by negligence of or breach of any agreement by said persons, but only to the extent that insurance proceeds are received in compensation for such loss. Further, each policy shall comply with the requirements of CRS 38-33.3-313(4).

    9.3   Liability and Other Insurance. The Association shall have the power to and shall obtain comprehensive public liability insurance, including medical payments and malicious mischief, with coverage of at least $1,000,000.00 (if available at reasonable rates and upon reasonable terms) for any single occurrence, insuring against liability for bodily injury, death and property damage arising from the activities of the Association or with respect to property under its jurisdiction, including, if obtainable, a cross liability endorsement insuring each Member against liability to each other Member and to the Association and vice versa. The Association may also obtain Worker's Compensation insurance and other liability insurance as it may deem desirable, insuring each Member and the Association and its Board of Directors and officers, from liability in connection with the Common Elements, the premiums for which shall be Common Expenses and included in the assessments made against the Members. The Association may also obtain such other insurance as the Board deems appropriate. All insurance policies shall be reviewed at least annually by the Board of Directors and the limits increased in its discretion. The Board may also obtain such errors and omissions insurance, indemnity bonds, fidelity bonds and other insurance as it deems advisable, insuring the Board, the officers of the Association, the Members or any management company engaged by the Association against any liability for any act or omission in carrying out their obligations hereunder, or resulting from their membership on the Board or any committee thereof. At a minimum, however, there shall be blanket fidelity bonding of anyone (compensated or not) who handles or is responsible for funds held or administered by the Association, with the Association to be an obligee thereunder. Such bonding shall cover the maximum funds to be in the hands of the Association or management company during the time the bond is in force. In addition, the fidelity bond coverage must at least equal the sum of three (3) months of regular assessments, plus all reserve funds.

9.4 <u>Maintenance by Owners</u>.

(a)   Each Owner shall be responsible for the following maintenance and repair of the following portions of such Owner's Condominium Unit:

(i) the maintenance and repair of the interior and exterior doors and windows (except for the painting of exterior doors and windows which shall be an Association expense) of such Owner's residence;

(ii) the maintenance and repair of the water, sewer, electrical, natural gas, telephone and other utility services located within such Owner's Residence; and

(iii) the maintenance and repair of the Limited Common Elements allocated to the interior of such Owner's residence, including, but not limited to the maintenance, repair or replacement of heat exchanges, hot tubs, chimneys or flues or other mechanical devices serving that unit only. If any such Limited Common Element is assigned to more than one Unit, such expense shall be shared equally among the Units to which it is assigned. Each Unit Owner shall be responsible for removing all snow and debris from all patios and balconies which are Limited Common Elements appurtenant to his or her Unit. If any such Limited Common Element is appurtenant to more than one Unit, the Owners of those Units will be jointly responsible for such removal.

(b)   In performing the maintenance or repair required by Section 9.4 (a) hereof, no Owner shall do any act or work which impairs or otherwise affects the Common Elements. If, in the reasonable judgment of the Association, an Owner has failed to maintain those portions of such Owner's Unit, which such Owner is required to maintain in a clean, safe, attractive and sightly condition and in good repair consistent with the high standards of The Ledges, the Association may, after 10 days notice to such Owner, perform all work deemed necessary by the Association to place such Unit in conformity with the foregoing standards and shall have access to such Unit for such purposes. The Association shall be reimbursed by the Owner who or which failed to adequately maintain such Owner's Unit for all costs of the work performed by the Association pursuant to the authorization contained in the preceding sentence, for interest on such costs from the date incurred at the annual rate of 18 percent and for all costs of collection of the amounts to be reimbursed, including reasonable attorneys' fees.

9.5 <u>Maintenance by the Association</u>.

(a)   The Association shall be responsible for the following maintenance and repair:

(i) those portions of the Units which are not required by Section 9.04 (a) hereof to be maintained by the Owners, and

(ii) the Common Elements.

(iii) the Parking Spaces.

(b)   the costs of the maintenance and repair required by Section 9.05 (a) hereof shall be a Common Expense. If, however, the need to perform such maintenance results from the negligence or intentional act of an Owner or such Owner's Permittees, such Owner shall reimburse the Association for all costs of such maintenance and repair, for interest on such costs from the date incurred at the annual rate of 18 percent and for all costs of collection of the amounts reimbursed including, without limitation, reasonable attorneys' fees.

10.   DAMAGE OR DESTRUCTION

10.1.   <u>Damage or Destruction to Common Elements Improvements</u>. In the event of any damage or destruction to any improvements included within the Common Elements which are not a part of the residences by fire or other casualty, the Association shall promptly cause such improvements to be repaired and restored, utilizing available insurance proceeds therefor, and if such improvements must be substantially rebuilt, the design of such improvements shall be substantially similar to the original design of such improvements. If the proceeds of insurance are insufficient to pay all costs of repairing and restoring such improvements, the difference between the insurance proceeds and such costs will be a Common Expense.

10.2.   <u>Less Than Catastrophic Damage to the Residences</u>. Any damage to any improvements comprising a residence which the Association reasonably estimates will involve costs of repair or restoration in excess of 75 percent of the insured value of the residence as shown on the schedule of insured values attached to the policy of property damage insurance described in Section 10.1 hereof shall be referred to in this Section as "catastrophic." In case of any damage to any residence by fire or other casualty which is less than catastrophic, the Association shall promptly cause the residence to be repaired and restored, utilizing available insurance proceeds therefor, and, if the residence must be substantially rebuilt, the design of the residence shall be substantially similar to the original design of the residence. If the proceeds of insurance are insufficient to pay all costs of repairing and restoring the residence, the difference between the insurance proceeds and such costs shall be a Common Expense.

10.3.   Catastrophic Damage to or Destruction of Residences. In case of any catastrophic damage to or destruction of any residence or residences by fire or other casualty, the Association shall not take any action to repair or restore the residence for a period of one month after the occurrence of such fire or other casualty except for such actions as may be required to protect the safety of Owners and Permittees. If the Association receives written directions from all Owners and first mortgagees during such one month period directing the Association not to rebuild the residence or residences, the Association shall cause the residence or residences to be razed and the land which constitutes the Property to be graded to a reasonably attractive condition and the Association shall sell the Property in accordance with the provisions of Section 10.04 hereof. If the Association does not receive such written directions from all Owners and first mortgagees during such one month period, the Association shall promptly cause such residence or residences to be repaired and restored in accordance with the provisions of Section 10.02 hereof.

10.4.   Sale of Property. If the Association is required to sell the land which constitutes the Property pursuant to the provision of Section 10.03 hereof, or any portion thereof, the Association (as attorney-in-fact for the Owners) shall execute and record in the real estate records of Carbon County, Colorado, a notice of such facts, and thereafter shall sell the Property or portion thereof free and clear of the provisions of the Declaration. In the event of such sale, the proceeds of insurance and the proceeds of such sale, to the extent paid over to the Association, shall be applied first to the payment of expenses of the Association incurred to make safe and raze the residence or residences, to grade such land and to conduct such sale. The net amount of such proceeds shall then be apportioned by the Association among the Owners based upon the relative insured values of the Units as determined from the schedule of insured values attached to the policy of property damage insurance described in Section 10.1 hereof; or, if such policy does not contain such insured values, such proceeds shall be apportioned among the Owners in accordance with their sharing ratios. The net amount of such proceeds so apportioned shall be held by the Association on account for the Owners in a separate account for each Unit to be applied (without contribution from one account to another) by the Association for the following purposes in the order indicated: (i) for payment of taxes and special assessment liens in favor of any assessing entity; (ii) for payment of the balance of the indebtedness secured by the lien of a first mortgagee; (iii) for payment of unpaid assessments, charges and other amounts due the Association; (iv) for payment of junior liens and encumbrances in the order of and to the extent of their priority; and (v) the balance remaining, if any, shall be paid to the Owners.

10.5.   First Mortgagees. Promptly after the occurrence of any fire or other casualty which causes damage to any residence or residences or any other improvements included within the Common Elements which, in either case, the Association estimates will cost $10,000 or more to repair, the Association shall deliver written notice thereof to all first mortgagees. The delivery of such written notice shall not be construed as imposing any liability whatever on any first mortgagee to pay all or any part of the costs of repair or restoration. Further, the provisions of Section 10.4 hereof shall not be construed as limiting in any way the right of a first mortgagee (in case the proceeds allocated under Section 10.4 shall be insufficient to pay the indebtedness held by such first mortgagee) to assert and enforce the personal liability for such deficiency of the person or persons responsible for payment of such indebtedness.

11.   RESTORATION AND TERMINATION OF THE LEDGES

11.1.   Restoration. If at any time the Owners entitled to vote at least 80 percent of the votes of the Association and all first mortgagees shall agree that all Units have become obsolete and shall approve a plan for their renovation or restoration, the Association (as attorney-in-fact for the Owners) shall promptly cause such renovation or restoration to be made according to such plan. All Owners shall be bound by the terms of such plan and the costs of the work shall be a Common Expense.

11.2.   Termination. If at any time an agreement to terminate The Ledges is obtained from Owners entitled to vote at least 80 percent of the votes of the Association and all first mortgagees in accordance with the provisions of Section 218 of the Act, the Association (as attorney-in-fact for the Owners) shall promptly undertake the action required of the Association under the provisions of Section 218 of the Act.

12.   CONDEMNATION

12.1.   Entire Taking. Subject to the terms of any first deed of trust, if the entire Property shall be taken under any statute, by right of eminent domain, or by purchase in lieu thereof, or if any part of the Property shall be so taken and the part remaining shall not permit the continuance of any of the uses of the Property prior to such taking, the Association (as attorney-in-fact for the Owners) shall collect the award made in such taking and shall sell the part of the Property remaining after the taking, if any, free and clear of the provisions of this Declaration which shall wholly terminate and expire upon the recording of a notice by the Association setting forth all of such facts. The award and the proceeds of such sale, if any, shall be collected, apportioned and applied by the Association in the manner provided in Section 10.04 hereof.

12.2.   Partial Taking. Subject to the terms of any First Lien, if a taking occurs other than a taking specified in Section 12.01 hereof and within one month after the date of such taking the Owners entitled to vote at least 80 percent of the votes of the Association and all first mortgagees agree to restore the portion of the Property not so taken, then the Association (as attorney-in-fact for the Owners) shall collect the award made in such taking and shall promptly cause the portion of the Property not so taken to be restored as nearly as possible to its conditions prior to the taking, applying such award to that purpose. In the event of such restoration, the difference between the award made in such taking and the costs of such restoration shall be a Common Expense. In the event of such restoration, the difference between the award made in such taking and the costs of such restoration shall be a Common Expense. In the event of such restoration any part of the award not required for such restoration shall be apportioned among the Owners on the same basis as insurance proceeds are apportioned among the Owners pursuant to Section 10.4 hereof. In the event of a partial taking and in further event such restoration is not required as set forth in the first sentence of this Section, the Association (as attorney-in-fact for the Owners) shall collect the award made and apply such award in the same manner as net insurance and sales proceeds are distributed pursuant to Section 10.04 hereof. In the event of a partial taking of any Unit, the sharing ratios of all Units shall be adjusted by the Association on any reasonable basis and in accordance with the provisions of Section 107 of the Act.

13.   MORTGAGEE PROTECTION

The following provisions are added hereto (and to the extent these added provisions conflict with any other provisions of the Declaration, these added provisions shall control):

(a)   The Association shall be required to make available to all Owners and Mortgage Lenders, and to insurers and guarantors of any first mortgage, for inspection, upon request, during normal business hours or under other reasonable circumstances, current copies of this Declaration (with all amendments), the Articles of Incorporation, the Bylaws, any rules and regulations and the books and records of the Association. Furthermore, such persons shall be entitled, upon written request, to (i) receive a copy of the Association's financial statement for the immediately preceding fiscal year, (ii) receive notices of and attend the Association meetings, (iii) receive notice from the Association of an alleged default by an Owner in the performance of such Owner's obligations under this Declaration, the Articles of Incorporation or the Bylaws of the Association, which default is not cured within thirty (30) days after the Association learns of such default, and (iv) receive notice of any substantial damage or loss to the Common Properties.

(b)   Any holder, insurer or guarantor of a mortgage on a Unit shall have, if first requested in writing, the right to timely written notice of (i) any condemnation or casualty loss affecting a material portion of the Common Properties, (ii) a sixty (60) day delinquency in the payment of the Assessments on a mortgaged Unit, (iii) the occurrence of a lapse, cancellation or material modification of any insurance policy or fidelity bond maintained by the Association, and (iv) any proposed action which requires the consent of a specified number of mortgage holders.

14.   GENERAL PROVISIONS

14.1 Duration. The covenants and restrictions of this Declaration shall run with and bind The Ledges and shall inure to the benefit of and be enforceable by the Declarant, the Association, the Town of Oro, and the Owner of any Unit subject to this Declaration, and their respective legal representatives, heirs, successors and assigns, for a term of ninety-nine (99) years from the date this Declaration is recorded, after which time said covenants shall be automatically extended for successive periods of ten (10) years each unless an instrument signed by the then Owners of 75% of all the Units subject hereto (and 100% of the mortgagees of those supporting termination) has been recorded, agreeing to revoke said covenants and restrictions; provided, however, that no such agreement to revoke shall be effective unless made and recorded three (3) years in advance of the effective date of such revocation, and unless written notice of the proposed agreement is sent to every Owner at least ninety (90) days in advance of any signatures being obtained.

14.2 Notice. Any notice required to be sent to any Member or Owner under the provisions of this Declaration shall be deemed to have been properly sent when personally delivered or mailed, postage prepaid, to the last-known address of the person who appears as Member or Owner on the records of the Association at the time of such mailing.

14.3 Enforcement. Enforcement of these covenants and restrictions shall be accomplished by any proceeding at law or in equity against any person or persons violating or attempting to violate any covenant or restriction, either to restrain violation or to recover damages, and against the Units to enforce any lien created by these covenants; and failure to enforce any covenant or restriction herein contained shall in no event be deemed a waiver of the right to do so thereafter. The prevailing party in any action to enforce these covenants shall be entitled to receive, from the non-prevailing party or parties, all attorneys' and paralegals' fees and court costs actually incurred by the prevailing party, including those for any appeals.

14.4 Severability. Invalidation of any one of these covenants or restrictions or any part, clause or word hereof, or the application thereof in specific circumstances, by judgment or court order shall not affect any other provisions or applications in other circumstances, all of which shall remain in full force and effect.

14.5 Amendment. In addition to any other manner herein provided for the amendment of this Declaration, the covenants, restrictions, easements, charges and liens of this Declaration may be amended, changed, deleted or added to at any time and from time to time, in whole or in part, by approval at a meeting of Owners holding not less than 66-2/3% vote of the entire membership in the Association (as opposed to only those Members represented at a meeting of the Association). Further no provision of this Declaration may be amended if such provision is required to be included herein by the Town of Oro. The foregoing sentence may not be amended.

14.6 <u>Effective Date</u>. This Declaration shall become effective upon its recordation in the Public Records of the County.

14.7 <u>Conflict</u>. This Declaration shall take precedence over any conflicting provisions in the Articles of Incorporation and Bylaws of the Association and the Articles shall take precedence over the Bylaws.

14.8 <u>Standards for Consent, Approval, Completion, Other Action and Interpretation</u>. Whenever this Declaration shall require the consent, approval, completion, substantial completion, or other action by the Declarant or its affiliates or the Association, such consent, approval or action may be withheld in the sole and unfettered discretion of the party requested to give such consent or approval or take such action, and all matters required to be completed or substantially completed by the Declarant or its affiliates or the Association shall be deemed so completed or substantially completed when such matters have been completed or substantially completed in the reasonable opinion of the Declarant or Association, as appropriate. This Declaration shall be interpreted by the Board of Directors and an opinion of counsel to the Association rendered in good faith that a particular interpretation is not unreasonable shall conclusively establish the validity of such interpretation.

14.9 <u>Easements</u>. Should the intended creation of any easement provided for in this Declaration fail by reason of the fact that at the time of creation there may be no grantee in-being, having the capacity to take and hold such easement, then any such grant of easement deemed not to have been so created shall nevertheless be considered as having been granted directly to the Association as agent for such intended grantees for the purpose of allowing the original party or parties to whom the easements were originally intended to have been granted the benefit of such easement and the Owners designate hereby the Declarant and the Association (or either of them) as their lawful attorney-in-fact to execute any instrument on such Owners' behalf as may hereafter be required or deemed necessary for the purpose of later creating such easement as it was intended to have been created herein. Formal language of grant or reservation with respect to such easements, as appropriate, is hereby incorporated in the easement provisions hereof to the extent not so recited in some or all of such provisions.

14.10 <u>Arbitration</u>. Any disputes between the Declarant and the Association and any deadlock within the Board of Directors shall be resolved through binding arbitration. Unless it is otherwise agreed, arbitration shall be conducted in accordance with the commercial arbitration rules of the American Arbitration Association.

14.11 <u>Blasting and Other Activities</u>. ALL OWNERS, OCCUPANTS AND USERS OF THE LEDGES ARE HEREBY PLACED ON NOTICE THAT DECLARANT AND/OR ITS AGENTS, CONTRACTORS, SUBCONTRACTORS, AND LICENSEES MAY BE, FROM TIME TO TIME, CONDUCTING BLASTING, EXCAVATION, CONSTRUCTION AND OTHER ACTIVITIES WITHIN OR IN PROXIMITY TO THE LEDGES. BY THE ACCEPTANCE OF THEIR DEED OR OTHER CONVEYANCE OR MORTGAGE, LEASEHOLD, LICENSE OR OTHER INTEREST, AND BY USING ANY PORTION OF THE LEDGES, EACH SUCH OWNER, OCCUPANT AND USER AUTOMATICALLY ACKNOWLEDGES, STIPULATES AND AGREES (i) THAT NONE OF THE AFORESAID ACTIVITIES SHALL BE DEEMED NUISANCES OR NOXIOUS OR OFFENSIVE ACTIVITIES, HEREUNDER OR AT LAW GENERALLY, (ii) NOT TO ENTER UPON, OR ALLOW THEIR CHILDREN OR OTHER PERSONS UNDER THEIR CONTROL OR DIRECTION TO ENTER UPON (REGARDLESS OF WHETHER SUCH ENTRY IS A TRESPASS OR OTHERWISE) ANY PROPERTY WITHIN OR IN PROXIMITY TO THE LEDGES WHERE SUCH ACTIVITY IS BEING CONDUCTED (EVEN IF NOT BEING ACTIVELY CONDUCTED AT THE TIME OF ENTRY, SUCH AS AT NIGHT OR OTHERWISE DURING NON-WORKING HOURS), (iii) DECLARANT AND THE OTHER AFORESAID RELATED PARTIES SHALL NOT BE LIABLE FOR ANY AND ALL LOSSES, DAMAGES (COMPENSATORY, CONSEQUENTIAL, PUNITIVE OR OTHERWISE), INJURIES OR DEATHS ARISING FROM OR RELATING TO THE AFORESAID ACTIVITIES, (iv) ANY PURCHASE OR USE OF ANY PORTION OF THE LEDGES HAS BEEN AND WILL BE MADE WITH FULL KNOWLEDGE OF THE FOREGOING, AND (v) THIS ACKNOWLEDGEMENT AND AGREEMENT IS A MATERIAL INDUCEMENT TO DECLARANT TO SELL, CONVEY, LEASE AND/OR ALLOW THE USE OF THE APPLICABLE PORTION OF THE LEDGES.

14.12 <u>Covenants Running With The Land</u>. Anything to the contrary herein notwithstanding and without limiting the generality (and subject to the limitations) of Section 14.1 hereof, it is the intention of all parties affected hereby (and their respective heirs, personal representatives, successors and assigns) that these covenants and restrictions shall run with the land. Without limiting the generality of Section 14.4 hereof, if any provision or application of this Declaration would prevent this Declaration from running with the land as aforesaid, such provision and/or application shall be judicially modified, if at all possible, to come as close as possible to the intent of such provision or application and then be enforced in a manner which will allow these covenants and restrictions to so run with the land; but if such provision and/or application cannot be so modified, such provision and/or application shall be unenforceable and considered null and void in order that the paramount goal of the parties affected hereby (that these covenants and restrictions run with the land as aforesaid) be achieved.

14.13 <u>Disclaimer of Warranties</u>. TO THE MAXIMUM EXTENT LAWFUL AND UNLESS CLEARLY AND ABSOLUTELY PROHIBITED BY LAW, ALL IMPLIED WARRANTIES OF FITNESS FOR A PARTICULAR PURPOSE, MERCHANTABILITY AND HABITABILITY, ANY WARRANTIES IMPOSED BY STATUTE AND ALL OTHER IMPLIED WARRANTIES OF ANY KIND OR CHARACTER ARE SPECIFICALLY DISCLAIMED. DECLARANT HAS NOT GIVEN AND OWNER HAS NOT RELIED ON OR BARGAINED FOR ANY SUCH WARRANTIES. AS TO ANY IMPLIED WARRANTY WHICH CANNOT BE DISCLAIMED ENTIRELY, ALL

SECONDARY, INCIDENTAL AND CONSEQUENTIAL DAMAGES ARE SPECIFICALLY EXCLUDED AND DISCLAIMED (CLAIMS FOR SUCH SECONDARY, INCIDENTAL AND CONSEQUENTIAL DAMAGES BEING CLEARLY UNAVAILABLE IN THE CASE OF IMPLIED WARRANTIES WHICH ARE DISCLAIMED ENTIRELY ABOVE). ALL OWNERS, BY VIRTUE OF THEIR ACCEPTANCE OF TITLE TO THEIR RESPECTIVE UNITS (WHETHER FROM THE DECLARANT OR ANOTHER PARTY) SHALL BE DEEMED TO HAVE AUTOMATICALLY WAIVED ALL OF THE AFORESAID DISCLAIMED WARRANTIES AND INCIDENTAL AND CONSEQUENTIAL DAMAGES.

    14.14 <u>Liability of the Association</u>. NOTWITHSTANDING ANYTHING CONTAINED HEREIN OR IN THE ARTICLES OF INCORPORATION, BYLAWS, ANY RULES OR REGULATIONS OF THE ASSOCIATION OR ANY OTHER DOCUMENT GOVERNING OR BINDING THE ASSOCIATION (COLLECTIVELY, THE "ASSOCIATION DOCUMENTS"), THE ASSOCIATION SHALL NOT BE LIABLE OR RESPONSIBLE FOR, NOR IN ANY MANNER BE DEEMED A GUARANTOR OR INSURER OF, THE HEALTH, SAFETY OR WELFARE OF ANY OWNER, OCCUPANT OR USER OF ANY PORTION OF THE LEDGES, INCLUDING, WITHOUT LIMITATION, RESIDENTS AND THEIR FAMILIES, GUESTS, INVITEES, AGENTS, SERVANTS, CONTRACTORS, MEMBERS' PERMITTEES OR SUBCONTRACTORS OR FOR ANY PROPERTY OF ANY SUCH PERSONS. WITHOUT LIMITING THE GENERALITY OF THE FOREGOING:

    (a) IT IS THE EXPRESS INTENT OF THE ASSOCIATION DOCUMENTS THAT THE VARIOUS PROVISIONS THEREOF WHICH ARE ENFORCEABLE BY THE ASSOCIATION AND WHICH GOVERN OR REGULATE THE USES OF THE LEDGES HAVE BEEN WRITTEN, AND ARE TO BE INTERPRETED AND ENFORCED, FOR THE SOLE PURPOSE OF ENHANCING AND MAINTAINING THE ENJOYMENT OF THE LEDGES AND THE VALUE THEREOF; AND

    (b) THE ASSOCIATION IS NOT EMPOWERED, AND HAS NOT BEEN CREATED, TO ACT AS AN ENTITY WHICH ENFORCES OR ENSURES THE COMPLIANCE WITH THE LAWS OF THE UNITED STATES, STATE OF COLORADO, THE COUNTY OF CARBON, THE TOWN OF ORO, AND/OR ANY OTHER JURISDICTION OR THE PREVENTION OF TORTIOUS ACTIVITIES.

    EACH OWNER (BY VIRTUE OF HIS ACCEPTANCE OF TITLE TO HIS UNIT) AND EACH OTHER PERSON HAVING AN INTEREST IN OR LIEN UPON, OR MAKING ANY USE OF, ANY PORTION OF THE LEDGES (BY VIRTUE OF ACCEPTING SUCH INTEREST OR LIEN OR MAKING SUCH USES) SHALL BE BOUND BY THIS SECTION AND SHALL BE DEEMED TO HAVE AUTOMATICALLY WAIVED ANY AND ALL RIGHTS, CLAIMS, DEMANDS AND CAUSES OF ACTION AGAINST THE ASSOCIATION ARISING FROM OR CONNECTED WITH ANY MATTER FOR WHICH THE LIABILITY OF THE ASSOCIATION HAS BEEN DISCLAIMED IN THIS SECTION.

    AS USED IN THIS SECTION, "ASSOCIATION" SHALL INCLUDE WITHIN ITS MEANING ALL OF THE ASSOCIATION'S DIRECTORS, OFFICERS, COMMITTEE AND BOARD MEMBERS, EMPLOYEES, AGENTS, CONTRACTORS (INCLUDING MANAGEMENT COMPANIES), SUBCONTRACTORS, SUCCESSORS AND ASSIGNS. THE PROVISIONS OF THIS SECTION SHALL ALSO INURE TO THE BENEFIT OF THE DECLARANT AND ALL PARTIES RELATED THERETO, ALL OF WHICH SHALL BE FULLY PROTECTED HEREBY.

    Executed by the parties the day and year first above written.

                          _____
                          Thomas Kamasuka

                          ACME CONSTRUCTION COMPANY, a
                          Colorado corporation

                          By:_____
                          President

ATTEST:

_____
Secretary

                      [Acknowledgement]

Figure 4-6
Party Wall Agreement

PARTY WALL AGREEMENT

WHEREAS, ACME DEVELOPMENT COMPANY, a corporation, organized and existing by and under the laws of the State of Delaware, is the owner in fee simple of the following described real estate situate in the Town of Anytown, State of Anywhere;

Lots A and B, Block 1, ACME SUBDIVISION, Town of Anytown, County of Anycounty and State of Somewhere;

and

WHEREAS, said owner has constructed on said premises a multiple dwelling unit composed of two dwellings connected by a division wall between said dwellings, to be known as Sunnyside Court; and

WHEREAS, the common wall placed equally divided on the common boundary separating Lot A from Lot B, the footings underlying and the portion of roof over such wall is collectively referred to herein as the "Party Wall," and it is intended by the undersigned to create, in favor of each purchaser, an easement covering said party wall;

NOW, THEREFORE, the undersigned, ACME DEVELOPMENT COMPANY, in order to protect each and every purchaser, his successors and assigns, of any lot or parcel of said premises, the following easements on building structures and party walls located on said premises are hereby created, to-wit:

1. **Party Wall Declaration.** Said dividing wall is hereby declared to be a Party Wall between the adjoining residences erected on said premises. To the extent not inconsistent with this Declaration, the general rules of law regarding party walls and liability for damage due to negligence, willful acts or omissions shall apply to the Party Wall.

2. **Maintenance of Party Wall.** The cost of maintaining said party wall shall be borne equally by the owners on either side of said wall.

3. **Damage to Party Wall.** In the event of damage or destruction of said wall from any cause, other than the negligence of either party thereto, the then owners shall, at joint expense, repair or rebuild said wall, and each party, his successors and assigns, shall have the right to the full use of said wall so repaired or rebuilt. If either party's negligence shall cause damage to or destruction of said wall, such negligent party shall bear the entire cost of repair or reconstruction. If either party shall neglect or refuse to pay his share, or all of such cost in case of negligence, the other party may have such wall repaired or restored and shall be entitled to have a mechanic's lien on the premises of the party so failing to pay, for the amount of such defaulting party's share of the repair or replacement costs.

4. **Drilling Through Party Wall.** Either party shall have the right to break through the party wall for the purpose of repairing or restoring sewerage, water, utilities, subject to the obligation to restore said wall to its previous structural condition at his own expense and the payment to the adjoining owner of any damages negligently caused thereby.

5. **Destruction of Dwelling Unit.** No dwelling located on said premises shall, at any time, extend beyond two stories in height; and in the event of a destruction of said multiple dwelling unit or any portion thereof, the dwelling so destroyed shall be restored at the joint and equal expense of the adjoining owners, according to a uniform architectural plan and finish; and if any dwelling is but partially destroyed so that the cost of restoring it is not equal to that of restoring the adjoining dwelling, then the amount shall be apportioned according to the individual cost.

6. **Easement.** Neither party shall alter or change said Party Wall in any manner, interior decoration excepted, and said party wall shall always remain in the same location as when erected. The owners of either unit shall have a perpetual easement in and to that part of the other unit on which the Party Wall is located, for party wall purposes, including mutual support, maintenance, repair and inspection. In the event of damage to or destruction of the Party Wall from any cause, then the owners shall at joint expense, repair or rebuild said party wall, and each owner shall have the right to the full use of said party wall so repaired and rebuilt. Notwithstanding anything contained above to the contrary, if the negligence, willful act or omission of any owner, his family, agent or invitee, shall cause damage to or destruction of the Party Wall, such owner shall bear the entire cost of repair or reconstruction, and an owner who by his negligent or willful act causes the Party Wall to be exposed to the elements shall bear the full cost of furnishing the necessary protection against such elements.

7. **Landscaping, Service Facilities and Parking.** (A) The owners from time to time shall undertake such landscaping and general outdoor improvements including but not limited to driveway and parking areas as they may mutually and unanimously deem proper for the harmonious improvement of both units in a common theme, and each owner shall be solely responsible for all expenses, liabilities and general upkeep responsibilities with respect to such landscaping and outdoor improvements on the Parcel of that owner. The owner of one Parcel shall not unreasonably damage the value of the other Parcel such as by shoddy upkeep outside, but both owners shall make all reasonable efforts to preserve a harmonious common appearance of the units.

(B) Common utility or service connections or lines, common facilities or other equipment and property located in or on either of the units but used in common with the other unit, if any, shall be owned as tenants in common of equal undivided one-half interests by the owners of each unit and, except for any expense or liability caused through the negligence or willful act of any owner, his family, agent or invitee, which shall be borne solely by such owner, all expenses and liabilities concerned with such property shall be shared proportionately with such ownership. The owner of the unit on which such property is not located shall have a perpetual easement in and to that part of such other unit containing such property as is reasonably necessary for purposes of maintenance, repair and inspection.

(C) The area identified on the Map as Access Easement shall be a common access to facilities on both Parcels. There is hereby created a reciprocal easement and right-of-way for each owner over, across and through the Access Easement. The owners shall have equal right to the use of such Access Easement and no owner shall hinder or permit his invitees to hinder reasonable access to the other owner's unit or park or permit his invitees to park any vehicle on the Access Easement in a manner which will prevent access to the other unit. It is presumed that snowplowing, heating, and other necessary maintenance of the Access Easement will be required from time to time, the costs of which will be shared by the owners. Other maintenance, repair or improvements of the Access Easement may be required from time to time, and the same shall be undertaken upon the unanimous agreement of the owners who shall share all expenses.

(D) The space allotted for parking shall be exclusively for passenger automobiles belonging to the owners and their guests, and shall be limited to one automobile per owner, and at no time shall one automobile be parked thereon for more than seventy-two (72) hours without being moved.

8. **Alteration, Maintenance and Repairs.** (A) In addition to maintenance provided for, the owners shall, at their own individual expense with respect to each respective unit, provide exterior maintenance and exterior repair upon the units and the unimproved portions of the parcels upon which the units are located including, but not limited to, the exterior walls and the roof housing the units; repair, replacement or cleaning of exterior windows shall be considered interior maintenance.

(B) No owner shall make or suffer any structural or design change (including a color scheme change), either permanent or temporary and of any type or nature whatsoever, upon any part of his unit without first obtaining the prior written consent thereto from the other owner. The units shall be painted in the same color scheme and at the same time, and both units shall be maintained in the same manner. In the case of damage or destruction of any unit or any part thereof by any cause whatsoever, the owner of such unit shall cause with due diligence the unit to be repaired and restored, applying the proceeds of insurance, if any, for that purpose. Such unit shall be restored to a condition comparable to that prior to the damage and in a harmonious manner to promote the common theme of both units.

9. **Allocation of Expenses.** Costs and expenses of landscaping, service facilities, parking, alteration, maintenance and repairs, except as caused by the negligence or willful act of an owner, shall be allocated in the following proportions: Lot A - 50%; Lot B - 50%.

10. **All Owners Responsible - Ultimate Control Resolution.** Both parcel owners shall be mutually responsible for the administration and management of the obligations created hereunder. However, in the event both owners cannot mutually agree when a decision is required by this Declaration, the impasse shall be resolved as follows:

(A) Decision required in year 1995 and every second year thereafter: Lot A owner's decision is binding.

(B) Decision required in year 1996 and every second year thereafter: Lot B owner's decision is binding.

11. **Override.** In the event any owner believes, based on the standard of the reasonable person, (i) that an impasse decision has been made incorrectly or contrary to the Declaration as (ii) the owner in ultimate control is guilty of mis-, mal-, or non-feasance with respect to this Declaration, then the aggrieved owner may petition the Anycounty District Court for a judicial determination of the controversy, which decision shall be binding upon both owners. The Court may assess costs and any reasonable attorney fees as may have been incurred by the parties based upon the merits of the case in favor of the prevailing party.

12. **Covenants Running with Land.** The easements hereby created are and shall be perpetual and construed as covenants running with the land and each and every person accepting a deed to any lot in said multiple unit shall be deemed to accept said deed with the understanding that each and every other purchaser is also bound by the provisions herein contained, and each and every purchaser, by accepting a deed to any lot shall thereby consent and agree to be bound by the covenants herein contained to the same extent as though he had signed this instrument. The undersigned, in executing and delivering deeds to said lots shall insert in said conveyances, by reference, that the same are made subject to the terms, conditions, reservations and covenants herein contained, designating the book and page of the record in which this instrument and the attached plat are recorded.

IN WITNESS WHEREOF, the undersigned has executed this instrument on the 21st day of September, 1995.

[Signature]

[Acknowledgement]

Chapter 4 Quiz

Fill in each blank with the most correct word or phrase.

1. Multiunit dwellings owned by a corporation are called: _____.

2. A corporation which owns multiunit dwellings provides for costs of acquisition and maintenance and the use of common areas by means of a(n) _____ agreement.

3. Each owner of a condominium unit owns a defined _____ within the structure and is a tenant in common in the _____ of the condominium.

4. The basic governing document of a condominium regime is the _____.

5. A preemptive right granting each owner a first right to purchase other units sold to third parties is a(n) _____.

6. A common interest community that is not a condominium or a cooperative is a(n) _____, which covers the type of ownership associated with clustered developments and multiplexes.

7. Within a planned unit development, guidelines for such things as building height limitations and clothes lines are established by _____.

Circle the most correct answer.

8. True or False. The concept of condominium ownership is a creature of statute.

9. True or False. As of 1995, the Uniform Common Interest Ownership Act had been adopted in only a few states.

10. True or False. Cooperative ownership has proven extremely popular nationwide because of the ease in obtaining financing.

11. True or False. Condominium declarations specify which common elements are limited and which are general.

12. True or False. Owners in cooperatives own shares of stock in a corporation and not individual apartments.

13. True or False. Condominiums, by their nature, must be part of a larger building, such as a high-rise building.

14. True or False. Each condominium unit owner assumes liability for any purchase money loan obtained by any other unit owner in the building.

15. True or False. To protect the investment of all the owners of condominium units, the condominium association is responsible for the cost of maintenance and repair of each individual unit.

16. True or False. The condominium association is responsible for management of the common elements.

17. True or False. The condominium declaration may provide certain rights to the developer, such as the right to expand the complex.

18. True or False. Costs of operating common recreational facilities are common expenses, which are assessed against each unit owner.

19. True or False. Unpaid condominium assessments became a lien against the unit and may be foreclosed.

20. True or False. Liens for condominium assessments usually are a first lien, subject only to tax liens and a first mortgage or deed of trust.

21. True or False. An as-built condominium plat or map must be signed by the declarant and must be recorded along with the condominium declaration.

22. True or False. A subdivision map, articles of incorporation, bylaws, and protective covenants are necessary to establish a planned unit development.

23. True or False. The point at which the lots and contiguous portions of multiplex buildings join is called a party wall.

24. True or False. A party wall agreement or declaration is signed and recorded by the developer, and subsequent owners of the various units become bound by it.

25. True or False. A common form of time share ownership is a leasehold.

26. True or False. Time share ownership can exist only with appropriate legislation.

Answer each of the following questions based on the condominium declaration for The Ledges at Figure 4-5 of this chapter.

27. Maria is the owner of Unit C-11 at The Ledges Condominium. Maria often walked her cat Cleo on the sidewalks at The Ledges. The cat always was on a leash, but still managed to destroy the young plants along the sidewalks. The Ledges Condominium Homeowners Association replaced the plants and billed Maria for the cost of the plants. Maria objected to the action of the Homeowners Association. She maintained that the plants were part of the common elements, and the cost of maintaining and repairing the common elements is the responsibility of the Association. She also objected on the grounds that by keeping her pet on a leash, she had complied with all requirements of the Association and could not be singled out for an assessment for the benefit of all the owners.

    Does the Condominium Declaration allow such an assessment against one owner? If so, cite the provision(s) that apply. If not, cite the provisions that support Maria's position.

28. At his death in December, Ali owned Unit C-12 of The Ledges Condominium. The monthly assessment for Ali's unit had been fixed properly by the Association at $100 a month, and the proper monthly notices had been sent. On April 1, the personal representative for Ali's estate asked for an account of the amounts owing for monthly assessments. The Association provided the following statement:

    THE LEDGES CONDOMINIUM ASSOCIATION
    Statement for the Month of April - Unit C-12

January Assessment	$100.00
Late Charge for three months at $10.00 a month	30.00

February Assessment	100.00
Late Charge for two months at $10.00 a month	20.00
March Assessment	100.00
Late Charge for one month at $10.00 per month	10.00
Total Amount Past Due	$360.00
Interest at 18% per annum on past due balance - $5.40 a month for three months	16.20
Total Past Due Plus Interest	$376.20
April Assessment	100.00
BALANCE DUE UPON RECEIPT	$476.20

What provision(s) of the Condominium Declaration authorizes assessments?

Is the bill accurate? Why or why not?

29. Kim, who lived in Unit D-26 of The Ledges, had a green thumb. She hung planter boxes from the railing along the balcony outside her unit and filled them with white petunias. Everyone who passed by seemed to enjoy them and commented on how lovely they were. Park, who lived downstairs, also enjoyed them; but he explained to Kim that when she watered them, water and dirt dripped onto his deck below. Kim told Park that the manager had given her permission to plant the flowers, and there was nothing she could do about the dripping. Two days later, employees of the Association removed the planter boxes and flowers from the railing on Kim's balcony without her permission. Kim accused the Association of trespass and theft.

What defense will the Association assert?

What is Kim's most viable assertion?

30. Maria, after the unfortunate incident with her cat, decided to sell her unit. Since the purchase price was well below the unit's appraised value, she soon found a buyer. Park, the owner of D-25, served notice on Maria, the buyer, and the Condominium Association that he was exercising his right of first refusal as an owner and would purchase the unit on the same terms and conditions as the prospective buyer.

What section(s), if any, of the Condominium Declaration provide for a right of first refusal?

31. What is the importance of the *Owner Control Date* in the Condominium Declaration?

32. Under the Condominium Declaration, catastrophic damage is that which will exceed _____ percent of the insured value of the residence.

Chapter 5
LANDLORD AND TENANT

Chapter 2 reviewed the freehold estates, that is, those estates which combine possession and ownership (seisin). Freehold estates include the fee simple, the fee tail, and the life estate. This chapter reviews the nonfreehold estates or leasehold estates.

Nonfreehold Estates

The nonfreehold estates, or *leasehold* estates, are characterized by an exclusive right to possession without ownership. The common law recognizes four such estates: (1) the *tenancy for years*, (2) the *periodic tenancy*, (3) the *tenancy at will*, and (4) the *tenancy at sufferance*. These estates are now governed by statute as well as by common law rules.

Tenancy for Years　　　　The tenancy for years is a lease for a fixed period of time. It may be for one day, for one month, for 99 years, or for some longer period. Tenancies which last for extended periods and which involve unimproved land, such as 50 years or the traditional 99 years, may allow the construction of permanent improvements. These are called ***ground leases***. Since a tenancy for years ends on a certain date, no notice is required for its termination on that date. The Statute of Frauds requires that leases for more than one year be in writing. Otherwise, any lease may be either oral or written.

Periodic Tenancy　　　The periodic tenancy is a lease from day to day, from month to month, from year to year, or other agreed time, but without any agreement as to when the lease will end. The operative date for this type of tenancy ordinarily is determined by the date when the rent must be paid. Thus, if rent must be paid on the first of each month, a tenancy from month to month is created. Whether or not the rent is paid, the tenancy automatically renews on the operative date (such as the first of the month).

Notice must be given to terminate a periodic tenancy, either by the landlord or by the tenant. At common law, the amount of notice required was equal to the length of the tenancy period, for example, one month for a month-to-month tenancy. State statutes now govern notice periods and generally require a shorter notice by the landlord than was required under common law rules. They sometimes require a longer notice by the tenant.

A periodic tenancy also may be terminated for failure to pay rent or for breach of the lease agreement terms by the tenant. Termination for either reason requires that the tenant be served with notice.

Tenancy at Will A tenancy at will is the lowest form of leasehold estate. It is treated as an estate because it confers the right of exclusive possession upon the tenant. It occurs when a person lawfully comes into possession without an agreement as to term or as to payment of rent. Thus, a tenancy at will arises when a tenant takes possession before agreement is reached concerning payment of rent; when the lease violates the Statute of Frauds (an oral lease for more than one year); or when a purchaser of property takes possession before closing. At common law, no notice was required to terminate a tenancy at will. State statutes now impose some period of notice.

Like the periodic tenancy, a tenancy at will can be terminated for failure to pay rent or for breach of the lease agreement terms by the tenant. If a tenancy at will is terminated for either of these reasons, the tenant must be served with notice.

Tenancy at Sufferance From a technical standpoint, the tenancy at sufferance is not a tenancy at all. It arises when a tenant for a term of years remains in possession (holds over) after the lease is ended. When that occurs, the landlord may commence an eviction or may allow the hold-over tenant to remain either as a periodic tenant or, until agreement is reached as to the terms of the tenancy, as a tenant at will.

Unless the lease agreement provides otherwise, death does not terminate the tenancy for years or the periodic tenancy. The interest of the tenant passes by will or inheritance as personal property, and the lease is enforceable against the decedent's estate. A tenancy at will depends upon the continuing agreement of both the landlord and the tenant that the leasehold should continue. The death of either party extinguishes the agreement of that party and, therefore, terminates the tenancy.

Figure 5-1
Comparison of Leasehold Characteristics

Type of Leasehold	Duration	Notice to Terminate
Tenancy for Years	Fixed term; need not be year(s) literally	No notice required; terminates at end of term fixed; death does not terminate without agreement to the contrary
Periodic Tenancy	Renewing term, with no termination date	Notice required per state statute; death does not terminate without agreement to the contrary
Tenancy at Will	No agreement regarding term or payment of rent	Notice required per state statute; death of either party terminates the tenancy
Tenancy at Sufferance	Occurs when tenant holds over the term; no agreement regarding term or payment of rent during holdover period	Notice required per state statute; death of either party terminates the tenancy

Rights, Duties, and Liabilities of the Tenant

In the absence of a statute, the tenant has few rights. However, a tenant does have the right of *quiet enjoyment* of the leasehold. This means the tenant has exclusive possession during the lease term and may not be disturbed in that possession by the landlord or by anyone holding a superior title. The tenant has a duty to pay rent, which duty is terminated only by an actual or constructive eviction.

An actual or constructive eviction of the tenant by the landlord (or by someone with a title superior to that of the landlord) is a breach of the tenant's right of quiet enjoyment. The ancient common law rule was that an actual eviction was necessary. In other words, it was required that the landlord enter the premises and expel the tenant. The more modern common law rule is that any disturbance of the tenant's possession by the landlord (or by someone acting under his authority) which renders the premises unfit for occupancy or which effectively deprives the tenant of the beneficial enjoyment of the premises, amounts to a constructive eviction if the tenant abandons possession within a reasonable time afterward.

What constitutes a constructive eviction depends upon the circumstances, although the general rule is that the tenant must prove the landlord acted with intent to interfere with the tenant's possession. It generally is not enough that an act or omission of the landlord renders the property uninhabitable if the act or omission was not accompanied by that intention. For example, a constructive eviction likely would be found if the landlord agreed to provide heat and if no heat was provided, making it necessary for the tenant to vacate the premises. Constructive eviction also exists if a landlord allows the common areas to deteriorate to the extent that members of the public are unwilling to enter the tenant's commercial space.

Courts are divided on the issue of whether infestation by vermin constitutes a constructive eviction. Some courts have taken the position that when an intolerable condition exists, which was neither caused by nor can be remedied by the tenant, a constructive eviction should be found. Other courts have taken a more traditional view that there is no warranty of habitability; and unless the infestation was caused by an intentional act of the landlord, no constructive eviction can be found.

If the property is subject to a mortgage when the tenant takes possession under the lease, the mortgage is superior to the rights of the tenant. If the mortgage is later foreclosed, the covenant of quiet enjoyment is breached; and the tenant is justified in terminating the tenancy. On the other hand, if the property is mortgaged after the tenant takes possession, the rights of the tenant prevail over the rights of the mortgagee. If that mortgage is later foreclosed, only the reversion of the landlord passes to the mortgagee. The tenant remains obligated on the lease, and the new landlord is obligated to respect the rights of the tenant under the lease. For this reason, most written leases provide that they are subordinated to (made subject to) any mortgage entered into after the tenant takes possession.

Similarly, the lease terminates if the property is taken by a governmental authority through eminent domain or condemnation. If less than all of the property is taken, however, or if the property is taken only temporarily, the lease remains in effect. The tenant may have an interest in any condemnation award if the value of the interest taken exceeds the remaining amount of rent owed. In the case of a temporary taking for a period of time less than the tenancy, the tenant is entitled to the entire amount of the award.

The tenant's common law duty to pay rent may not be extinguished for any reason, including any breach of the lease by the landlord (short of actual or constructive eviction). At common law, the duty to pay rent continued even when the premises was destroyed so long as any part of it remained and could be occupied. If both the land and its improvements were leased, a complete destruction of the improvements did not terminate the duty to pay rent. The rule today, either by decision or by statute, more often is that destruction of the premises allows the tenant to terminate the lease.

At common law as well as today, subject to statutory changes, the tenant has a duty not to commit *waste*. Thus, the tenant may not commit **active waste** by damaging the premises, by altering its appearance, by changing the fundamental purpose of the premises, or by affecting the premises in a vital and substantial way. Neither may the tenant commit **passive waste** by failing to make the repairs necessary to prevent damage by the elements.

The tenant at common law had no duty to maintain the property in good repair, apart from the obligation not to commit waste. In other words, without a provision in a written lease, the tenant was obligated to make only those repairs needed to protect the property from the elements or to repair damages caused by that tenant. The landlord likewise had no obligation to keep the premises in repair. Dilapidation of the property through ordinary wear and tear was not a breach of either party's obligations.

Today, state statutes or the lease agreement frequently requires the landlord to maintain the leased property. Breach of that obligation may permit the tenant to make the repairs and to deduct their cost from the rent. Local building codes also impose duties on both tenant and landlord to prevent code violations from occurring. Ordinarily, the primary obligation imposed by a building code falls upon the landlord as the owner; but the code does not allow the tenant to make the repairs and to deduct their cost from the rent.

Since the tenant has an exclusive right to possess the leased property, the tenant generally is the only person with a duty to third parties (whether invitees, licensees, or trespassers). Therefore, the tenant is liable for damages sustained by these individuals unless a statute or local code provides differently.

Rights, Duties, and Liabilities of the Landlord

The landlord has the right to be paid rent for the duration of the lease term. The amount of rent usually is fixed by the lease. If it is not fixed for some reason, an amount of rent equal to a fair rental value will be implied. A capitalized rate (income multiplied by a number of years) may be used for commercial property. Ordinarily, rent is payable in advance. Commercial leases frequently contain an *escalator clause* by which the rent may be increased to correspond with increases in the cost of living index. In the case of a periodic tenancy, the rent may be increased if notice is given equal to the notice required for termination.

The landlord also has the right to have the property returned in the same condition at the end of the lease term, subject to reasonable wear and tear. In other words, the property must be free of active or passive waste. A landlord generally also has the right to enter the property to make repairs when the tenant fails to do so, although she has no obligation to make repairs in the absence of statute or a provision in the lease.

At common law, the covenants of both the landlord and the tenant were independent. Short of eviction, no breach of the landlord's obligations excused the tenant from payment of rent. Similarly, the failure of the tenant to pay rent did not permit the landlord to expel the tenant. The landlord's only remedy was to enforce the covenant breached, such as by suing to collect the rent.

In many states today, the rule remains that the tenant is not excused from payment of rent unless he is evicted without cause by the landlord. In many other states, that rule has been modified to permit the tenant certain remedies, such as the right to correct defects and to deduct the cost of repair from the rent. Contrary to the common law rule, it is now the rule everywhere that the tenant's failure to pay the rent gives rise to the landlord's right to evict the tenant.

The landlord has a duty to deliver possession to the tenant at the inception of the lease. If the landlord remains in possession, the tenant either may file suit to gain possession or may terminate the lease.

> On August 1, Larry signed a lease with Tim, leasing Apartment A to Tim for one year. The lease was to begin on September 1. Tim is unable to move into Apartment A on September 1 because Larry still lives there. Tim may sue for possession of the premises, or he may terminate the lease and look elsewhere.

If a third person with a title paramount to the landlord is in possession, the tenant may sue to recover damages or may terminate the lease and, in either event, sue the landlord for damages. Whether the tenant may recover possession from the third party depends on whether the title of the third party was created before or after the lease was made. Issues of notice will be involved as well.

> On August 1, Lila signed a lease with Terri, leasing Apartment A to Terri for one year. The lease was to begin on September 1. Terri is unable to move into Apartment A on September 1, because Theresa is in possession. If Theresa leased from Lila before August 1, Terri may terminate the lease, look elsewhere, and sue Lila for damages. If Theresa leased from Lila on September 1, Terri also may be able to sue for possession, but only if Theresa had notice of Terri's prior right. Theresa had such notice if Lila told Theresa she already had leased the apartment or if Terri had recorded the lease before September 1.

If the third person is in possession without fault of the landlord (a trespasser, for example), the tenant may recover possession. Under the "American Rule," that is the sole remedy of the tenant. Under the "English Rule," which is followed in several states, the tenant has the alternative remedy of terminating the lease.

> If, in the last example, Theresa had entered into a lease with Franklin (who had no interest in the apartment but who defrauded Theresa into thinking that he had), either Lila or Terri could sue to evict Theresa so that Terri could take possession. Under the American Rule, that would be Terri's only remedy.

The warranty of habitability did not exist at common law. That being so, there could be no expectation that the premises were tenantable, fit, or suitable for the use for which the tenant required them. Absent fraud or misrepresentation, the tenant took the property "as is," with all existing defects which were known to the tenant or which could be ascertained by reasonable inspection. To hold the landlord liable for a defect in the premises, the tenant had to show that the defect was latent (hidden) and that it was known to and concealed by the landlord.

The rule of no warranty of habitability has been changed by statute in many states. In addition, an increasing number of courts have found that an implied warranty of habitability exists, based on the requirement that landlords comply with building codes. Where statutory provisions exist, the same provisions may determine the effect of their breach. For example, the tenant might be permitted to correct the defect and to deduct the cost from the rent. Where a warranty of habitability is implied by the courts, the effect usually is to permit a reduction in rent equal proportionately to the reduction in the rental value of the property caused by the landlord's breach.

> Theodore leased commercial space from Lolita. When Theodore applied for a building permit to make exterior alterations, he was informed that the electrical wiring did not conform with the

Uniform Electrical Code then in effect and that the premises would
have to be rewired completely. Lolita recently had bought the
building as an investment, without inspection, and had no
knowledge of the defect. At common law, Theodore has no remedy
against Lolita. By statute in some states, he would be permitted
to deduct the cost of repair from the rent.

Similarly, in the absence of agreement to the contrary, the landlord was
under no common law duty to the tenant or to members of the public to make
repairs to the premises or to keep the premises safe during the lease term. At
common law, the duty to keep the premises in good repair fell to the tenant; and
the tenant could be held liable for a breach of that duty, either to the landlord or
to visitors to the premises.

On the other hand, the landlord does have a duty to maintain common
areas under her control (hallways, stairways, laundry rooms, recreation rooms,
and similar facilities used by all tenants). The landlord may be liable in tort for
negligent maintenance of those areas. Recent cases have expanded that liability
to include failure to provide security when the failure results in assaults on
tenants and visitors.

Even though the common law imposes no such duty, a lease may impose
a duty on the landlord to keep the premises in repair. In this case, the landlord
must use reasonable care to make the repairs or the landlord will be liable to the
tenant or to guests of the tenant for any injuries that result. The landlord also
may be liable in tort to the tenant or to guests of the tenant for damages caused
by a failure to repair if a repair was requested by the tenant but was not
performed by the landlord. The fact that the landlord may be liable, however,
does not eliminate the liability of the tenant to visitors. The tenant has
possession of the property and must maintain it in a way that does not risk harm
to others.

Patti was a guest in Tina's apartment, which Tina leased from
Linda. Patti was injured when she tripped over a board that was
warped from inadequate care. Tina tried to help Patti get up, but
Tina tripped over the same board and was injured. Linda came to
Tina's apartment later that day to collect rent. As she was leaving,
Linda tripped over the warped board and was injured.

At common law, Patti has a claim against Tina only (the tenant); and Linda
likewise has a claim against Tina. However, if the lease places the duty of repair
on Linda and if Tina had asked Linda to repair the board, Patti's claim then
would be against both Tina and Linda. Tina also has a claim against Linda in
this situation, provided Linda was notified of the defect.

The landlord always is liable for injuries that result from latent (hidden) defects in the premises which were known to the landlord and which were not disclosed to the tenant. The landlord's liability is based on a theory of fraud. However, the duty is only to disclose the defect, not to correct it. In a few jurisdictions, the landlord is liable for defects even when they were not known to the landlord if they could have been discovered through a reasonable inspection. That rule imposes an additional duty on the landlord to inspect the premises being leased and, based upon the inspection, to disclose any defects discovered.

Uniform Residential Landlord and Tenant Act   Fifteen states (Alaska, Arizona, Florida, Hawaii, Iowa, Kansas, Kentucky, Mississippi, Montana, Nebraska, New Mexico, Oklahoma, Oregon, South Carolina, and Tennessee) have adopted the Uniform Residential Landlord and Tenant Act, with varying degrees of modification.

The Act requires landlords of residential property to maintain it in a fit and habitable condition, to keep it clean and safe, and to maintain the utilities in good and safe working order, including maintenance of running water and reasonable amounts of hot water. The tenant, on the other hand, is obligated to keep the occupied premises in as safe and clean a condition as possible and not to damage the premises or to disturb neighbors. The Act permits a tenant to terminate a residential lease upon a thirty-day notice for any breach of the landlord's maintenance obligations that materially affects the tenant's health and safety. The Act also allows damages for breach of the lease by the landlord as well as for injunctive relief and for abatement of rent. If the cost of correcting a noncomplying condition is less than $100 or one-half the amount of the monthly rent, whichever is greater, the tenant may correct the condition and may deduct the cost from the rent. Under some circumstances, the tenant may be justified in obtaining substitute housing at the landlord's expense, and noncompliance with the lease may be raised as a defense to an action to collect unpaid rent.

Finally, the Act provides that if the premises are destroyed by fire or other casualty, substantially impairing the enjoyment of the premises, the tenant may vacate the premises on a fourteen-day notice.

Landlord's Remedies   At common law, the landlord was entitled to seize the personal property of the tenant for nonpayment of rent. State statutes today generally provide for a landlord's lien that may be foreclosed for nonpayment of rent. Notice and public sale of the property ordinarily are required.

It is customary for a landlord to require a security deposit or damage deposit at the time the tenant takes possession. It is customary as well for any balance of the deposit to be returned to the tenant at the end of the tenancy (after deduction of any unpaid rent and of any costs incurred to restore the premises to a condition of good repair). Security deposits frequently are subject to statutory rules, which may require payment of accrued interest and written notice of the reasons if a deposit is withheld.

Upon breach of any lease term today, including payment of rent, the landlord may initiate statutory eviction proceedings. The landlord cannot resort to *self-help*, such as changing the locks, turning off the water, or using other means to force the tenant to abide by the lease terms. Because the obligations of the landlord and of the tenant are independent, the breach of those obligations by one does not excuse performance by the other. In fact, self-help tactics may subject the landlord to significant liability.

Eviction proceedings generally are commenced by serving a demand for possession or *notice to quit* (see Figure 5-2).

Figure 5-2
Notice to Quit

NOTICE TO QUIT OR PAY RENT

TO: JANE DOE
      123 County Highway No. 2
      Anytown, Anystate 00000

TAKE NOTICE that demand is made of you for the payment to the undersigned of the sum of $2000.00 now due it for rent and use of the premises at 123 County Highway No. 2, Anytown, Anystate, now occupied by you under a lease from it, or, if said rent is not paid within Three (3) days, demand is made of you for possession of said premises on or before April 30, 1997.

DATED this 25th day of April, 1997.

ACME CORPORATION, INC.

By:_____

If the tenant fails to quit (vacate) the premises, the landlord must initiate a proceeding in *unlawful detainer* or for a *writ of restitution* to remove the tenant from the property. In most jurisdictions, the notice to quit is a prerequisite to begin eviction proceedings. The eviction proceeding typically is joined with a claim for past due rent. Eviction proceedings usually are a type of summary action, intended as an alternative to the cumbersome ejectment suit. This alternative is provided to discourage landlords from using self-help measures to evict tenants, thereby breaching the peace. A *writ of restitution* ultimately may be issued, ordering the tenant's physical removal either by the sheriff or by some other public official.

When service of notice is required before an eviction proceeding can be filed (such as the notice required to terminate a periodic tenancy or a tenancy at will), the notice may be given in different ways, depending on state statute. Personal notice always will suffice, and posted notice usually is provided as the alternative. In the absence of personal service, the summons or other paper initiating the eviction proceeding must be mailed as well as posted under the decision of the United States Supreme Court in <u>Greene v. Lindsay</u>, 456 U.S. 444 (1982).

When a written lease exists, it controls the rights of the parties upon breach of the lease agreement. Typically, eviction of the tenant or vacation of the premises by the tenant does not relieve the tenant from liability for rent. In fact, the rent may be accelerated, causing the entire amount owing under the lease to be due. Thus, if the lease is for one year and if the tenant is evicted at the end of six months, the tenant will be liable not only for past due rent but also for the rent covering the remaining six months.

The prevailing rule in most jurisdictions is that the landlord has no duty to minimize her damages by reletting the premises and may allow them to stand vacant. Thus, when the tenant abandons the premises, he remains liable for the rent for the balance of the lease term. Most lease agreements provide that if the landlord relets the premises for the same or for a greater amount of rent, the tenant is relieved from further liability after deduction of the costs of reletting.

When a tenant fails to pay rent, the landlord may be faced with a tricky decision. She must choose whether to commence the eviction process or to serve a demand for payment of rent or for possession. The latter demand, in turn, gives the tenant the choice of vacating the premises or of paying the rent to remain in possession. If the tenant chooses to vacate the premises, he may be relieved from payment of the rental balance on a waiver theory. In other words, by accepting return of the premises, the landlord may waive the right to future rent.

The landlord also may be faced with a tricky decision when a tenant simply vacates possession. The landlord may treat this as a surrender of possession, particularly if there is a symbolic surrender, such as return of the keys to the landlord. In that case, the landlord is justified in having the locks changed. However, if a court concludes there is no surrender (the tenant might return and demand possession), a formal eviction proceeding is the preferable, more conservative course.

The problem is that a lease grants a nonfreehold, possessory interest which technically must be reconveyed or released to the landlord if the lease is terminated short of its full term. For that reason, a formal eviction more likely will be necessary when there is a written lease for an unexpired term. When a periodic tenancy is involved, a clear surrender of possession may be more easily relied upon. If a surrender can be shown, the courts will treat it as a surrender of possession by operation of law, which can serve as a substitute for a surrender deed.

Assignment and Subletting

A tenancy for years or a periodic tenancy is a nonfreehold interest in real property and, therefore, is freely *alienable* or transferable. Written leases may contain restrictions on transfer, which restrictions generally are strictly construed as a restraint on alienation. For example, a prohibition against assignment will be construed not to prohibit subletting.

A restriction might condition transfer on the consent of the landlord; and if so, the lease is likely to add that the landlord's consent may not be withheld unreasonably. The landlord, then, is held to a standard of reasonable conduct. She may withhold consent for commercially justifiable reasons but not for arbitrary reasons, such as the ethnic background of the assignee. The courts are divided when the lease provides only that the landlord may withhold consent and does not also provide that the consent may not be withheld unreasonably. The traditional rule is that consent then may be withheld for any reason. The more modern trend conditions the withholding of consent on reasonable grounds, as if that provision were contained in the lease.

According to the rules used most often, whether a particular transfer is an assignment or a sublease depends on whether the entire interest of the tenant is transferred. If less than the entire interest is transferred (whether extent of the premises or extent of the term), the transfer is a sublease. According to the minority rule, the intent of the parties governs: this most often means that the court will determine the transfer is an assignment if the parties call it an assignment and a sublease if the parties call it a sublease.

Figure 5-3
Assignment of Lease

ASSIGNMENT

The assignment, made the 2nd day of December, 1996, between JANE DOE, hereinafter referred to as "Assignor," and RICHARD ROE, hereinafter referred to as "Assignee," witnesseth:

WHEREAS, the Assignor is presently the lessee under a certain lease (hereinafter designated "Prime Lease") dated December 1, 1996, between ACME CORPORATION, INC., as Lessor and said JANE DOE as Lessee, a true copy of which is annexed hereto and made a part hereof and marked Exhibit "A;" and

WHEREAS, the Assignor and Assignee have agreed upon an assignment of the lease of said premises on the terms and conditions hereinafter specified;

NOW, THEREFORE, the Assignor hereby assigns all her right, title and interest to said "Prime Lease" to the Assignee and Assignee hereby assumes all rights and obligations of the Assignor under said "Prime Lease" and in the premises described therein; said premises to be used and occupied by the Assignee for his primary residence and for no other purpose, for a term to commence on January 1, 1997 and to end on June 30, 1997.

All covenants, terms and conditions of said Prime Lease shall be binding upon the parties hereto, their heirs, personal representatives, successors and assigns in their respective capacities; i.e., those binding the Lessor in said Prime Lease shall bind the Assignor herein, and those binding the Lessee in said Prime Lease shall bind the Assignee herein, EXCEPT:

The rent shall be Five Hundred Dollars per month payable to the Assignor on the 1st day of each month, commencing January 1, 1997, and continuing until June 1, 1997.

The Assignee agrees to deposit with the Assignor, concurrently with the execution of this Assignment, the sum of Five Hundred Dollars as security for the performance by the Assignee of all the covenants, terms and conditions on his part to be performed.

In Witness Whereof, the parties have executed this Assignment the day and year first above written.

[Signatures and Acknowledgements]

An *assignment of lease* is a transfer by the tenant to a third party of the tenant's interest in the entire premises for the entire term. The extent to which the assignee becomes bound to the terms of the lease depends on various factors. If the assignee expressly assumes the obligations of the lease, he is bound by them. If he does not expressly assume those obligations, he may or may not be bound by them, depending on whether they can be classified as *covenants running with the land*. If the assignee assumes the terms of the original lease, a new privity of estate is created between the assignee and the landlord, permitting the landlord to look to the assignee to perform those terms. In no event, however, is the original tenant relieved of liability.

Figure 5-4
Sublease

SUBLEASE

The sublease, made the 2nd day of December, 1996, between JANE DOE, hereinafter referred to as "Sublessor," and RICHARD ROE, hereinafter referred to as "Sublessee," witnesseth:

WHEREAS, the Sublessor is presently the lessee under a certain lease (hereinafter designated "Prime Lease") dated December 1, 1996, between ACME CORPORATION, INC., as Lessor and said JANE DOE as Lessee, a true copy of which is annexed hereto and made a part hereof and marked Exhibit "A;" and

WHEREAS, the Sublessor and Sublessee have agreed upon a subletting of said premises on the terms and conditions hereinafter specified;

NOW, THEREFORE, the Sublessor hereby leases and demises to the Sublessee and Sublessee hereby hires and takes from the Sublessor, the premises described in said Prime Lease, to be used and occupied by the Sublessee for his primary residence and for no other purpose, for a term to commence on January 1, 1997 and to end on March 31, 1997.

Except as hereinafter specified, all covenants, terms and conditions of said Prime Lease shall be binding upon the parties hereto, their heirs, personal representatives, successors and assigns in their respective capacities; i.e., those binding the Lessor in said Prime Lease shall bind the Sublessor herein, and those binding the Lessee in said Prime Lease shall bind the Sublessee herein. Said exceptions are:

(1) Paragraph I. of the Prime Lease, specifying the rental, shall not apply to this Sublease.

(2) The provisions of Paragraph VI. of the Prime Lease relating to the security deposit to be paid shall not apply to this Sublease. All remaining provisions of Paragraph VI of said Prime Lease shall remain in full force and effect and shall apply to this Sublease.

The rent shall be Five Hundred Dollars per month payable to the Sublessor on the 1st day of January, 1997, the 1st day of February, 1997, and the 1st day of March, 1997.

The Sublessee agrees to deposit with the Sublessor, concurrently with the execution of this Sublease, the sum of Five Hundred Dollars as security for the performance by the Sublessee of all the covenants, terms and conditions on his part to be performed.

In Witness Whereof, the parties have executed this Sublease the day and year first above written.

[Signatures and Acknowledgements]

A *sublease*, on the other hand, is a transfer of less than the entire interest of the tenant to a third party. Even if the transfer is of a period of time only one day short of the original term, the transfer is a sublease. When a sublease exists, the original tenant becomes landlord to the new tenant. The original landlord, however, gains no rights related to the new tenant and may look only to the original tenant for enforcement of the lease. Any eviction proceeding, on the other hand, must be brought against both.

Depending upon the intention of the parties and upon the rule followed by a particular court, a transfer also may be a partial assignment. A *partial assignment* transfers less than the entire interest of the tenant but is governed by the rules applicable to assignments *(discussed above)*.

Drafting a Lease

The provisions that might be found in a lease agreement are as varied as the types of property that might be subject to lease. Because of this, each lease agreement is different All lease agreements, however, include topics that are fairly standard from one to the next and typically are drafted in the order of their importance.

Identity of the Parties   A lease first should identify the parties to the lease by name, together with their addresses.

Description of the Premises   Next, the property is described. This may be done by reciting the legal description if it is brief, by referring to a recorded plat, or by attaching to the lease an exhibit that contains the legal description of the premises leased. Some leases describe the premises only by square feet and attach a map of that area. So long as the location of the premises may be ascertained reasonably, the lease is enforceable. Certainly, the more specific the description is, the better.

Term   The lease next should set forth its term, including any options for extension of the original term.

Rent   The amount of rent typically is listed next. The lease should specify the *minimum rent* (the fixed, minimum dollar amount to be paid) and the times at which the rent must be paid. If additional rental amounts are to be paid, the details should be described. In a *net lease* (or a *triple net lease*, as it is more often known), additional rent consists of 1) the amount of taxes and special assessments paid by the landlord; 2) cost of maintaining the building and common areas; and 3) cost of utilities. As additional rent, some commercial leases provide for payment of a percentage of the revenues derived from the operation of the premises. Most commercial leases provide for an increase in rent in proportion to any increase in the Consumer Price Index. The lease also may impose an additional charge for late payment of rent. Ordinarily, a deposit is required to cover damages and the last month's rent.

Maintenance of the Premises   The lease should specify what items of maintenance are the responsibility of the tenant and what items of maintenance are the responsibility of the landlord, apart from who pays those costs. The tenant usually is responsible to maintain only the premises leased, while the landlord usually is responsible to maintain the building and the common areas. From the tenant's point of view, it is desirable that the lease require the landlord to bear the cost of any capital improvements to the premises.

Use of the Premises   A commercial lease typically specifies the purpose for which the property will be used and requires that any change in its use be approved by the landlord. The lease also sets restrictions on signs and advertising.

Alterations and Additions   Leases generally provide that the tenant may not alter or make additions to the leased premises without the consent of the landlord.

Insurance   The lease typically requires that both landlord and tenant carry insurance. In the usual lease, the cost of the landlord's insurance is added to the rent and is made payable by the tenant on a monthly basis.

Destruction of the Premises and Eminent Domain   Commercial   leases address the issue of damage to or destruction of the premises and generally give the tenant the option to terminate the lease if the premises are substantially destroyed or if the damage occurs near the end of the lease term. Otherwise, the landlord may be obligated to repair any damage to the extent of insurance proceeds available. Similar provisions address the issue of the taking of all or a part of the leased premises through the power of eminent domain. In that event, the lease may be terminated or the amount of the rent proportionately reduced.

Assignment and Subletting Assignment and subletting generally are permitted only with the consent of the landlord.

Sale or Foreclosure   A lease typically provides for *attornment* in the event of the sale of the premises by the landlord voluntarily or through foreclosure of any mortgage existing when the lease is created. In other words, the tenant is required by the lease to accept the new owner as landlord. The original landlord likely will be released from liability in this event. The lease may require the tenant to provide an affidavit, sometimes known as an *estoppel certificate (see Figure 5-5)*, to any prospective purchaser to the effect that the landlord is not in default.

Figure 5-5
Estoppel Certificate

TENANT ESTOPPEL CERTIFICATE

TO: ACME DEVELOPMENT COMPANY
        0001 First Street
        Anytown, Anystate

RE: 0002 First Street, Anytown, Anystate

The undersigned hereby warrants and represents with respect to the above referenced property:

1.   There is presently in existence a valid Lease dated July 1, 1995, between the undersigned, as Tenant, and Blank Development Company, as Landlord, pertaining to a certain area on the property known as Suite 300, on the third floor.

2.   Said Lease is in full force and effect.

3.   No advance rentals, prepaid rent, trade-offs for rent or deposits have been paid or made under said Lease except: A security deposit in the amount of $5,000.

4.   There have been no modifications or amendments to said Lease other than: NONE

5.   Landlord has performed all obligations under said Lease and is not presently in default thereunder.

6.   Rent is due in advance on the 1st day of each month and has been paid to July 1, 1996.

7.   All construction and improvements to be performed by Landlord have been completed and accepted by Tenant.

8.   The term of the Lease expires on July 1, 1998. Tenant does not have an option to renew.

9.   Tenant has no option or right of first refusal to purchase the premises.

The undersigned understands that you are relying upon this Certificate in consummating the purchase of the premises.

Dated at Anytown, Anystate, this 25th day of June, 1996.

_____
                                    Tenant

Default   Instances of default by the tenant usually involve 1) failure to pay rent, 2) breach of any affirmative obligation of the lease when the breach is not cured after notice, 3) bankruptcy or assignment for benefit of creditors, or 4) vacation of the premises. Generally, the landlord has alternative remedies when the tenant defaults, including 1) termination of the lease or 2) re-entry by the landlord without terminating the lease. The landlord is granted the right to relet the premises and, if they are relet, to collect from the tenant the expenses of reletting as well as any shortage of rent realized after the reletting.

Some commercial leases do not address default by the landlord at all. If they do, they generally are limited to the breach of any affirmative obligation of the lease. The lease typically provides for a lien on furniture, fixtures, and equipment of the tenant and provides for sale of those items upon default by the tenant.

Figure 5-6 illustrates a lease agreement for residential property, which contains many of the provisions discussed in this chapter.

One cannot be too careful in drafting or in reviewing a lease. The common law rules that relate to the obligations of the landlord and the tenant often differ from modern expectation of landlords and tenants. On the other hand, particularly in jurisdictions where the Uniform Residential Landlord and Tenant Act has been adopted, statutes or case law may swing the pendulum farther in the direction of the tenant than many landlords would wish. For these reasons, it is important that the rights and obligations of each party be stated carefully and in detail.

Figure 5-6
Form of Lease

Residential Lease Agreement

This Residential Lease Agreement is made and entered into as of and effective the 1st day of December, 1996, between ACME CORPORATION, INC., which shall hereinafter be referred to as "Lessor" and JANE DOE, of _____, who shall hereinafter be referred to as "Lessee",

NOW WITNESSETH:

I.   Description of the Property. The Lessor leases to the Lessee the following described real property in Anycounty, Anystate:

Lot 1, STARSHINE ADDITION, Filing 1, according to the plat thereof

recorded in the Office of the Anycounty Clerk and Recorder,

also known as 123 County Highway # 2, Anytown, Anystate, together with all improvements thereon, all fixtures and appliances attached to or located on the premises, all of which hereinafter shall sometimes be referred to as the "Property".

II.   Term and Consideration. The lease shall be for the term of six months, from the 1st day of January, 1997, to and including the 30th day of June, 1997. The rental for the Property shall be One Thousand Dollars ($1,000.00) per month, payable in advance, the rental payment for the first month being payable upon execution of this Residential Lease Agreement. The rental of One Thousand Dollars per month shall continue until changed by Lessor upon not less than thirty days notice to Lessee. Rentals for terms other than the first month and the last month (which shall be paid as set forth in Paragraph III) shall be paid in the following manner, unless otherwise agreed by the parties in writing: either by hand delivery to Lessor's headquarters east of Anytown, Anystate, or by depositing said payment in the United States Mail, sufficient postage affixed thereto, addressed to Lessor at Post Office Box 0000, Anytown, Anystate 00000. Under either method of payment, such payment shall be payable to Acme Corporation, Inc., by check or money order, and shall occur on or before the 1st day of the month for which the payment is due.

III. Delivery of Possession of the Property. Possession of the Property shall be delivered to Lessee at 12:01 A.M. on the 1st day of January, 1997.

IV.   Covenants of Lessee. The Lessee agrees:

A.   That she will pay the said rent at the times and in the manner aforesaid;

B.   That she will promptly pay all gas, electricity, waste disposal, water rates or other utility charges which may become payable during the continuance of this lease for gas, electricity, waste disposal, water and other utilities, if any, serving the property;

C. That she will not injure, overload, or deface or suffer to be injured, overloaded, or defaced the property or any part thereof;

D.   That she will permit no more than two (2) adults and no (0) children to reside upon the Property at any time during the term of this Lease Agreement; the Lessee may not increase the number of occupants of said premises, except for casual visitors, without the written consent of the Lessor. In the event additional persons reside on the property without the written consent of the Lessor the Lessee, in addition to being in default, shall owe an additional rent of $500.00 per person per month or portion thereof;

E.   That she will permit no more than four (4) horses and no other animals to be present on the property during the terms of this Lease Agreement;

F. That she will not make or suffer any unlawful, improper or offensive use of the property, or any use or occupancy thereof contrary to any law of the state or any regulation of any political subdivision now or hereafter made, or which shall be injurious to any person or property, or which shall be liable to endanger or affect any insurance on the said property or to increase the premium thereof;

G. That the Lessor or its representative at all reasonable times may enter to view the property and to make repairs which the Lessor or its representative may see fit to make;

H. That she will keep the Property in good repair, with the exception of structural repairs, which shall be the responsibility of the Lessor, and that, at the expiration of the said term, Lessee will peaceably yield up to the Lessor the property in the same condition as when she first entered the property, reasonable use and wear and damage by unavoidable casualties excepted. Lessee agrees not to make alterations or do or cause to be done any painting or wallpapering to said premises without the prior written consent of Lessor;

I. Lessee agrees to mow and water the grass and lawn, and keep the grass, lawn, flowers, and shrubbery thereon in good order and condition, to replace in a neat and workmanlike manner all glass and doors broken during occupancy thereof, to use due precaution against freezing of water or waste pipes and stoppage of same in and about said premises and that in case water and waste pipes are frozen or become clogged by reason of neglect of Lessee, the Lessee shall repair the same at her own expense as well as all damage caused thereby. Lessee shall keep any decks reasonably clear of ice and snow;

J. The Lessee agrees not to sublet said premises nor assign this lease nor any part thereof without the prior written consent of Lessor;

K. Pets. No pets of any kind shall reside at subject property during the term of the lease without the express written consent of Lessor. In the event any pets are permitted, Lessee agrees to repair any damages done by such pet(s) in a timely manner when requested by Lessor or Lessor's agent during the term of this agreement. Such animal(s) will be the responsibility of the Lessee, who accepts full liability for damage or injury caused by or to the animal(s), to anyone or any object during the term of the tenancy and Lessee agrees to hold Lessor harmless from any such liability. The Lessee shall not be entitled to any recovery from the Lessor as the result of any damage or injury suffered by any horse, pet or other animal on the Property under this agreement; and

L. That no assent, express or implied, by the Lessors to any breach of any of the Lessee's covenants shall be deemed to be a waiver of any succeeding breach of the same or any other covenant.

V.   Covenants of Lessor. The Lessor covenants that the Lessee shall be permitted to peaceably hold and enjoy the property. Except as otherwise provided herein, the Lessee shall be permitted to make repairs which she deems necessary and desirable to the property, which repairs shall not adversely affect the appearance or condition of the property.

VI.   Security and Damage Deposit. At the time of or before the Lessee occupies the Property, but not later than the 1st day of January, 1996, in addition to the payment for the first installment of rent, the Lessee shall deposit with the Lessor the sum of $1,000.00 as a partial security deposit, and Lessee shall deposit with the Lessor additional payments of $500.00 each on or before the 1st day of January, 1997 and the 1st day of February, 1997, the latter two of which payments shall be applied toward the final months rent subsequent to any thirty day notice of termination given by either party. All or a portion of such deposit may be retained by Lessor and a refund of any portion of such deposit is conditioned as follows:

A. Lessee shall occupy said premises for term agreed to above:

B. Lessee shall clean, repair, and restore said residence and return the same to Lessor in its initial condition, except for reasonable wear and tear:

C. Lessee shall surrender to Lessor the keys to premises:

D. Any refund from deposit, as by itemized statement shown to be due to Lessee, shall be returned to Lessee within sixty (60) days after termination of this tenancy and vacation of the premises:

E. Lessee acknowledges that any unpaid late fees or charges or other amounts due Lessor may be deducted from any deposits held by Lessor, and that Lessor may take into its possession and have a lien against the property of Lessee for any amount owed Lessor.

VII. <u>Termination upon Breach.</u> If either of the parties or their successors in interest shall neglect or fail to perform and observe any covenant relating to the lease which on such party's part is to be performed, and the same is not corrected after ten days written notice, then the Lessor, if it is the terminating party, may thereafter terminate this agreement, enter into and upon the property or any part thereof, and repossess the same as of its former estate, and the Lessee, if the terminating party, may thereafter terminate this agreement and recover any and all unearned rentals paid hereunder. In the event of such termination, all rights and obligations under this Lease Agreement accruing prior to such termination or resulting from such termination shall be unaffected by such termination.

VIII. <u>Costs and Attorney's Fees.</u> If, by reason of any default or breach on the part of the Lessee in the performance of any of the provisions of this agreement, a legal action is instituted, the Lessee agrees to pay all reasonable costs and attorney's fees in connection therewith. It is agreed that the venue of any legal action brought under the terms of this lease may be in the county in which the premises are situated.

IX. <u>Non-Liability of Lessor.</u> Lessee covenants that the Lessor and Lessor's agents shall not be held liable for any damage or injury to the Lessee, the Lessee's agents, guests, or employees or to any person entering the premises or the building or property of which the transferred premises are a part (whether to person or property) and Lessee agrees to indemnify and hold harmless the Lessor and Lessor's agents from any such claims.

X. <u>Remedies.</u> The Lessee promises and agrees that if default be made in the payment of rents or in the performance of any other conditions under this lease, that this lease may be forthwith terminated at the election of the Lessor and the Lessee will immediately surrender and deliver up possession of the leased premises to the Lessor upon receiving written notice from the Lessor stating the breach of the conditions of this lease. Upon the election of the Lessor to so terminate the lease the Lessor shall be entitled to recover from the Lessee all unpaid rent whether or not accrued to date of termination (less any amount for which the Lessor may rent out the premises subsequent to the default during the term) and court costs and other expenses incurred collecting the amount due. In the event that it shall become necessary for the Lessor to employ an attorney to enforce any of the provisions hereof or to enforce the collection of any rents due under the term of this lease, Lessor shall be entitled to recover all costs together with reasonable attorney's fees. In the event of such termination, it is understood and agreed that any advance rental payments and the security, rental and cleaning deposit herein made shall be retained by the Lessor as damages for the breach of this lease, in addition to other legal remedies which the Lessor may have for such breach.

XI. <u>No Waiver.</u> The failure of the Lessor to insist in any one or more instances, upon a strict compliance of any of the obligations, covenants, and agreements herein contained or the failure of the Lessor in any one or more instances to exercise any option, privilege or right herein contained shall in no wise be construed to constitute a waiver or relinquishment or release of such obligation, covenant, or agreement, and no forbearance by the Lessor or any default hereunder shall in any manner be construed as constituting a waiver of such default by the Lessor.

XII. _Interest_. Lessee and Lessor acknowledge that any interest earned on prepaid rents or damage deposits shall belong to Lessor as additional compensation.

XIII. _Notices_. All notice and deliveries hereunder shall be made by depositing same in the United States Mail, postage prepaid, addressed,

If to Lessor, to

Acme Corporation, Inc.
P. O. Box 000
Anytown, Anystate 00000

If to Lessee, to

Jane Doe
P. O. Drawer XXX
Anytown, Anystate 00000

unless otherwise directed by the recipient party.

XIV. _Entirety of Agreement._ This document represents the entire agreement of the parties with respect to the subject matter hereof, and all agreements entered into prior hereto are revoked and superseded by this agreement. This agreement may not be changed, modified or rescinded except in writing, signed by all parties hereto, and any attempt at oral modification of this agreement shall be void and of no effect.

XV. _No Participation of Real Estate Brokers._ The parties covenant and agree that no real estate broker or sales person is involved in the within Lease Agreement or entitled to any commission hereunder.

XVI. _Governing Law._ This agreement shall be deemed to be made under, and shall be construed in accordance with and shall be governed by, the laws of Anystate, and any action arising therefrom shall be commenced in Anycounty, Anystate.

XVII. _Interpretation_. It is agreed that all words used herein in the singular number shall include the plural and the present tense shall include the future and the masculine gender shall include the feminine and neuter. Paragraph titles are for convenience only and shall neither limit nor broaden the contents thereof.

XVIII. _Binding Effect._ All the covenants, stipulations, and agreements in this lease and option agreement shall extend to and bind the parties and their successors in interest respectively, by and to whom the same have been made.

In witness whereof, the parties have executed this Residential Lease Agreement as of the date first noted above.

ACME CORPORATION, INC.

By:_____   _____
      Lessor   Lessee

Chapter 5 Quiz

Fill in each blank with the most correct word or phrase.

1.   Nonfreehold estates are characterized by an exclusive right to _____, without _____.

2.   Common law recognizes four nonfreehold estates: _____, _____, _____, and _____.

3.   A tenancy for a fixed period of time is a(n) _____.

4.   A(n) _____ does not require notice for termination.

5.   A(n) _____ is treated as an estate in real property, because it confers the right of exclusive possession on the tenant and is the lowest form of leasehold estate.

6.   A(n) _____ arises when a tenant for a term of years remains in possession after the termination of the lease.

7.   A tenancy from month to month, but without an agreed termination date, is a(n) _____.

8.   Any action by the landlord or one acting under her authority effectively to deprive the tenant of the beneficial enjoyment of the premises, together with the intent to so deprive, amounts to _____.

Circle the most correct answer.

9.   True or False. A ground lease may allow for construction of permanent improvements.

10.   True or False. Under the Statute of Frauds, leases for six months or longer must be in writing to be enforceable.

11.   True or False. A lease which begins at 1:00 a.m. on May 1, 1998 and ends at 1:00 a.m. on May 2, 1998 creates a periodic tenancy.

12.   True or False. A periodic tenancy is renewed automatically whether or not the rent is paid.

13. True or False. A tenancy at will or a periodic tenancy may be terminated without notice if the rent is not paid or if the tenant breaches the terms of the lease.

14. True or False. The death of either the landlord or the tenant extinguishes a tenancy at will.

15. True or False. The interest of the tenant in a tenancy for years or in a periodic tenancy passes by will or inheritance as personal property.

16. True or False. At common law, a tenant has few rights beyond the right of quiet enjoyment.

17. True or False. Courts universally have held that infestation of the premises by rats will provide a basis for constructive eviction.

18. True or False. A mortgage is superior to the rights of a tenant if the mortgage was given before the landlord leased the premises.

19. True or False. A temporary taking through the power of eminent domain for a period of time that is less than the tenancy entitles the tenant to the entire amount of the condemnation award.

20. True or False. A tenant who leased both the land and the improvements had a duty at common law to pay rent even if the improvements were entirely destroyed; today, the rule often allows the tenant to terminate the lease if the premises are destroyed.

21. True or False. Local building codes give the tenant the right to make repairs required under the codes and to deduct the costs from the rent.

22. True or False. Generally speaking, only the tenant is liable to invitees, licensees, or trespassers.

23. True or False. A tenant may not commit active or passive waste.

24. True or False. Under the common law doctrine of independent covenants, a tenant was not excused from payment of rent even if the landlord breached his obligations under the lease.

25. True or False. The warranty of habitability is a creation of statutes and courts; it was not present at common law.

26. True or False. A landlord has the duty to disclose a defect but has no duty to repair it.

27. True or False. The Uniform Residential Landlord and Tenant Act imposes obligations upon the landlord to maintain utilities in good and safe working order.

28. True or False. Under the URLTA, a tenant may obtain substitute housing at the landlord's expense in some instances.

29. True or False. At common law, a landlord could seize a tenant's personal property for nonpayment of rent.

30. True or False. A landlord may change the locks to the premises if the tenant is more than 90 days late in payment of rent but must provide secured storage for the personal possessions of the tenant.

31. True or False. A notice to quit is the first step in eviction proceedings.

32. True or False. The manner of service of a notice terminating a periodic tenancy is governed by statute.

33. True or False. In most jurisdictions, when a tenant abandons the premises under lease, the landlord has no duty to mitigate her damages by reletting the premises.

34. True or False. Vacation of a leased premises by the tenant before the expiration of the term relieves the landlord from proceeding with a formal eviction process.

35. True or False. The determination of whether a transfer is an assignment or a sublease turns on whether the entire estate is transferred.

36. Jennifer owned a vacation cottage on the Outer Banks. When Jennifer was transferred to Ireland, she and her friend Carol agreed that Carol would rent the cottage for $500 a month beginning May 1, 1996 and ending May 1, 1998. Carol paid $500 due for the first month plus a $1,000 security deposit, and they formalized the agreement with a handshake. What type of tenancy was created?

    1. Periodic tenancy

2. Tenancy at will
3. Tenancy at sufferance
4. Tenancy for years

Review the Residential Lease Agreement at Figure 5-6 and answer the following questions.

37. In April 1977, the temperature in Anytown, Anystate fell to -40° F, a record low that exceeded the previous record of -10° F set in 1801. Sewer pipes in the basement of the leased premises froze and broke and damaged the pipe, walls, and floor of the basement. What provision(s) of the lease govern(s)?

What position(s) can each party advance to place liability with the other party?

38. After obtaining the written consent of the Lessor, Jane moved her two draft horses onto the premises and housed them in a preexisting barn. The horses were used to pull a circus wagon, which Jane used to advertise her gardening business. From time to time, she used the horses for other tasks, such as pulling machinery. Over time, the horses damaged the floor and one wall of the barn, causing it to collapse. The Lessor demanded that Jane repair the damage. She refused. What provision(s) of the lease govern(s)?

What arguments can Jane make to support her refusal?

39. What obvious error appears in paragraph VI of the lease?

40. Review the portion of the chapter which lists items typically covered in a residential lease agreement. What significant item is omitted from the lease at Figure 5-6?

Chapter 6
SERVITUDES
AND
OTHER LAND USE LIMITATIONS

A *servitude* is a burden or restriction on the ownership of real property, which burden exists for the benefit of another. The common law servitudes are: 1) the *profit*, 2) the *easement*, and 3) the *license*.

Along with rents, the common law servitudes are the *incorporeal* or intangible interests in real estate. Compare these with *corporeal* or tangible interests (the freehold estates and the leasehold estates). The profit, easement, and license are interests in real property; but they are not possessory interests like freehold estates and leasehold estates. They are a right of use, rather than a right of possession.

Also included in this chapter are real covenants, sometimes called restrictive covenants or protective covenants. Although they are not common law servitudes, restrictive covenants are similar. They act as burdens upon property ownership for the benefit of another or for the benefit of the public in general. They are not interests in property but, rather, are contractual rights. Like the common law servitudes, restrictive covenants are enforceable in equity, usually by injunction. The English common law called them equitable servitudes.

Common Law Profits

In the early days of common law, land generally was cultivated through a common field system. Each *villein* (tenant of the lord) was given a particular part of the manor to farm, together with certain other *profits a prendre* or **rights** *of commons* with respect to common areas of the manor. These rights were so called because they amounted to rights to take a part of the land. Rights of commons survive today in the form of public commons or town square of some communities.

Profits are an interest in land and are governed by the Statute of Frauds, which means they must be in writing. They are more than a license because they permit the removal of something from the land. They usually are personal, that is, for the benefit of a particular person; but they may also be *appurtenant to* (for the benefit of) some other estate. When they are personal, profits terminate with the death of that person.

The common law profits were the *turbary profit* (the right to remove fuel), the *piscary profit* (the right to fish), *estovers* (the right to cut timber) and the *right of pasture*. Today, any right to enter upon and to remove something from the property of another falls within the definition of a profit. Probably the most common profits are fishing rights and hunting rights.

Easements

An *easement* is an interest in property that gives the holder (owner) of the easement the right to use of the property of another in some way, whether below, on, or above the surface. An easement is a nonpossessory right, which means the holder of the easement has a right of use but not a right of possession. Easements came into existence during the Industrial Revolution as the manorial system broke down and was replaced after the Statute Quia Emptores (1290) by the modern system of individual land ownership. Easements were born of necessity. For example, if Able could reach Northern Estates only by passing through Southern Estates, it was necessary that Able have an easement of *ingress* and *egress* for that purpose across Southern Estates.

Today, of course, municipal and state road systems provide ingress and egress for most of us. Thus, we can distinguish between a private easement and a public right-of-way. *Right-of-way* is a general term and may connote a fee interest in a strip of land, within which a public road is constructed. Or, it may connote what truly is an easement, that is, a nonpossessory right to use the land of another, which is granted by the owner of the land to a municipal entity for the benefit of the public in general.

Public rights-of-way can be created in a variety of ways. As we shall see later, easements may be created by *prescription* (long-term use). It may be correct to say that most of the roads on which we travel, particularly in rural areas, originally came into being through prescription. In other words, they have been there for such a long time that no one, including the owner of the land over which they pass, questions the right of the public to use them.

In addition to prescription, public ways can be created by the combined acts of dedication and acceptance. A *dedication* can occur either by deeding a right-of-way or by subdividing property. A subdivision map typically contains a certificate of dedication by which the developer or subdivider dedicates to public use each right-of-way and easement shown on the map. *Acceptance* is the act of the local jurisdiction, usually a city or a county, in accepting the dedication. The local jurisdiction's acceptance may occur by signing the subdivision map or may occur by formal action, such as a resolution. Acceptance also may occur by action of the local jurisdiction in maintaining the right-of-way.

Public ways also may be acquired when a municipal, state, or federal entity exercises its right of **eminent domain**. The eminent domain or condemnation proceeding is discussed at length in a later chapter. For present purposes, it is sufficient to say that federal, state, county, and municipal governments generally possess a constitutional or statutory right to acquire private land for public use. After negotiation, the landowner may choose to convey the easement or right-of-way voluntarily by deed or grant of easement; or the governmental entity may have to obtain a court order vesting it with ownership of the land or the easement. The due process clauses of the state and federal constitutions require that the landowner be paid fair compensation for the land.

By comparison, private easements are classified either as *appurtenant* or *in gross*. An **appurtenant easement** exists for the benefit of another parcel of land (the dominant estate). Thus, an easement for ingress and egress granted by the owner of Western Estates to Eastern Estates is an appurtenant easement.

Western Estates	Eastern Estates

The easement in this example is appurtenant to Eastern Estates, which is the dominant estate or dominant tenement. Western Estates is the servient estate or servient tenement.

Figure 6-1
Appurtenant Easement

GRANT OF EASEMENT

THIS INDENTURE, made the 22nd day of August, 1996, between JOHN DOE, Grantor, and JANE ROE, Grantee.

Whereas, the Grantor is seised of an estate in fee simple of a parcel of land described as the North Half of Section 1, Township 1 South, Range 75 West of the 3rd Principal Meridian, County of Any and State of Anywhere, and marked Exhibit "A" attached hereto across which there runs a private road shown on Exhibit "A" by the dotted lines between point A, where the road opens into Smith Road and point B, where it opens into County Road No. 1; and

Whereas, Grantee is seised in fee simple of another parcel of land described as the South Half of Section 1, Township 1 South, Range 75 West of the 3rd Principal Meridian, County of Any and State of Anywhere, upon which is erected a private dwelling house; and

Whereas, for the consideration hereinafter mentioned, the Grantor has agreed to grant to the Grantee such easement and right of way over said private road as hereinafter expressed;

WITNESSETH, that in pursuance of said agreement and in consideration of the sum of Five Hundred Dollars ($500) paid by the Grantee to the Grantor, the receipt whereof is hereby acknowledged, the Grantor hereby grants to the Grantee, her heirs and assigns:

Full and free right and liberty for her and them; her and their tenants, servants, visitors, and licensees, in common with all other persons having the like right, at all times hereafter, on foot or on horseback or in vehicles (but not with sheep, cattle, pigs, or other animals) to pass and repass along the said private road from said Smith Road to County Road No. 1 for all lawful purposes connected with the use and enjoyment of said premises of the Grantee as a single private dwelling house, but for no other purposes.

To have and to hold said right of way hereby granted to the Grantee, her heirs and assigns, as appurtenant to her said premises.

In Witness Whereof, the Grantor has hereunto set his hand and seal the day and year first above written.

_____
John Doe

[Acknowledgement]

An *easement in gross*, on the other hand, is appurtenant to nothing. The most common type of easement in gross is one granted to a utility company to erect poles or to lay underground cable, water, or sewer mains not serving any particular parcel of land.

Figure 6-2
Easement in Gross

GRANT OF EASEMENT TO LAY SEWER LINE

Mutual agreement, made this 6th day of April, 1996, between John Doe of the City of Oro, State of Anywhere, Grantor, and Acme Construction, Inc. of the City of Oro, State of Anywhere, Grantee,

WITNESSETH, that for and in consideration of the sum of One Dollar ($1.00) and other consideration hereinafter set out, the parties agree:

The Grantor gives and grants to the Grantee the right to construct and maintain a sewer line under and through his property located in Estates Subdivision, an addition to the City of Oro, County of Wherever, State of Anywhere, being Lot Nos. 1 through 6, inclusive, of said addition.

In consideration of said right, the Grantee agrees to lay said sewer line at sufficient depth not to interfere with the Grantor's use and enjoyment of said property; and to place an intake connection in said line for use of the Grantor at a point to be designated by him, and further agrees to pay to the Grantor any damage which may result to his property by reason of the laying, maintaining, repairing, and operation of said sewer line.

In Witness Whereof, the parties have executed this agreement on the day and year first above written.

_____
John Doe

ACME SEWER CONSTRUCTION, INC.

By_____
Its President

ATTEST:

_____
Its Secretary

[Acknowledgements]

An easement in gross exists in this situation as well:

Anita and her heirs are granted written permission to enter Barbara's property to swim in a stream flowing through Barbara's land so long as the property is owned by Barbara and her heirs.

Notice the difference between the right granted in the above example of an easement in gross and a piscary profit, where the holder of the right can remove something of value (fish) from the stream.

Whether an easement is appurtenant or in gross is determined by the intent of the parties, although courts will endeavor to construe the easement as appurtenant.

> Andrew owned both Western Estates and Eastern Estates in the diagram above. Andrew conveyed Western Estates to Beatrice, reserving "an easement for ingress and egress for the benefit of Andrew."

A court likely would conclude that the easement in this example is appurtenant to Eastern Estates rather than for the benefit of Andrew personally.

The distinction between an appurtenant easement and an easement in gross is important. An appurtenant easement *runs with the land*. Continuing with the same example above, if Andrew thereafter conveyed Eastern Estates to Cynthia, the right of ingress and egress also would be conveyed to Cynthia as part of the ownership of Eastern Estates, even if there is no mention of it in the deed.

An easement in gross, on the other hand, does not run with the land. Using the same example, if the court had concluded the easement was in gross and personal to Andrew, it would not be conveyed to Cynthia as a part of her ownership of Western Estates. Andrew cannot convey the easement in gross to anyone. It is entirely personal to him. An exception exists only in the case of certain commercial easements, such as easements for public utilities. As a practical matter, utility easements must be transferable.

Easements are further classified as either affirmative or negative. An *affirmative easement* gives its owner the right to do something on the servient estate that otherwise would constitute a trespass (swim, for example). By contrast, a *negative easement* prohibits the owner of the servient estate from doing something she otherwise would have a right to do. Negative easements are always appurtenant easements and never easements in gross. They always must benefit a particular parcel of land.

> Austin owned Southern Estates and Northern Estates. Austin conveyed Southern Estates to Bruno by a deed containing this language: "provided Southern Estates shall be used for residential purposes and for no other purpose."

In this example, Southern Estates is subject to a negative easement in favor of Northern Estates, not unlike a defeasible estate. A negative easement is different from a defeasible estate or an estate subject to condition subsequent, however. Continuing with the same example to illustrate, Austin does not retain a reversion or right of entry. Rather, he may enforce the restriction only by injunction, specific performance, or damages. In other words, the estate never will revest in Austin as the grantor. Whether a particular instrument creates a negative easement or a defeasible estate is determined by the intent of the parties.

Other types of negative easements are easements for light and air as well as easements for an unobstructed view. In both of these circumstances, the servient tenement agrees not to erect a structure in a manner that encroaches on the dominant tenement. For example, Austin might convey Southern Estates to Bruno, "provided no structure shall be constructed on Southern Estates so as to obstruct the view of Pointy Peak from Northern Estates" or "provided no structure shall be constructed on Southern Estates so as to cast a shadow on Northern Estates."

Figure 6-3
Light Easement

GRANT OF EASEMENT OF LIGHT

THIS INDENTURE, made the 22nd day of August, 1996, between AUSTIN DOE, Grantor, and MARY ROE, Grantee;

WITNESSETH: that in consideration of the sum of One Hundred Thousand Dollars paid by the Grantee to the Grantor, the receipt whereof the Grantor hereby acknowledges, the Grantor hereby grants to the Grantee and her heirs:

Full and free right to the uninterrupted access, transmission, and enjoyment of light (to the extent of ___ degrees from the zenith) over and across all that parcel of land described as Southern Estates, Estate Filing No. 1, Carbon County, State of Anywhere, more particularly described on Exhibit "A," attached hereto and therein colored red, to the existing windows of the dwelling house erected upon a parcel of land of the Grantee adjoining the said first-mentioned parcel of land on the north side thereof, and more particularly described and delineated on said Exhibit and therein colored blue.

To hold said easement hereby granted unto the Grantee, her heirs and assigns.

In Witness Whereof, the Grantor has hereunto set his hand and seal the day and year first above written.

_____(SEAL)
AUSTIN DOE
[Acknowledgement]

Finally, easements are classified as either exclusive or nonexclusive. Easements generally are nonexclusive, that is, the grantor of the easement has a right of use in common with the grantee.

Anna grants to Bertha an easement for ingress and egress over an existing road through Western Estates. Anna may use the road in common with Bertha and even can grant an easement to Cassandra, an adjacent property owner, to use the road as well.

As a general rule, an easement is exclusive only when it expressly says so. In the example, the grant is not expressly exclusive and, therefore, is construed to be nonexclusive.

Easements may be created by grant, reservation, or other agreement (an express easement); by implication; by necessity; or by prescription. The instrument creating the easement must describe the dominant estate, the servient estate, and the dimensions of the easement with reasonable certainty. Grant of an easement requires all the formalities of a deed. It must be in writing signed by the grantor and, like other instruments concerning land, must be acknowledged before a notary public or other officer empowered to administer oaths. If the easement fails to meet any of these formal requirements, only a license results.

An *easement by reservation* occurs when a parcel of land is deeded to another, with the grantor reserving a right of ingress and egress or reserving some other right to continue to use the land or some portion of it. The common law experienced difficulty with easements by reservation. At first, they were not permitted. Once permitted, they were allowed to exist only in favor of the grantor of the deed that contained the reservation. Today, easements may be reserved in favor of third parties as well.

Easements also may be created by other documents. For example, adjacent property owners may enter into a mutual easement agreement to provide for ingress and egress over each other's property. In addition, easements may be created in documents such as condominium declarations and party wall agreements.

An *easement by implication* arises under certain, special circumstances when a grantor divides a tract of land and sells one or more parts of it to others. For an easement by implication to arise, there first must be unity of ownership, followed by a severance of that ownership. Second, there must be an apparent, actual use of one part of the property for the benefit of some other part of the property.

> Andrew (see earlier diagram) owned both Western Estates and Eastern Estates. He owned a home on Eastern Estates and gained access to the home by a road crossing Western Estates. If Andrew conveys Western Estates to Beatrice without reserving an easement for ingress and egress, such a reservation probably will be implied over the existing road for the benefit of Andrew.

Grant of an easement also may be implied. If Andrew conveyed Eastern Estates with the house to Beatrice, for example, an easement for ingress and egress over the existing road for the benefit of Beatrice probably would be implied as part of the conveyance. The easement would run with the land for as long as Eastern Estates and Western Estates were owned by different individuals.

Before an easement will be implied in either case, however, the court will require a showing that the preexisting use (sometimes called a *quasi-easement*) has certain characteristics. In general, the quasi-easement must be apparent (either visible or discoverable through reasonable inspection). The preexisting use must be permanent or continuous rather than merely temporary or casual. Finally, the court must be convinced that a genuine benefit is gained by the dominant parcel that makes it necessary to imply the easement. Courts are more reluctant to find reserved, implied easements simply because the grantor had full opportunity to make an express reservation and did not do so.

An *easement by necessity* also can be created. Again, unity of ownership, followed by severance, is required. Rather than implying the easement from actual use, however, it is implied solely as a matter of necessity. It is implied based upon public policy and not upon the intent of the parties.

> Alicia owns Northacre and Southacre, neither of which contains any improvements. Northacre connects to the state highway, but Southacre has no highway frontage. Alicia conveys Southacre to Bradford, causing Bradford to be landlocked, that is, without access except over Northacre.

A *way of necessity* or easement by necessity will be found to exist on these facts. This is not because of any intent of the parties but, rather, because of public policy that land not be landlocked. Unlike an easement implied from existing use, an easement by necessity is not permanent. It continues only as long as the necessity continues. If Bradford in the example obtains an easement across another adjacent parcel or if a new highway is constructed that provides access to Southacre, the prior easement by necessity will cease to exist.

Finally, a review of easements must include the *easement by prescription*. As mentioned previously, a right-of-way or easement may be created in favor of the public by prescription. A private easement may be created by prescription as well. In either case, creating an easement by prescription is a function of the statute of limitations. In every jurisdiction, a statute of limitations establishes a period of time (sometimes fifteen to twenty years) after which one dispossessed from real property may not recover possession. When a private roadway has been in use for the period of the statute, for instance, the roadway becomes a public roadway by prescription.

The requirements to create an easement by prescription are the same as the requirements for adverse possession, which are discussed in greater detail in a later chapter. Briefly, those requirements are that the adverse use or prescriptive use be open, continuous, and uninterrupted for the period defined in the statute of limitations.

> Beatrice owns Western Estates, and Andrew owns Eastern Estates. Beatrice never has granted an easement to Andrew. However, for more years than required by the statute of limitations, Andrew has openly, continuously, and without interruption used an existing road across Western Estates. Beatrice never has complained or objected.

An easement by prescription is created on the facts stated in the example. The extent of the easement is limited to that portion of the property which is used. If the portion used is only five feet wide, the prescriptive easement is only five feet wide. It cannot be widened without the consent of the owner of the servient estate or, in the case of a public way, by consent or by exercise of the power of eminent domain.

Easements may be transferred without regard to how they were created. Appurtenant easements run with the land and follow the ownership of the dominant estate. The grantee of the servient estate, whether the easement is appurtenant or in gross, takes title subject to the easement. Easements in gross generally are not assignable, since they are considered personal. Commercial easements in gross, such as the easements of public utilities, are assignable because of their significant benefit.

Questions may arise concerning whether the dominant estate (the holder of the easement) may expand the use of an easement. For example, suppose an easement for ingress and egress had been reserved by Abe at a time when Abe used the dominant estate only occasionally and only for recreational purposes. Later, however, Abe may decide to develop and to subdivide the dominant parcel in such a way that the easement becomes continuously used by many persons. The question to be answered is whether the increased use is a violation of the easement. To answer that question, courts look to the express language of the grant or reservation and to the circumstances surrounding its creation. A rule of reasonableness generally is applied. If the increased use is reasonable considering the circumstances of the grant or reservation and if it is not prohibited by the language of the grant or reservation, the increased use likely will be permitted. A different rule is used, however, when the easement is either implied or prescriptive. When that is the case, courts are more reluctant to permit an increased use.

A question similarly may arise concerning whether the owner of the servient estate may use his or her property in such a fashion as to encroach upon the easement. For example, may the owner of the servient estate build over an underground sewer easement? Or may she use the airspace over an access easement? The answer to those questions generally is that the servient estate may not be used in a way that interferes unreasonably with the dominant tenement's use of the easement. Temporary buildings may be placed over an underground easement, for example, but permanent buildings probably cannot. The airspace may be used by the servient estate to the extent that it does not interfere with the dominant estate's right of passage.

Other than easements by necessity, easements usually are permanent. However, they can be terminated or extinguished in a number of ways. Easements may be terminated by *merger* when the dominant and servient estates are combined into own ownership. They may be terminated by *express release*. In other words, the owner of the dominant estate may release the servient estate of the burden of the easement by quit claim deed or by other document.

An easement may be released orally if the *oral release* is accompanied by nonuse or by significant acts indicating an intent to extinguish the easement. In the same vein, an easement may be terminated by oral statements of the dominant tenant which are relied upon by the servient tenant to his detriment, such as the expenditure of money by the servient tenant. In this situation, the dominant tenant will be estopped from reasserting the easement.

An easement also may be abandoned by nonuse if the nonuse is accompanied by an intent to abandon and if it continues for the period defined by the statute of limitations. Generally speaking, however, there is no requirement that the dominant tenant exercise his or her rights under the easement.

Easements are enforceable by any remedy available to a court. Most often, when an easement is interfered with in some way, the rights of the holder of the easement will be enforced by injunction, including mandatory relief. For example, if the owner of the servient estate erects a fence across an easement for ingress and egress, the court will order it removed and will enjoin the owner of the servient estate from further interference with the easement.

Licenses

Generally speaking, when the grant of a right to enter upon the land of another for some purpose lacks one or more of the requirements of an easement, it will be construed to be a license. A license is not an interest in land but, rather, merely is the right of one person to do something on the land of another which otherwise would be a trespass. A license is temporary and personal. It generally cannot be assigned or transferred. It terminates upon death of the licensee or upon conveyance of the servient estate to a third party.

Figure 6-4
License to Use Real Estate

LICENSE TO FISH

I, the undersigned, in consideration of the sum of Ten Dollars, the receipt of which is hereby acknowledged, do hereby grant to MARY SMITH full license and authority with a rod and line to fish for and to take and carry away fish of every kind in that portion of the Beaver Brook, so called, which crosses my farm in Any County, and also to traverse and use the banks of said brook for any purpose necessary to the proper exercise of this license, and to pass and repass on foot over said farm between said brook and County Road 1, from the first day of March of every year, commencing with the year 1997, until the first day of October of every year until such license is revoked by me.

DATED this 4th day of November, 1996.

_____

Sonja Smith

A license may be revoked by the licensor except when it is *coupled with an interest*. For example, an oral or implied right of ingress and egress coupled with a right to remove timber cannot be terminated until the timber is removed or until the right to remove the timber is terminated. Also, if money is spent in reliance on a license with knowledge of the grantor of the license, the granter may be estopped to terminate it. In this situation, the license is said to have ripened into an easement.

If a license is in writing and is described as perpetual or irrevocable, it probably will be construed to be an easement.

Drafting Nonpossessory Rights

When drafting documents to grant nonpossessory rights, the language varies according to the specific right to be granted. This section includes examples of language that may be used for easements, for a license, and for a profit.

Grant of Appurtenant Easement   Alicia grants to Bruno an easement described as follows: *(Describe the extent of the easement by metes and bounds, for example)* over and across Lot 1, Buena Vista Estates, for the benefit of Lot 2, Buena Vista Estates, for the purpose of ingress and egress. The easement is nonexclusive.

In this example, Lot 1 is the servient estate; and Lot 2 is the dominant estate.

Reservation of Appurtenant Easement   Aaron conveys Lot 1, Buena Vista Estates, to Beatrice, reserving an exclusive easement described as follows: *(Describe the extent of the easement by metes and bounds)* over and across said Lot 1, Buena Vista Estates, for the benefit of Lot 2, Buena Vista Estates, for the purpose of ingress and egress.

Once again, Lot 1 is the servient estate, and Lot 2 is the dominant estate. This easement is exclusive, however.

Grant of Easement in Gross   Gina grants to the City of Metropolis an easement for utilities described as follows: *(Describe the extent of the easement by metes and bounds)* under, over, and across Lot 1, Buena Vista Estates.

The purpose of the easement is described differently in this example for purpose of clarity and for no other reason. Notice that the easement is granted under the lot as well as over and across it, since the utilities may be placed underground. The easement is for the benefit of no particular person or property and, therefore, is an easement in gross.

Grant of License   Larry grants to Luisa a license for ingress and egress over and across the following described parcel: *(Describe the parcel affected by the license by metes and bounds).*

The interest granted in this example is for the benefit of no particular parcel, but it is for the benefit of a particular person. It is therefore a license.

Grant of Profit   George grants to Georgia the right to pasture up to one hundred head of cattle in the Northwest Quarter, Section 1, R8W, T5W of the 2nd P.M., Grand County.

In this example, the cattle will graze the land, removing the crop of natural grass. The interest is, therefore, a profit.

Real Covenants

The term *covenant* is borrowed from the law of contracts. Simply stated, a *covenant* is an agreement or contract; but in the context of the law of real property, a *real covenant* is an agreement or a contract relating to real property. Real covenants differ from the covenants of contract law in that real covenants may be imposed unilaterally (by a developer, for example). They are not agreed to in the usual sense. Rather, the purchaser impliedly agrees to a real covenant by purchasing the property and taking title.

Covenants may be either affirmative or restrictive, although they usually are restrictive. An *affirmative covenant* requires the promisor (covenantor) to do something affirmative, such as to maintain a party wall. By contrast, a *restrictive covenant* prohibits or restricts the promisor (covenantor) from doing something related to the use of land.

Real covenants came into being at a time when the law courts conservatively declined to expand the use of easements beyond their traditional boundaries. Easements then and now were required to describe specifically the area affected by the easement as well as the dominant and servient estates. Since easements in gross were not binding on successors at common law, their use was limited to such things as ingress and egress.

To impose additional and more extensive burdens on real estate, landowners turned to the law of contracts, seeking to impose the burden of a promise (covenant) on real estate itself and not merely on the promisor.

From the point of view of the law courts, the problem with using a covenant to bind real property was that contract law required *privity* to enforce the promise. A contract is enforceable at law only by the parties *privy* to it, that is, the persons who signed the contract and third party beneficiaries. Law courts, therefore, were reluctant to enforce a promise against a successor owner of land.

Alistair owned Lots 1 and 2, Farview Estates. He wanted to sell Lot 2 to Brenda. However, he wanted to be certain that the use of Lot 2 was limited to residential purposes to assure the continuing value of Lot 1. He could convey either a determinable fee or a fee subject to condition subsequent to Brenda, but he had no interest in regaining ownership of Lot 2 in the future. He could not reserve an easement because the use of easements was far too restricted. All he could do, therefore, was to obtain an agreement from Brenda that she would restrict use of Lot 2 to residential purposes.

The problem with Alistair's solution is that an agreement is enforceable only by the parties to it, together with their heirs and personal representatives. How does Alistair ensure that the agreement also is enforceable by and against his and Brenda's assigns, in other words, by and against subsequent owners?

That was the legal question in the landmark case of Tulk v. Moxhay, 2 Phillips 774, 41 Eng. Rep. 1143 (1848). In that case, an affirmative covenant was enforced against a remote grantee, creating the concept in English law of the *equitable servitude*. The facts of that case were that Tulk, the owner of Leicester Square in London, sold Leicester Square Garden, including its equestrian statue, to one Elms by a deed containing a covenant that Elms as well as his heirs and assigns forever would maintain the garden in proper repair.

The same property ultimately was conveyed to Moxhay, but without the covenant. Although Moxhay had notice of the covenant contained in the original deed, he announced his plans to redesign the square and to build upon it. Tulk brought suit in the Chancery Court, seeking to enjoin Moxhay from carrying through with his plans and to enforce the covenant of the original deed against him. The Chancellor readily granted the relief requested, reasoning that "nothing could be more inequitable than the original purchaser should be able to sell the property the next day for a greater price, in consideration of the assignee being able to escape from the liability which he had himself undertaken."

American courts were more ready to enforce real covenants at law than were the English courts. Using the example above, the promise not to use Lot 2 for other than residential purposes will be enforced against successors and assigns of the original parties to the agreement (actually, the parties to the deed) if the agreement (the covenant) *runs with the land*. We call such a covenant a real covenant. The English, on the other hand, call it an equitable servitude.

Of course, with today's merger of law and equity, there is no practical distinction between a real covenant and an equitable servitude. A promise of the parties to a deed, whether benefit or burden, will be enforced against and in favor of their successors if it is a covenant running with the land and if it has been recorded.

To find that a particular covenant runs with the land, a court must determine that the parties so intended and that the covenant *touches and concerns* the land. If the language of the covenant is that it "shall be binding upon successors and assigns," the court easily may conclude that the parties intended it to run with the land. For the covenant to satisfy the *touch and concern* test, the court must determine that the covenant benefits the property either physically or economically.

Returning to the example, a covenant running with the land might be created as follows:

> Alistair grants and conveys Lot 2, Farview Estates, to Brenda, it being agreed by Brenda, that Lot 2 shall forever be used for residential purposes, and that such agreement shall be binding upon her heirs and assigns.

From the language, it is apparent that Brenda intends her agreement to bind her successors and assigns. In other words, it runs with the land. The touch and concern test is also met because the agreement relates to use of the land. The covenant is, therefore, a real covenant; and if it is recorded, it will run with the land and forever will be enforceable at law and in equity, unless it is terminated at some future time.

Assume, for example, that Brenda later conveyed Lot 2 to Charles and that Charles began construction of a shopping mall. Alistair may bring the project to a halt by injunction. Or Alistair may maintain a suit against Charles for damages, in which case Charles probably would be required to pay Alistair for the damage resulting to his property. Even if Alistair is not damaged or even if Alistair's property is benefitted (possibly Lot 1 will become more valuable if there is an increased demand for other commercial uses), Alistair always may maintain a suit for an injunction and may bring the project to a halt.

The type of real covenant described in the example is a restrictive or *protective covenant*. Such covenants often are found in land use planning. Thus, a new residential area may be created by multiple deeds rather than by a subdivision plat. Some or all of the deeds in the subdivision may contain protective covenants that contain restrictions on the use of the parcels conveyed, such as minimum building size, minimum construction cost, setbacks from streets, side lot lines, and so forth. When a subdivision is created in this manner, the grantor and all grantees of the deeds generally have a right to enforce the covenants with respect to all the lots which are so restricted. These types of covenants sometimes are known as neighborhood covenants or neighborhood restrictions.

> Diana is the developer of Diana's Estates. She conveys Lot 1,
> Diana's Estates, to Paul. It is covenanted in the deed that all lots
> in Diana's Estates shall be used solely for residential purposes.

Diana and Paul have both a benefit and a burden. The benefit is the assurance that no lot in Diana's Estates will be used in such a way as to reduce the value of another lot. The burden is that the use of any lot is restricted. The benefit of the covenant will be enforceable by later purchasers as assignees of Diana. Similarly, Diana may enforce the burden of the covenant against later purchasers because they took title from her with notice of the restriction to which she agreed.

Using the same example, later purchasers will be entitled to enforce the covenants of earlier deeds on a third party beneficiary theory. The covenants contained in the various deeds also may be treated as implied, reciprocal equitable servitudes, which sometimes is called the *common scheme of development* theory. For instance, if Diana agrees in her deed to Paul to restrict all land under her ownership to residential use, equity will imply an undertaking on her part, as the developer or common grantor, whether or not the deeds to other purchasers contain the same express restrictions.

The courts will more readily enforce neighborhood restrictions if a common plan or common scheme of development can be shown for the subdivision. A common scheme may be found in other documents recorded in connection with the subdivision or may be found in the physical appearance of buildings constructed within the subdivision.

More frequently, restrictive covenants are contained in a document separate from the deeds, usually called a Declaration of Protective Covenants. Assuming it is recorded before any deeds are delivered by the developer, such a declaration binds successive purchasers. The declaration generally states who may enforce its provisions, usually the developer, owners of property in the subdivision, and occasionally the governmental entity where the subdivision is located. Sometimes the declaration of protective covenants is contained in another document, such as a condominium declaration.

Figure 6-5
Protective Covenants

DECLARATION OF RESTRICTIVE COVENANTS

KNOW ALL MEN BY THESE PRESENTS That Acme Development Company, a corporation duly established under the laws of the State of Massachusetts, being the owner of all that certain real estate situate in Any County, Massachusetts, being known and designated as:

[legal description]

does hereby impress all of the property described above with the following restrictions:

1. No building, other than private dwellings arranged for the occupancy for not more than one family and consisting of not less than 1,800 square feet of living space exclusive of any garage and breezeway, and private garages for not more than three automobiles to be used in connection with such dwelling houses, shall be erected and maintained on any lot. Unless attached to the dwelling, no garage shall be erected nearer than sixty-five (65) feet from the front street line.

2. No building or structure, or any part thereof, shall be erected or placed thereon nearer than forty (40) feet to any street line nor nearer than fifteen (15) feet to the side lines of any building plot upon which a single residence is to be erected.

3. All such private dwelling houses shall be of Colonial architecture, with a height minimum of one and one-half stories.

4. No noxious or offensive activity shall be carried on upon any lot, nor shall anything be done thereon which may be or become an annoyance or nuisance to the neighborhood.

In Witness Whereof said Acme Development Company has caused its corporate seal to be hereto affixed and these presents to be signed, acknowledged and delivered in its name and behalf by its President, this 12th day of December, 1996.

Signed and sealed in the presence of:_____

ACME DEVELOPMENT COMPANY, a
Massachusetts corporation

By:_____
Its President

[acknowledgment]

Covenants intended for illegal purposes will not be enforced in today's courts, although they may have been fully enforceable at common law. For example, covenants which have the effect of excluding members of a minority group from a neighborhood will not be enforced. Today's courts have determined that this type of covenant violates the due process clauses of the state and federal constitutions. Covenants which have the effect of restraining trade in violation of the antitrust laws also cannot be enforced. For example, the owner of a grocery store might have difficulty enforcing a covenant which prohibits construction of grocery stores on other lots. An argument could be made that the grocery store owner's attempt to enforce such a covenant amounted to a monopoly in violation of federal law.

A particular covenant may be found unconscionable and, therefore, unenforceable. For example, an argument could be made that a covenant against couples with children should not be enforced for reasons of public policy.

Covenants can be terminated by agreement of all parties entitled to enforce them, by abandonment, or by a change of circumstances. Occasionally, a developer will create a subdivision using protective covenants or neighborhood covenants to guide future development; and purchasers thereafter ignore the covenants in the course of building their homes. When that happens, a court may conclude that the owners are prevented from enforcing the covenants against others under the equitable doctrines of estoppel, laches (delay), and unclean hands. Under the doctrine of *unclean hands*, a person may not obtain equitable relief when she has committed similar violations.

A change of circumstances may terminate restrictive covenants. For example, restrictive covenants recorded in the 1960s may have established minimum construction cost that became outdated after the inflation of the 1970s and 1980s. Using its equity powers, a court may be willing to modify the covenants, even though all the persons bound by the covenants do not agree to their change.

Common law rules establish additional restrictions or limitations on the use of private property. The law of nuisance protects adjacent landowners. The rights of lateral and subjacent support protect adjacent landowners as well as owners of surface estates. Today, private property is subject to airspace rights and limitations.

Nuisance

A property owner cannot use his or her property in a way that creates either a public or private nuisance.

A *public nuisance* is an interference with the rights of the public. Specific nuisances are defined in statutes or in municipal or county ordinances and are treated as petty offenses. However, the legislative enumeration is not binding on a court, which is free to identify additional nuisances as they arise. Examples of public nuisances are air pollution, noise pollution, criminal activity (including prostitution and illegal drugs), maintaining vicious or excessive numbers of animals, and storing of explosives.

A *private nuisance* is analogous to a civil trespass; it is a violation of the property rights of another. Commission of a private nuisance is a tort that can result in an award of damages. According to the Restatement of Torts (Second), a private nuisance is the intentional and unreasonable use of land or the unintentional but reckless or dangerous use of land. To the extent that they impact neighboring land, public nuisances are private nuisances as well. The distinction between the two relates more to the remedy than to the substance of the right. A public nuisance can be enjoined by a public authority with jurisdiction, usually the city or the county. A private nuisance may be enjoined only by the person damaged by the nuisance, usually a neighbor.

Lateral and Subjacent Support

At least in its natural, unimproved state, any parcel of land is entitled to the duties of lateral and subjacent support. *Lateral support* is the support given by the adjacent land. The right of lateral support is violated, for example, if an excavation for a foundation causes the subsidence (cave-in) of the neighboring parcel. The right does not exist, however, when the neighboring parcel has been altered by the construction of improvements that weaken it. The right to lateral support is an absolute, strict-liability right and is not dependent upon proof of negligence. On the other hand, the presence of negligence will cause liability even when the neighboring parcel has been altered.

The right of *subjacent support* is similar to the right of lateral support. The right of subjacent support is violated when property is undermined, for example, when the mineral estate has been severed and is separately owned. A tunnel or drift created below the surface must be shored up so that the surface does not collapse, at least in its natural state.

Airspace

At common law, the owner of a parcel of land owned the airspace as well, without limitation. Thus, if someone built a balcony extending over his neighbor's land, the neighbor could compel removal of the encroachment, even though the land itself was not touched.

An owner of land can convey interests in the airspace above her or his land. For example, the Waldorf Astoria in New York City is built in airspace above the subterranean tracks of the Pennsylvania Railroad. A landowner similarly may grant an easement for light over her land. When such an easement exists, the owner of the land that is servient to the easement cannot construct a building which obstructs sun and light directed at the dominant estate.

The development of aviation has qualified the rule that a landowner owns "to the sky." Today, the right of overflight is recognized by federal law, restricting the landowner's use of his land to that which is reasonably needed to use the surface. However, an airplane cannot fly at an altitude so low that it causes a nuisance. Thus, in an early case, a farmer was awarded damages caused by low-flying aircraft that caused his chickens not to lay eggs. Under such circumstances, the property owner may have a claim against the government if it owns the airport. The property owner may seek abatement of the nuisance or, if the value of the land is affected, for *inverse condemnation*. In other words, the property owner may recover the diminution in value of her property caused by the overflights.

To prevent disputes of this type, the planners of airports ordinarily negotiate a special form of easement called an *avigation easement* from adjacent landowners. An avigation easement releases the airport owner from claims for damage from low-flying aircraft. It also may limit the height of buildings, other structures, and even trees within the area of the easement. The easement is obtained by paying a sum of money. Statutes authorizing the construction of airports generally grant the public body the authority to obtain avigation easements through the power of eminent domain if they cannot be acquired voluntarily.

Figure 6-6
Airspace Easement

AVIGATION AND HAZARD EASEMENT

WHEREAS, JANE DOE, hereinafter called the "Grantor," is the owner in fee of that certain parcel of land situated in the City of Oro, County of Carbon, and State of Anywhere, more particularly described as follows:

[description of property]

hereinafter called "Grantor's property," and outlined on the map attached hereto as Exhibit "A."

NOW, THEREFORE, in consideration of the sum of Ten Dollars ($10) and other good and valuable consideration, the receipt and sufficiency of which is hereby acknowledged, the Grantor, for herself, her heirs, administrators, personal representatives, successor and assigns, does hereby grant, bargain, sell and convey unto the City of Oro, State of Anywhere, hereinafter called the "Grantee", its successors and assigns, for the use and benefit of the public, an easement and right of way, appurtenant to Oro International Airport, for the unobstructed passage of all aircraft, ("aircraft" being defined for the purposes of this instrument as any contrivance now known or hereafter invented, used or designed for navigation of or flight in the air) by whomsoever owned and operated, in the air space above Grantor's property above a Mean Sea level of 200 feet, to an infinite height above said Grantor's property, together with the right to cause in all space above the surface of the Grantor's property such noise, vibrations, fumes, dust, fuel particles, and all other effects that may be caused by the operation of aircraft and all other effects that may be caused by the operation of aircraft landing at, or taking off from, or operating at or on said Oro International Airport; and Grantor does hereby fully waive, remise and release any right or cause of action which they may now have or which they may have in the future against Grantee, its successors and assigns, due to such noise, vibrations, fumes, dust, fuel particles, and all other effects that may be caused or may have been caused by the operation of aircraft landing at, or taking off from, or operating at or on said Oro International Airport.

The easement and right of way hereby granted includes the continuing right in the Grantee to prevent the erection or growth upon Grantor's property of any building, structure, tree or other object extending into the air space above said Mean Sea level of 200 feet, and to remove from said air space, or at the sole option of the Grantee, as an alternative, to mark and light as obstructions to air navigation, any such building, structure, tree or other object now upon, or which in the future may be upon Grantor's property, together with the right of ingress to, egress from, and passage over Grantor's property for the above purposes.

To have and to hold said easement and right of way, and all rights appertaining thereto unto the Grantee, its successors and assigns, until said Oro International Airport shall be abandoned and shall cease to be used for public airport purposes.

And for the consideration hereinabove set forth the Grantor, for herself, her heirs, administrators, personal representatives, successor and assigns, does hereby agree that for and during the life of said easement and right of way, she will not hereafter erect, permit the erection or growth of, or permit or suffer to remain upon Grantor's property any building, structure, tree or other object extending into the aforesaid prohibited air space, and that she shall not hereafter use or permit or suffer the use of Grantor's property in such a manner as to create electrical interference with radio communication between any installation upon said airport and aircraft, or as to make it difficult for flyers to distinguish between airport lights and others, or as to impair the visibility in the vicinity of the airport, or as otherwise to endanger the landing, taking off or maneuvering of aircraft, it being understood and agreed that the aforesaid covenants and agreements shall run with the land.

In Witness Where, the Grantor has set her hand and seal this ____ day of _____, 1996.

[signature and acknowledgment]

Chapter 6 Quiz

Fill in each blank with the most correct word or phrase.

1. Common law servitudes are the _____, the _____, and the _____.

2. Restrictive covenants may be characterized as _____ because they are burdens upon real property ownership for the benefit of the public or others.

3. The holder of an easement has the right of _____ but not the right of _____.

4. An _____ easement "runs with the land."

5. Easements may be created by _____, by _____, by _____, or by _____.

6. The holder of the easement is the _____.

7. Easements are enforceable by _____, by an action for _____, and by an action for _____.

8. A license is _____ and _____ in its nature and _____ be assigned.

9. To meet the "touch and concern" test, a covenant must benefit the property either _____ or _____.

Circle the most correct answer.

10. True or False. An easement is a possessory right.

11. True or False. An appurtenant easement relates to a distinct parcel of land.

12. True or False. An easement in gross is a personal right to do something on someone else's land, for example, to lay sewer mains not serving any particular parcel of land.

13. True or False. An easement in gross does not run with the land, but the holder may convey it to a third party.

14. True or False. Negative easements always are appurtenant easements.

15. True or False. The estate in a negative easement never reverts to the grantor.

16. True or False. A grant of an easement which lacks the formalities of a deed results not in an easement, but in a license.

17. True or False. At common law, easements could be reserved in favor of third parties; today, they cannot.

18. True or False. To create an easement by implication or by necessity, there first must be a unity of ownership, followed by its severance.

19. True or False. An easement by necessity is based upon whether the parties intended that an easement be created.

20. True or False. An easement by necessity is not permanent, unlike an easement implied by existing law.

21. True or False. Requirements for an easement by prescription are the same as for adverse possession; however, the extent of the easement is only that which is used.

22. True or False. The dominant tenant may not expand his use of the easement if the easement was made by grant.

23. True or False. The Statute of Frauds requires that an easement may be terminated only in writing regardless of how it was created.

24. True or False. A dominant tenant need not exercise her rights under an easement to maintain them.

25. True or False. A license is an interest in land that grants the right to do something which otherwise would be a trespass.

26. True or False. Conveyance of the servient estate to a third party terminates a license.

27. True or False. A license may be revoked by the licensor at will unless it is coupled with an interest.

28. True or False. A license may ripen into an easement if the grantor is estopped from terminating it.

29. True or False. A covenant is unenforceable against successors and assigns of the original parties unless it runs with the land.

30. True or False. A declaration of protective covenants usually binds successive purchasers.

31. Smith owned a large lot next to a park. In 1964, she orally gave Jones permission to use a "short cut" across her lot to get to the park. She did not designate a particular path to use and set no time limit. Jones used the path daily. Jones was so grateful that he wrote a note to Smith, telling her how much he appreciated being allowed to cut across her lot and assuring her that he would vary his route so as not to harm the vegetation. The statutory time for adverse possession in the state is 20 years. Smith conveyed her lot to Dover in 1995. Dover refused to let Jones cross the lot. Can Dover do this?

    1. No. Once a valid easement is granted, the grantee must consent to its extinguishment.
    2. No. Jones's prescriptive easement would have been disclosed by an inspection of the premises.
    3. No. Easements which run with the land need not be mentioned in subsequent conveyances.
    4. Yes. A license binds only the person who gives it; it does not bind subsequent owners.

32. True or False. Easements usually are nonexclusive; the grantor retains the right to use the easement in common with the grantee.

Chapter 7
PLANNING AND ZONING

At the beginning of the twentieth century, a discussion of the restrictions on ownership and use of real property would have been concluded at the end of the last chapter. Since that time, however, a vast, statutory system of regulation has developed, known as the law of planning and zoning or land use law. Topics included under that rubric are zoning regulation, including the master planning process; subdivision regulation; design review; and building code enforcement. Because these regulations restrict the use of private property, they raised various constitutional issues in their early years. Many of those issues now have been put to rest, however.

The Master Plan

Most communities today have taken control of land use through the planning and zoning process, which supersedes the use of restrictive or protective covenants. The first step in the process is a community's adoption of a *master plan*, sometimes called a comprehensive plan. The purpose of the master plan is to establish long-range goals to develop all or a portion of the community. It also can be used to maintain an already developed community. The master plan itself has no binding effect on landowners within the community. Rather, specific zoning regulations must be adopted. To be valid, however, the zoning regulations must relate to and be supported by the master plan.

Euclidean Zoning

Zoning as a restriction on the use of property was held to be a constitutional exercise of the police power of local government in <u>Village of Euclid v. Ambler Realty Co.</u>, 272 U.S. 365 (1926). Accordingly, the traditional forms of zoning sometimes are described as *Euclidean zoning*. This section discusses only that form of zoning.

A zoning ordinance and its accompanying zoning map typically divide a community into geographic areas called *zone districts*: residential zone districts, commercial zone districts, industrial zone districts, and so forth. Each zone district may be further divided. For example, a residential zone district may be further divided into single-family residential zone districts and multi-family residential zone districts. Each district may be characterized by density as well. For instance, a high density residential zone district would allow a greater number of dwelling units for each acre of land than a low density residential zone district would allow.

There may be other types of zone districts as well, depending upon the nature and location of the particular community. A community which has open space, such as parks and recreation land, may preserve that open space through open space zone districts. Communities that accommodate tourists and business travelers may do so in an accommodation zone district in which the principal use is hotels, motels, and other forms of accommodation units. Other than the human imagination, there is no limit on the numbers and types of zone districts that can be created as part of the zoning plan.

Within each zone district is a list of permitted uses (uses by right) as well as a list of special review (conditional) uses. Permitted uses or uses by right usually are the higher forms of property use. Thus, single-family residences are permitted as a use by right in a residential zone district. One who wishes to build a single-family residence within a residential district may do so by obtaining a building permit; no other zoning permission is required. The selected zoning ordinances and maps at Figure 7-1 provide examples of zoning districts that can be established, provisions of a residential zoning district, and the criteria and procedure to obtain a conditional use permit.

Figure 7-1
Selected Zoning Ordinances and Map (Vail, Colorado)

Chapter 18.06
DISTRICTS ESTABLISHED
Sections:
18.06.010 Designated.
18.06.020 Permitted Uses.

18.06.010. Designated. The following Zoning Districts are established:
A. Hillside Residential District (HR);
B. Single-Family Residential District (SFR);
C. Two-Family Residential District (R);
D. Primary/Secondary Residential District;
E. Residential Cluster District (RC);
F. Low-Density Multiple-Family District (LDMF)
G. Medium-Density Multiple Family District (MDMF);
H. High-Density Multiple-Family District (HDMF);
I. Public Accommodation District (PA);
J. Commercial Core 1 District (CC1);
K. Commercial Core 2 District (CC2);
L. Commercial Core 3 District (CC3);
M. Commercial Service Center District (CSC);
N. Arterial Business District;
O. Heavy Services District (HS);
P. Agricultural and Open Space District (A);
Q. Parking District (P);
R. General Use District (GU);
S. Natural Area Preservation District (NAP);
T. Ski Base/Recreation District;
U. Special Development District (SP). (Ord. 94-21 (1994):Ord. 32(1988) § 2: Ord 23 (1987) § 1: Ord. 30(1986) § 1: Ord. 30(1977) § 2.

18.06.020 Permitted uses.
A. The listing of any use as being a permitted use in any particular district shall be deemed an exclusion of such use from any other district unless expressly permitted as a permitted use, conditional use or accessory use.
B. The permitted uses, conditional uses, and accessory uses in the particular districts shall be deemed to be exclusive uses for those districts, and any use not specifically permitted as a permitted use is prohibited unless a determination of similar use is made in accordance with Section 18.66.040. (Ord. 50 (1978) § 21.)

Chapter 18.08
ZONING MAP
Sections:
18.08.010 Adopted.
18.08.020 Filing.
18.08.030 Changes.
18.08.040 Replacement.
18.08.050 Interpretation of boundaries.
18.08.060 Property without a zone designation.

18.08.010 Adopted. The Town is divided into districts as shown on the Official Zoning Map which, together with explanatory material thereon, is adopted by reference and declared to be of this Title. (Ord. 8(1973) § 1.202.)

18.08.020 Filing. The Official Zoning Map shall be filed in the office of the Town Clerk and shall be identified by the signature of the Mayor, attested by the Town Clerk, and bear the Seal of the Town under the following words: "This is to

certify that this is the Official Zoning Map referred to in Section 18.08.010 of the Zoning Title, Town of Vail, Colorado," together with the date of the adoption of the ordinance codified in this Title and the date of the most recent change in district boundaries shown thereon. (Ord. 8(1973) § 1.202.)

18.08.030 Changes. No change shall be made in the district boundaries or other matter shown on the Official Zoning Map except by appropriate action of the Town Council in accord with Sections 18.66.110 through 18.66.160. Any change adopted by the Town Council shall be entered on the Official Zoning Map promptly, together with an entry noting the date of the change and a brief description of the nature of the change, which entry shall be attested by the Town Clerk. The date of the most recent change shall at all times be indicated on any copies of the Official Zoning Map subsequently reproduced. (Ord. 8(1973) § 1.203.)

18.08.040 Replacement. In the event that the Official Zoning Map becomes damaged, destroyed, lost, or difficult to interpret or reproduce because of the nature or number of changes and additions, the Town Council may, by resolution, adopt a new Official Zoning Map, which shall supersede the prior Official Zoning Map. The new Official Zoning Map may correct drafting or other errors or omissions in the prior map and may add or revise street locations, lot designations, or other like designations, but no such correction or addition shall have the effect of amending the Zoning Ordinance or revising the boundaries of districts shown on the prior Official Zoning Map. (Ord. 8(1973) § 1.204.)

18.08.050. Interpretation of boundaries. Where uncertainty exists as to the boundaries of districts as shown on the Official Zoning Map, the following rules shall apply:
A. Boundaries indicated as approximately following the centerline of streets or roads shall be construed to follow the centerlines;
B. Boundaries indicated as approximately following plotted lot lines shall be construed as following the lot lines;
C. Boundaries indicated as approximately following the Town limits shall be construed as following the Town limits;
D. Boundaries indicated as parallel to or extensions of centerlines, lot lines, Town limits, or similar geographic lines shall be so construed;
E. Distances not specifically indicated on the Official Zoning Map shall be determined by the scale of the Map;
F. Where physical or cultural features existing on the ground are at variance with those shown on the Official Zoning Map or in circumstances not covered by subsections A through E of this Section, the Town Council shall interpret the district boundaries. (Ord. 8(1973) § 1.205.)

18.08.060 Property without a zone designation. Any land, lot, or site within the Town of Vail Municipal boundary which, according to the Official Zoning Map, does not have a designated zone district, shall be designated Natural Area Preservation Zone District. Newly annexed property will not be so designated for a period of not more than ninety (90) days or an additional period of time agreed upon between the property owners of said property and the Town for the imposition of zoning. (Ord. 6(1987) § 1.)

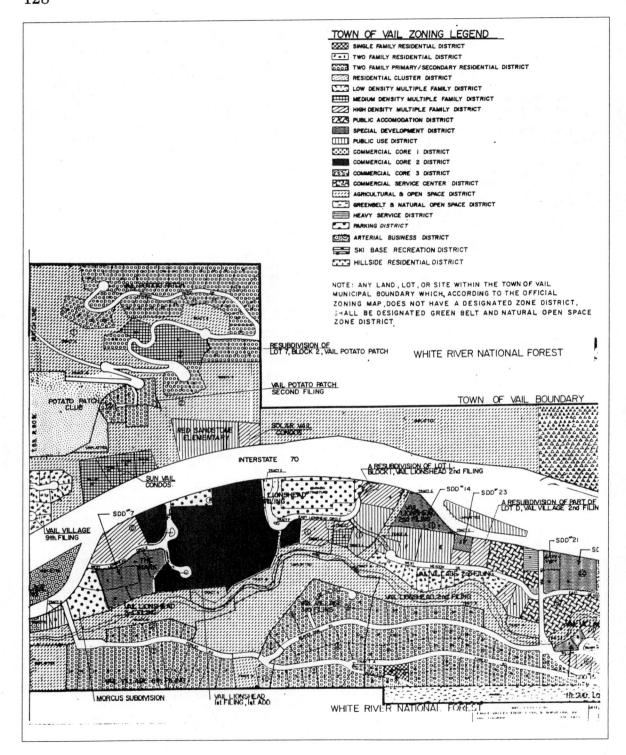

TOWN OF VAIL ZONING LEGEND

- SINGLE FAMILY RESIDENTIAL DISTRICT
- TWO FAMILY RESIDENTIAL DISTRICT
- TWO FAMILY PRIMARY/SECONDARY RESIDENTIAL DISTRICT
- RESIDENTIAL CLUSTER DISTRICT
- LOW DENSITY MULTIPLE FAMILY DISTRICT
- MEDIUM DENSITY MULTIPLE FAMILY DISTRICT
- HIGH DENSITY MULTIPLE FAMILY DISTRICT
- PUBLIC ACCOMODATION DISTRICT
- SPECIAL DEVELOPMENT DISTRICT
- PUBLIC USE DISTRICT
- COMMERCIAL CORE 1 DISTRICT
- COMMERCIAL CORE 2 DISTRICT
- COMMERCIAL CORE 3 DISTRICT
- COMMERCIAL SERVICE CENTER DISTRICT
- AGRICULTURAL & OPEN SPACE DISTRICT
- GREENBELT & NATURAL OPEN SPACE DISTRICT
- HEAVY SERVICE DISTRICT
- PARKING DISTRICT
- ARTERIAL BUSINESS DISTRICT
- SKI BASE RECREATION DISTRICT
- HILLSIDE RESIDENTIAL DISTRICT

NOTE: ANY LAND, LOT, OR SITE WITHIN THE TOWN OF VAIL MUNICIPAL BOUNDARY WHICH, ACCORDING TO THE OFFICIAL ZONING MAP, DOES NOT HAVE A DESIGNATED ZONE DISTRICT, SHALL BE DESIGNATED GREEN BELT AND NATURAL OPEN SPACE ZONE DISTRICT.

WHITE RIVER NATIONAL FOREST

RESUBDIVISION OF LOT 7, BLOCK 2, VAIL POTATO PATCH

VAIL POTATO PATCH SECOND FILING

TOWN OF VAIL BOUNDARY

POTATO PATCH CLUB

RED SANDSTONE ELEMENTARY

SOLAR VAIL CONDOS

INTERSTATE 70

SUN VAIL CONDOS.

A RESUBDIVISION OF LOT 1, BLOCK 1, VAIL LIONSHEAD 2nd FILING

SDD 14   SDD 23

A RESUBDIVISION OF PART OF LOT D, VAIL VILLAGE 2nd FILING

LIONSHEAD FILING

SDD 7

VAIL VILLAGE 9th. FILING

SDD 21

VAIL VILLAGE 2nd FILING

VAIL LIONSHEAD 2nd FILING

MORCUS SUBDIVISION

VAIL LIONSHEAD 1st FILING, 1st ADD.

WHITE RIVER NATIONAL FOREST

Chapter 18.10
SINGLE-FAMILY (SFR) DISTRICT

Sections:
18.10.010   Purpose.
18.10.020   Permitted uses.
18.10.020   Conditional uses.
18.10.040   Accessory uses.
18.10.050   Lot area and site dimensions.
18.10.060   Setbacks.
18.10.080   Height.
18.10.090   Density control.
18.10.110   Site coverage.
18.10.130   Landscaping and site development.
18.10.140   Parking.

18.10.010   Purpose.   The single-family residential district is intended to provide sites for low-density single-family residential uses, together with such public facilities as may be appropriately located in the same district. The single-family residential district is intended to ensure adequate light, air, privacy, and open space for each dwelling, commensurate with single-family occupancy, and to maintain the desirable residential qualities of such sites by establishing appropriate site development standards. (Ord. 8(1973) § 2.100.)

18.10.020   Permitted uses.   The following uses shall be permitted in the SFR district: Single-family residential dwellings. (Ord. 8(1973) § 2.200.)

18.10.030   Conditional uses.   The following conditional uses shall be permitted, subject to issuance of a conditional use permit in accordance with the provisions of Chapter 18.60:
A.   Public utility and public service uses;
B.   Public buildings, grounds, and facilities;
C.   Public or private schools;
D.   Public park and recreation facilities;
E.   Ski lifts and tows;
F.   Dog kennel;
G.   Bed and breakfast as further regulated by Section 18.58.310;
H.   Type II employee housing unit as set forth in Section 18.57.050 of this code.
(Ord. 8(1992) § 6: Ord. 31(1989) § 1: Ord. 20(1982) § 5: Ord. 8(1973) § 2.300.)

18.10.040   Accessory uses.   The following accessory uses shall be permitted in the SFR district:
A.   Private greenhouses, toolsheds, playhouses, garages or carports, swimming pools, patios, or recreation facilities customarily incidental to single-family uses;
B.   Home occupations, subject to issuance of a home occupation permit in accordance with the provisions of Section 18.58.130 through 18.58.190;
C.   Other uses customarily incidental and accessory to permitted or conditional uses, and necessary for the operation thereof.
(Ord. 8(1973) § 2.400.)

18.10.050   Lot area and site dimensions.   The minimum lot or site area shall be twelve thousand, five hundred square feet of buildable area. Each site shall have a minimum frontage of thirty feet. Each site shall be of a size and shape capable of enclosing a square eighty feet on each side within its boundaries. (Ord. 12(1978) § 3 (part).)

18.10.060   Setbacks.   In the SFR district, the minimum front setback shall be twenty feet, the minimum side setback shall be fifteen feet, and the minimum rear setback shall be fifteen feet. (Ord. 50(1978) § 2 (part).)

18.10.080   Height.   For a flat roof or mansard roof, the height of buildings shall not exceed thirty feet. For a sloping roof, the height of buildings shall not exceed thirty-five feet. (Ord. 37(1980) § 2 (part).)

18.10.090   Density control.   Not more than one dwelling unit shall be permitted on each site. The following GRFA shall be permitted on each site:
A.   Twenty-five square feet of GRFA for each one hundred square feet of the first twelve thousand five hundred square feet of site area; plus
B.   Ten square feet of GRFA for each one hundred square feet of site area over twelve thousand five hundred square feet.
   In addition to the above, four hundred twenty-five square feet of gross residential floor area (GRFA) shall be permitted for each allowable dwelling unit.
   No single-family residential lot except those located entirely in the red hazard avalanche zone or the flood plain shall be so restricted that it cannot be occupied by one single-family dwelling. (Ord. 37(1990) § 3: Ord. 12(1978) § 2 (part).)

18.10.110.   Site coverage.   Site coverage shall not exceed twenty percent of the total site area. (Ord. 41(1990) § 3: Ord. 19(1976) § 3 (part): Ord. 8(1973) § 2.507.)

18.10.130   Landscaping and site development.   At least sixty percent of each site shall be landscaped. The minimum width and length of any area qualifying as landscaping shall be ten feet, with a minimum area of not less than three hundred square feet. (Ord. 19(1976) § 3 (part): Ord. 8(1973) § 2.509.)

18.10.140   Parking.   Off-street parking shall be provided in accordance with Chapter 18.52. (Ord. 8(1973) § 2.510.)

Chapter 18.60
CONDITIONAL USE PERMITS

Sections:
18.60.010   Purpose—Limitations.
18.60.020   Application—Contents.
18.60.030   Fee.
18.60.040   Hearing.
18.60.050   Planning commission action.
18.60.060   Criteria—Findings.
18.60.070   Appeal to the town council.
18.60.080   Permit approval and effect.
18.60.090   Conflicting provisions.

18.60.010   Purpose—Limitations.   In order to provide the flexibility necessary to achieve the objectives of this title, specified uses are permitted in certain districts subject to the granting of a conditional use permit. Because of their unusual or special characteristics, conditional uses require review and evaluation so that they may be located properly with respect to the purposes of this title and with respect to their effects on surrounding properties. The review process prescribed in this chapter is intended to assure compatibility and harmonious development between conditional uses and surrounding properties and the town at large. Uses listed as conditional uses in the various districts may be permitted subject to such conditions and limitations as the town may prescribe to ensure that the location and operation of the conditional uses will be in accordance with development objectives of the town and will not be detrimental to other uses or properties. Where conditions cannot be devised to achieve these objectives, applications for conditional use permits shall be denied. (Ord. 8(1973) § 18.100.)

18.60.020   Application—Contents.   Application for a conditional use permit shall be made upon a form provided by the zoning administrator. The application shall be supported by documents, maps, plans, and other material containing the following information:

A.   Name and address of the owner and/or applicant and a statement that the applicant, if not the owner, has the permission of the owner to make application and act as agent for the owner;

B.   Legal description, street address, and other identifying data concerning the site;

C.   A description of the precise nature of the proposed use and its operating characteristics, and measures proposed to make the use compatible with other properties in the vicinity;

D.   A site plan showing proposed development of the site, including topography, building locations, parking, traffic circulation, useable open space, landscaped area, and utilities and drainage features;

E.   Preliminary building plans and elevations sufficient to indicate the dimensions, general appearance, scale, and interior plan of all buildings;

F.   Such additional material as the zoning administrator may prescribe or the applicant may submit pertinent to the application and to the findings prerequisite to the issuance of a conditional use permit as prescribed in Section 18.54.090;

G.   A list of the owner or owners of record of the properties adjacent to the subject property which is the subject of the hearing. Provided, however, notification of owners within a condominium project shall be satisfied by notifying the managing agent, or the registered agent of the condominium project, or any member of the board of directors of a condominium association. The list of owners, managing agent of the condominium project, registered agent or members of the

board of directors, as appropriate, shall include the names of the individuals, their mailing addresses, and the general description of the property owned or managed by each. Accompanying the list shall be stamped, addressed envelopes to each individual or agent to be notified to be used for the mailing of the notice of hearing. It will be the applicant's responsibility to provide this information and stamped, addressed envelopes. Notice to the adjacent property owners shall be mailed first class, postage prepaid. (Ord. 49(1969) § 1: Ord. 50(1978) § 15 (part): Ord. 30(1978) § 1: Ord. 16(1978) § 4(a): Ord. 8(1973) § 18.200.)

18.60.030   Fee.   The town council shall set a conditional use permit fee schedule sufficient to cover the cost of town staff time and other expenses incidental to the review of the application. The fee shall be paid at the time of the application and shall not be refundable. (Ord. 8(1973) § 18.400.)

18.60.040   Hearing.   Upon receipt of a conditional use permit application, the planning commission shall set a date for hearing in accordance with Section 18.66.070. Notice shall be given, and the hearing shall be conducted in accordance with Sections 18.66.080 and 18.66.090. (Ord. 8(1973) § 18.400.)

18.60.050   Planning commission action.   A. Within thirty days of the application for a public hearing on a conditional use permit, the planning commission shall act on the application. The commission may approve the application as submitted or may approve the application subject to such modifications or conditions as it deems necessary to accomplish the purposes of this title, or the commission may deny the application. A conditional use permit may be revocable, may be granted for a limited time period, or may be granted subject to such other conditions as the commission may prescribe.

Conditions may include, but shall not be limited to, requiring special setbacks, open spaces, fences or walls, landscaping or screening, and street dedication and improvement; regulation of vehicular access and parking, signs, illumination, and hours and methods of operation; control of potential nuisances; prescription of standards for maintenance of buildings and grounds; and prescription of development schedules.

B.   A conditional use permit shall not grant variances, but action on a variance may be considered concurrently with a conditional use permit application on the same site. Variances shall be granted in accordance with the procedure prescribed in Chapter 18.62. (Ord. 16(1978) § 4(b): Ord. 8(1973) § 18.500.)

18.60.060   Criteria—Findings.   A. Before acting on a conditional use permit application, the planning commission shall consider the following factors with respect to the proposed use:

1. Relationship and impact of the use on development objectives of the town;

2. Effect of the use on light and air, distribution of population, transportation facilities, utilities, schools, parks and recreation facilities, and other public facilities and public facility needs;

3. Effect upon traffic, with particular reference to congestion, automotive and pedestrian safety and convenience, traffic flow and control, access, maneuverability, and removal of snow from the streets and parking areas;

4. Effect upon the character of the area in which the proposed use is to be located, including the scale and bulk of the proposed use in relation to surrounding uses;

5. Such other factors and criteria as the commission deems applicable to the proposed use;

6. The environmental impact report concerning the proposed use, if an environmental impact report is required by Chapter 18.56.

7. Prior to the approval of a conditional use permit for a time-share estate, fractional fee or time-share license proposal, the applicant shall submit to the town a list of all owners of existing units within the project or building; and written statements from one hundred percent of the owners of existing units indicating their approval, without condition, of the proposed time-share, fractional fee or time-share license. No written approval shall be valid if it was signed by the owner more than sixty days prior to the date of filing the application for a conditional use. All buildings which presently contain time-share units would be exempt from this provision.
B. The planning commission shall make the following findings before granting a conditional use permit:
1. That the proposed location of the use is in accordance with the purposes of this title and the purposes of the district in which the site is located; detrimental to the public health, safety, or welfare, or materially injurious to properties or improvements in the vicinity;
2. That the proposed location of the use and the conditions under which it would be operated or maintained will not be detrimental to the public health, safety, or welfare, or materially injurious to properties or improvements in the vicinity;
3. That the proposed use will comply with each of the applicable provisions of this title.
(Ord. 36(1980) § 1: Ord. 8(1973) § 18.600.)

18.60.070 Appeal to the town council. A. An appeal to the town council may be made by the applicant, adjacent property owner, or by the town manager. The town council can also call up matters by a majority vote of those council members present.
B. For all appeals, the appeal must be filed in writing within ten days following the decision or must be called up by the town council at their next regularly scheduled meeting.
C. The council shall hear the appeal within thirty days of its being filed or called up, with a possible thirty-day extension if

the council finds that there is insufficient information. (Ord. 37(1980) § 11 (part).)

18.60.080 Permit approval and effect. Approval of a conditional use permit shall lapse and become void if a building permit is not obtained and construction is not commenced and diligently pursued toward completion or the use for which the approval has been granted has not commenced within two years from when the approval becomes final. (Ord. 48(1991) § 1: Ord. 15(1978) § 4(d).)

18.60.090 Conflicting provisions. In addition to the conditions which may be prescribed pursuant to this chapter, a conditional use also shall be subject to all other procedures, permits, and requirements of this and other applicable ordinances and regulations of the town. In event of any conflict between the provisions of a conditional use permit and any other permit or requirement, the more restrictive provision shall prevail. (Ord. 8(1973) § 18.900.)

As the sample zoning ordinances indicate, a special review or conditional use (also called special exception or conditional exception) requires more than a building permit. For example, a neighborhood business, such as a convenience store, may be permitted in residential zone districts but only as a conditional use. One who wishes to build a convenience store must apply for a conditional use permit. The permit is given only after a public hearing is held by a public body, usually called a planning commission. The permit may be subject to conditions (hence, the term conditional use), such as requiring landscaping to screen the use from view by neighbors. Once a permit is approved for a particular use at a particular location, that use ordinarily may be continued by successive owners until such time as the use is discontinued.

For a special review or conditional use procedure to be valid, the underlying ordinance must provide the planning commission with specific criteria against which the application may be judged. Typical criteria are impact on neighboring uses, impact on parking, impact on traffic circulation, and so forth. In judging an application against those criteria to determine whether or not the application should be granted, the planning commission engages in a quasi-judicial review process. Appeal generally is allowed to the governing body of the municipality (the town council, for example), after which judicial review of some type ordinarily is permitted. The parameters of judicial review in this type of case generally is similar to the judicial review provided for decisions of administrative agencies, such as public utilities commissions.

In addition to restrictions on property use, each zone district has certain area restrictions. For instance, minimum lot area restrictions may be imposed, requiring a lot to be a minimum size before it can be used for building. Such regulations range from requiring a lot size to be at least 2,000 square feet in an urban area, for example, to several acres in less populous areas. The purpose of area restrictions is to reduce density and to prevent the crowding of buildings.

Zoning regulations usually regulate the height of buildings as well. This type of regulation can vary according to topography and relates to building bulk. Thus, a *stepped building* may be permitted to be taller than a building that is not stepped because of the floor area that is included. Where the topography is steep, the height of the building may be measured from a low point, from a high point, or from some point in between.

Building bulk generally is regulated as a function of lot size. Regulations may require that buildings be set back a specific number of feet from the front, back, and side lot lines. They may limit floor area based on the size of the lot. The regulations also may depend on the buildable area of the lot, excluding areas within a flood area or areas which have a steep slope.

Each zoning ordinance also must deal with *nonconforming uses*, which are uses that existed before adoption of the ordinance and do not conform with the ordinance. Nonconforming uses are *grandfathered*, permitting their continued use. For example, a corner grocery will be permitted to continue its existence although the neighborhood is zoned for residential use only. The reason is that the corner grocery was there before the zoning was imposed. However, zoning ordinances typically do not permit nonconforming uses to be expanded in any way; and if a nonconforming use is destroyed or is discontinued for a set period of time, its revival will not be permitted.

Each zoning ordinance allows *variances* to give flexibility to the ordinance. There are two types of variances: use variances and area variances. *Use variances* permit a use that is different from those permitted by the ordinance. Using the example of the corner grocery, a use variance would be required to increase its size. Many zoning ordinances do not permit use variances, allowing only special or conditional uses. If use variances are permitted, they generally are granted only upon a showing that the property owner otherwise will suffer hardship. The property owner also must show that grant of the variance does not confer a special privilege (a privilege not granted to others).

The type of hardship needed to obtain a use variance is not easily shown. Financial hardship is not enough. Thus, the corner grocery cannot show the requisite hardship by demonstrating that it will be forced out of business unless the business is increased in size. Rather, the hardship must be a physical one, such as a change in government regulation that requires installation of additional equipment to reduce environmental hazards.

The rule against granting a special privilege is intended to prevent a single person or entity from being allowed to use property in a way allowed to no one else. In other words, some degree of consistency is required in administration of the regulations.

Area variances allow variations in the height and area of buildings, the amount of setback required; the amount of parking required; and other, similar nonuse regulations. Obtaining an area variance generally requires only a showing of practical difficulty rather than a showing of hardship. For example, an area variance routinely is granted when the configuration of a parcel of land does not permit strict compliance with the zoning regulations (such as reduction of setbacks when the parcel is particularly narrow) and when no objection is received from adjacent landowners. The property owner also must show that no special privilege is granted.

Applications for variances are heard by the planning commission or some other administrative board established either by the zoning ordinance or by some other ordinance of the municipality. As with conditional or special review uses, the application is judged against specific criteria; and appeals are permitted. The criteria typically involve impact on neighboring properties as well as the showings discussed above, including hardship, practical difficulty, and grant of special privilege.

Figure 7-2 illustrates provisions of zoning ordinances from Vail, Colorado related to nonconforming uses and variances, which are fairly typical of such ordinances in communities around the country that are similar in size.

Figure 7-2
Ordinances for Nonconforming Uses and Variances

Chapter 18.64
NONCONFORMING SITES, USES, STRUCTURES,
AND SITE IMPROVEMENTS

Sections:
18.64.010   Purpose.
18.64.020   Continuance.
18.64.030   Sites.
18.64.040   Uses.
18.64.050   Structures and site improvements.
18.64.060   Maintenance and repairs.
18.64.070   Discontinuance.
18.64.080   Change of use.
18.64.090   Restoration.

18.64.010   Purpose. This chapter is intended to limit the number and extent of nonconforming uses and structures by prohibiting or limiting their enlargement, their reestablishment after abandonment, and their restoration after substantial destruction. While permitting nonconforming uses, structures, and improvements to continue, this chapter is intended to limit enlargement, alterations, restoration, or replacement which would increase the discrepancy between existing conditions and the development standards prescribed by this title. (Ord. 8(1973) § 20.100.)

18.64.020   Continuance. Nonconforming sites, uses, structures, and site improvements lawfully established prior to the effective date of the ordinance codified in this title may continue, subject to the limitations prescribed in this chapter. Sites, uses, structures, and site improvements lawfully authorized by permits or regulations existing prior to the effective date of the ordinance codified in this title may continue, subject to such limitations as prescribed by such permits or regulations. (Ord. 8(1973) § 20.200.)

18.64.030   Sites. Sites lawfully established pursuant to regulations in effect prior to the effective date of the ordinance codified in this title which do not conform to the minimum lot area and dimension requirements prescribed by this title for the district in which they are situated may be continued and shall be deemed legally established building sites, subject to the site development standards prescribed by this title. No such site shall be further reduced in area or dimensions. (Ord. 8(1973) § 20.300.)

18.64.040   Uses. The use of a site or structure lawfully established prior to the effective date of the ordinance codified in this title which does not conform to the use regulations prescribed by this title for the district in which it is situated may be continued, provided that no such nonconforming use shall be enlarged to occupy a greater site area for building floor area than it occupied on the effective date of the ordinance codified in this chapter. Any subsequent reduction in site area or floor area occupied by a nonconforming use shall be deemed a new limitation, and the use shall not thereafter be enlarged to occupy a greater site area or floor area than such new limitation. (Ord. 8(1973) § 20.400.)

18.64.050   Structures and site improvements. Structures and site improvements lawfully established prior to the effective date of the ordinance codified in this title which do not conform to the development standards presented by this title for the district in which they are situated may be continued. Such structures or site improvements may be enlarged only in accordance with the following limitations:
A.   Structures or site improvements which do not conform to requirements for setbacks, distances between buildings, height, building bulk control, or site coverage may be enlarged, provided that the enlargement does not further increase the

discrepancy between the total structure and applicable building bulk control or site coverage standards; and provided that the addition fully conforms with setbacks, distances between buildings, and height standards applicable to the addition.
B.   Structures which do not conform to density controls may be enlarged, only if the total gross residential floor area of the enlarged structure does not exceed the total gross residential floor area of the preexisting nonconforming structure.
C.   Structures or site improvements which do not conform to requirements for useable open space or landscaping and site development may be enlarged, provided that the useable open space requirements applicable to such addition shall be fully satisfied, and provided that the percentage of the total site which is landscaped shall not be reduced below the minimum requirement.
D.   Structures or site improvements which do not conform to the off-street parking and loading requirements of this title may be enlarged, provided that the parking and loading requirements for such addition shall be fully satisfied and that the discrepancy between the existing off-street parking and loading facilities and the standards prescribed by this title shall not be increased. (Ord. 8(1973) § 20.500.)

18.64.060   Maintenance and repairs. Nonconforming uses, structures, and site improvements may be maintained and repaired as necessary for convenient, safe, or efficient operation or use, provided that no such maintenance or repair shall increase the discrepancy between the use, structure, or site improvement and the development standards prescribed by this title. (Ord. 8(1973) § 20.600.)

18.64.070.   Discontinuance. Any nonconforming use which is discontinued for a period of twelve months,

regardless of any intent to resume operation of the use, shall not be resumed thereafter, and any future use of the site or structures thereon shall conform with the provisions of this title. (Ord. 8(1973) § 10.700.)

18.64.080   Change of use. A nonconforming use shall not be changed to another nonconforming use unless permission has been granted by the town council. Prior to granting such permission, the council shall determine that the proposed use does not substantially differ from the existing nonconforming use in terms of compatibility with the character of the area in which it is located, and the council shall determine that the proposed use does not increase or aggravate the degree of nonconformity existing prior to any such change of use. (Ord. 8(1973) § 20.800.)

18.64.090   Restoration. Whenever a nonconforming use which does not conform with the regulations for the district in which it is located or a nonconforming structure or site improvement which does not conform with the requirements for setbacks, height, density control, building bulk control, or site coverage is destroyed by fire or other calamity, by act of God or by the public enemy, its use may be resumed or the structure may be restored, provided the restoration is commenced within one year and diligently pursued to completion. All new construction must conform to the applicable Uniform Building Code, Uniform Fire Code, and other relevant codes regarding safety and construction which are in effect at the time rebuilding is proposed. (Ord. 39(1982) § 1: Ord. 8(1973) § 20.900.)

Chapter 18.62
VARIANCES

Sections:
18.62.010   Purpose.
18.62.020   Application—Information required.
18.62.030   Fee.
18.62.040   Hearing.
18.62.050   Planning commission action.
18.62.060   Criteria and findings.
18.62.070   Appeal to the town council.
18.62.080   Permit approval and effect.
18.62.090   Related permits and requirements.

18.62.010   Purpose.   A.   In order to prevent or to lessen such practical difficulties and unnecessary physical hardships inconsistent with the objectives of this title as would result from strict or literal interpretation and enforcement, variances from certain regulations may be granted. A practical difficulty or unnecessary physical hardship may result from the size, shape, or dimensions of a site or the location of existing structures thereon; from topographic or physical conditions on the site or in the immediate vicinity; or from other physical limitations, street locations, or traffic conditions in the immediate vicinity. Cost or inconvenience to the applicant of strict or literal compliance with a regulation shall not be a reason for granting a variance.

B.   Variances may be granted only with respect to the development standards prescribed for each district, including lot area and site dimensions, setbacks, distances between buildings, height, density control, building bulk control, site coverage, useable open space, landscaping and site development, and parking and loading requirements; or with respect to the provisions of Chapter 18.52 governing physical development on a site.

Provided, however, notification of owners within a condominium project shall be satisfied by notifying the managing agent, or the registered agent of the condominium project, or any member of the board of directors of a condominium association. The list of owners, managing agent, registered agent, or members of the board of directors, as appropriate, shall include the names of the individuals, their mailing addresses, and the general description of the property owned or managed by each. Accompanying the list shall be stamped, addressed envelopes to each individual or agent to be notified to be used for mailing of the notice of hearing. It will be the applicant's responsibility to provide this information and stamped, addressed envelopes. Notice to the adjacent property owners shall be mailed first class, postage prepaid. (Ord. 49(1991) § 2: Ord. 50(1978) § 15 (part): Ord. 30(1978) § 2: Ord. 8(1973) § 19.200.)

18.62.030   Fee.   The town council shall set a variance fee schedule sufficient to cover the cost of town staff time and other expenses incidental to the review of the application. The fee shall be paid at the time of application and shall not be refundable. (Ord. 8(1973) § 19.300.)

18.62.040   Hearing.   Upon receipt of a variance application, the planning commission shall set a date for hearing in accordance with Section 18.66.070. Notice shall be given, and the hearing shall be conducted in accordance with Sections 18.66.080 and 18.66.090. (Ord. 8(1973) § 19.400.)

18.62.050   Planning commission action.   Within twenty days of the closing of a public hearing on a variance application, the planning commission shall act on the application. The commission may approve the application as submitted or may approve the application subject to such modifications or conditions as it deems necessary to accomplish the purposes of

C.   The power to grant variances does not extend to the use regulations prescribed for each district because the flexibility necessary to avoid results inconsistent with the objectives of this title is provided by Chapter 18.60, conditional use permits, and by Sections 18.66.100 through 18.66.160, amendments. (Ord. 8(1973) § 19.100.)

18.62.020   Application—Information required.
Application for a variance shall be made upon a form provided by the zoning administrator. The application shall be supported by documents, maps, plans, and other material containing the following information:

A.   Name and address of the owner and/or applicant and a statement that the applicant, if not the owner, has the permission of the owner to make application and act as agent for the owner;

B.   Legal description, street address, and other identifying data concerning the site;

C.   A statement of the precise nature of the variance requested, the regulation involved, and the practical difficulty or unnecessary physical hardship inconsistent with the objectives of this title that would result from strict or literal interpretation and enforcement of the specified regulation;

D.   A site plan showing all existing and proposed features on the site, and on adjoining sites if necessary, pertinent to the variance requested, including site boundaries, required setbacks, building locations and heights, topography and physical features, and similar data;

E.   Such additional material as the zoning administrator may prescribe or the applicant may submit pertinent to the application and to the findings prerequisite to the issuance of a variance as prescribed in Section 18.62.060;

F.   A list of the owner or owners of record of the properties adjacent to the subject property which is subject of the hearing.

this title, or the commission may deny the application. A variance may be revocable, may be granted for a limited time period, or may be granted subject to such other conditions as the commission may prescribe. (Ord. 8(1973) § 19.500.)

18.62.060   Criteria and findings.   A.   Before acting on a variance application, the planning commission shall consider the following factors with respect to the requested variance:

1. The relationship of the requested variance to other existing or potential uses and structures in the vicinity;

2. The degree to which relief from the strict or literal interpretation and enforcement of a specified regulation is necessary to achieve compatibility and uniformity of treatment among sites in the vicinity, or to attain the objectives of this title without grant of special privilege;

3. The effect of the requested variance on light and air, distribution of population, transportation and traffic facilities, public facilities, and utilities, and public safety;

4. Such other factors and criteria as the commission deems applicable to the proposed variance.

B.   The planning commission shall make the following findings before granting a variance:

1. That the granting of the variance will not constitute a grant of special privilege inconsistent with the limitations on other properties classified in the same district;

2. That the granting of the variance will not be detrimental to the public health, safety, or welfare, or materially injurious to properties or improvements in the vicinity;

3. That the variance is warranted for one or more of the following reasons:

a. The strict or literal interpretation and enforcement of the specified regulation would result in practical difficulty or unnecessary physical hardship inconsistent with the objectives of this title.

b. There are exceptional or extraordinary circumstances

or conditions applicable to the site of the variance that do not apply generally to other properties in the same zone.

    c. The strict or literal interpretation and enforcement of the specified regulation would deprive the applicant of privileges enjoyed by owners of other properties in the same district. (Ord. 8(1973) § 19.600.)

18.62.070 Appeal to the town council. A. An appeal to the town council may be made by the applicant, adjacent property owner, or by the town manager. The town council also can call up matters by a majority vote of those council members present.

B. For all appeals, the appeal must be filed in writing within ten days following the decision or must be called up by the town council at their next regularly scheduled meeting.

C. The council shall hear the appeal within thirty days of its being filed or called up, with a possible thirty-day extension if the council finds that there is insufficient information. (Ord. 37(1980) § 11 (part).)

18.62.080 Permit approval and effect. Approval of the variance shall lapse and become void if a building permit is not obtained and construction not commenced and diligently pursued toward completion within two years from when the approval becomes final. (Ord. 48(1991) § 2: Ord. 16(1978) § 5(c).)

18.62.090 Related permits and requirements. In addition to the conditions which may be prescribed pursuant to this chapter, any site or use subject to a variance permit also shall be subject to all other procedures, permits, and requirements of this and other applicable chapters and regulations of the town. In the event of any conflict between the provisions of a variance permit and other permit or requirement, the more restrictive provision shall prevail. (Ord. 8(1973) § 19.900.)

Amendment of Zoning Ordinances

Zoning ordinances provide methods for their amendment. Individual property owners may ask that a zoning ordinance related to their property be amended. For example, a property owner might ask that the allowed uses be changed to permit some new use desired by her or him. The ordinance also can be amended in general at the initiative of the municipality. For example, the municipality might want to place greater restrictions on density, an instance of *down-zoning*. If an amendment relates to a single parcel of land, notice usually must be given to adjoining property owners. In the case of a general amendment, published notice to the entire community usually will suffice.

In either case, a public hearing must be held and a determination made that the amendment is consistent with the master plan. If, in the case of an amendment related to a single parcel of land, the amendment has the effect of providing special zoning for that parcel, the amendment may be invalid as *spot zoning*. Spot zoning generally is disfavored; it disregards the master planning process and tends to grant a special privilege.

In connection with rezoning of individual lots, the process of *contract zoning* may be used. Using this process, the municipality and the landowner enter into negotiations, ultimately agreeing to rezone the property but only on certain conditions. It is similar to granting a conditional use. For example, a developer might be allowed to rezone land from agricultural to residential in exchange for the developer's agreement to mitigate the impacts of the rezoning by dedicating a portion of its land to park or recreational use. Many courts have found contract zoning to be invalid on the basis that it subverts what ought to be a legislative process by turning it into a process of negotiation. Other courts permit contract zoning as long as it is conducted in the course of public hearings where the amendment is allowed.

Planned Unit or Cluster Zoning

The cluster or planned unit development recently has emerged to introduce greater flexibility into the zoning process. The *planned unit development (PUD)* is a customized zone district, often containing an entirely new development. It sometimes is characterized by clustered dwelling units, which may include condominium ownership, and by extensive open space, including parks and hiking trails. Commercial uses, such as gasoline service stations and convenience stores, may be included as well.

A PUD often is treated as an amendment to existing zoning. For example, a PUD may be established by converting property from agricultural use to mixed residential/commercial use in the form of PUD zoning. Like other zoning amendments, compliance with the master plan must be shown. The existing zoning ordinances may establish particular criteria to form a PUD zone, generally relating to the impact of the development on adjoining land uses. As with other zoning amendments, public notice and hearing are required.

Constitutional Limitations on Zoning

As discussed earlier, the United States Supreme Court held in Village of Euclid v. Ambler Realty Co., 272 U.S. 365 (1926) that Euclidean zoning does not infringe constitutional limitations against taking property without compensating the property owner. That was true even though Ambler Realty experienced a significant reduction in the value of its commercial property by having it restricted to residential use.

On the other hand, if the landowner is deprived of all economically beneficial use of his property by zoning regulations or by other police power regulations, the courts will find an unconstitutional *taking* of the property. In other words, the effect of the zoning regulation is to condemn the property; and the owner must be compensated for the condemnation. <u>Lucas v. South Carolina Coastal Council</u>, 112 S.Ct. 2886 (1992). In that case, Lucas had bought two residential lots on a South Carolina barrier island, planning to build single family homes. However, after the lots were purchased, South Carolina enacted the Beachfront Management Act, the effect of which barred Lucas from erecting any habitable structure on the lots. The Supreme Court held that a taking had occurred, entitling Lucas to compensation.

Similarly, local governments cannot impose *exactions* in the zoning process. In other words, they cannot make the grant of favorable zoning subject to conditions that are unrelated to some necessity resulting from the zoning grant. An exaction occurs, for example, when a property owner is required to convey a portion of her property to the government, either outright or by way of easement, as a condition to obtain the zoning she desires. An exaction is not permitted unless some adverse impact of the zoning is mitigated by the exaction demanded.

In two recent cases, the United States Supreme Court established a two-step test to determine whether a particular condition of approval (exaction) of land use is permissible under the zoning power or whether the exaction is an impermissible taking under the Fifth Amendment, requiring compensation.

The first step, established in <u>Nollan v. California Coastal Comm'n</u>, 483 U.S. 825 (1987), involves determining whether a *nexus* or logical connection exists between some legitimate public interest and the permit condition exacted by the government. In <u>Nollan</u>, the Supreme Court held there was no nexus between a permit to demolish and rebuild a beachfront house and a requirement that the owner dedicate an access easement in front of the house. The Court rejected the theory that building a larger house would impact views of the beach. In the Court's view, there was no nexus between the house's interference with the public view of the beach and a public easement in front of the house that would permit people to walk along the beach.

If a nexus is found, however, <u>Dolan v. City of Tigard</u>, 114 S. Ct. 2309 (1994) establishes the next step to determine whether the condition of approval is valid. If a nexus exists, the court then must decide whether there is "rough proportionality" in the relationship between the exaction or condition and the public interest sought to be advanced. For example, the city in the <u>Dolan</u> case conditioned the teardown and reconstruction of a plumbing and electrical supply store on the applicant's 1) granting a floodplain easement to the city and 2) dedicating an additional 15-foot strip of land adjacent to the floodplain as a pedestrian/bike path. The theory of the city concerning the first requirement was that enlargement of the business and paving of the related parking lot would impact flooding by expanding impervious surfaces. The theory of the second requirement was that expansion of the business would impact traffic congestion. The Court found there was no "rough proportionality," stating:

> "No precise mathematical calculation is required, but the city must make some sort of individualized determination that the required dedication is related both in nature and extent to the impact of the proposed development." 114 S. Ct. at 2319-20.

As to the floodplain easement, the Court stated that the same purpose could have been accomplished by making the easement area open space and preserving the applicant's ownership, rather than by compelling the applicant to convey an easement across her property to the city. The Court reasoned that if the property belonged to the applicant, she could exclude the public and could retain that aspect of ownership. As to the pedestrian/bike path dedication, the Court concluded there was no showing that the path would eliminate traffic congestion in any way reasonably related to the impact of the store's expansion; rather, there was a finding only that creation of the pathway "could offset some of the traffic demand."

At issue in those cases was the philosophical question of whether the public at large should be required to carry the burden of such things as acquiring coastal and floodplain easements and such amenities as bike paths and hiking trails or whether the cost of such public projects may be shifted to developers who cause the need for them to arise. The answer seems to be that if the government can prove the developer caused the need, the developer will have to pay. Otherwise, the public at large must pay.

The question is particularly important in states like California, where constitutional limitations on taxation have caused local governments to look for other sources of revenue. By requiring the developer to dedicate land for uses such as recreation and schools, the financial impact of the development is shifted from the public to the developer. Alternatively, local ordinances may provide for payment of fees for that purpose in lieu of dedication of land. The money generated by these *impact fees* is used by the local government to acquire land for public purposes.

Subdivision Regulation

Subdivision regulations are another tool of the land use process. In essence, *subdivision regulations* establish rules for subdividing larger parcels of land into smaller ones, including the subdivision of parcels of land into condominium ownership. Large lot subdivisions or major subdivisions usually are treated separately from minor subdivisions. As a general rule, large lot subdivisions are entirely new developments; minor subdivisions involve the resubdividing of single, large lots into smaller lots.

Subdivision regulations typically are geared to a determination of the impact of any subdividing on the environment. Issues such as access, steep slopes, and availability of utilities must be addressed. Comments of public agencies frequently are solicited, along with public input. Additional requirements may be imposed based on this comment and input. Public notice and hearing are required, usually before the governing body of the municipality. The process is quasi-judicial, and judicial review is available.

As part of the approval process, the developer generally is required to enter into a *subdivision improvements agreement*. That agreement requires completion of subdivision improvements, such as street paving, curb and gutter construction, and utility placement. The agreement may require that completion of those improvements be guaranteed by a surety bond or by a letter of credit. The agreement also may require dedication of park land and school land to address the development's impact on recreation and schools. These requirements are subject to the same constitutional limitations that exist for zoning. Finally, the agreement obligates the municipality to accept the roads for maintenance when they are completed.

Figure 7-3 illustrates a portion of a subdivision map showing the configuration of the planned lots and a subdivision improvements agreement that might be used as part of this process.

Figure 7-3
Subdivision Improvements Agreement and Map

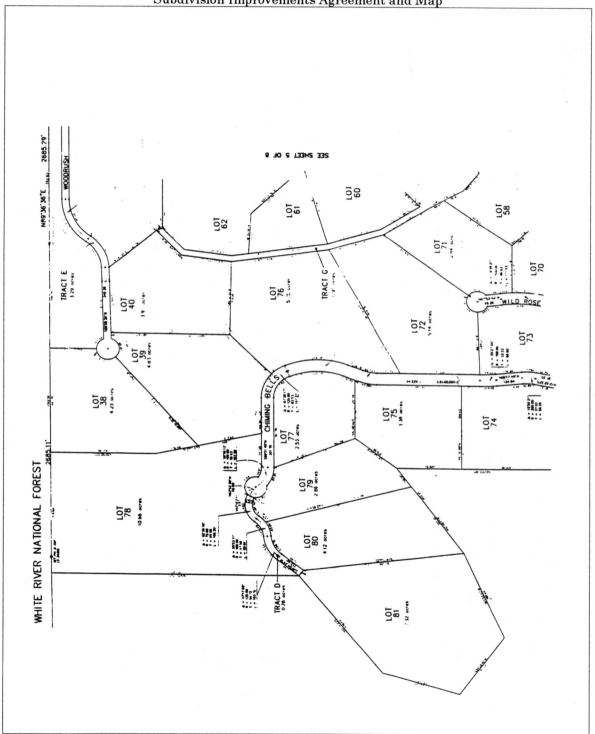

SUPPLEMENT TO
AMENDED AND RESTATED
SUBDIVISION IMPROVEMENTS AGREEMENT

THIS AGREEMENT, made and entered into this _____ day of _____, 1993, by and between Mountain Star Limited Liability company, a Wyoming limited liability company, hereinafter referred to as "Subdivider," and the Town of Avon, a Colorado Municipality, by and through its Council, hereinafter referred to as the "Town."

WITNESSETH:

WHEREAS, the parties entered into a certain Amended and Restated Subdivision Improvements Agreement dated May 27, 1993 and recorded on May 28, 1993, in book 610 at Page 129, real property records of Eagle County, Colorado (the "Amended Agreement"), relating to improvements for Mountain Star, a subdivision located in the Town of Avon, Eagle County, Colorado (the "Subdivision"), to establish the responsibilities for certain public improvements to the Subdivision as provided by Section 16.24.100 of the Avon Municipal Code, as amended; and

WHEREAS, the parties desire to supplement the Amended Agreement to make alternative provision for completion of the remaining public improvements ("Improvements") and to release the lien provided for in the Amended Agreement; and

WHEREAS, the Subdivider continues to agree to be responsible for the performance and completion of the Improvements.

NOW, THEREFORE, in consideration of the following mutual covenants, conditions, and promises, the parties hereby agree as follows:

1. The Amended Agreement is hereby supplemented as hereinafter set forth.

2. Subdivider agrees to furnish all equipment, labor, and material necessary to perform and complete, in a good and workmanlike manner, the Improvements. Subdivider further agrees that it will be responsible for all costs related to said work. All said work shall be performed substantially in accordance with the construction specifications and drawings heretofore or hereafter submitted to and approved by the Town. All work shall be done under the inspection procedures and standards established by the Town, shall be subject to the reasonable satisfaction of the Town and shall not be deemed complete until the reasonable approval and acceptance of the Improvements by the Town.

3. All improvements shall be completed by August 1, 1996.

4. To secure completion of the Improvements, Subdivider hereby agrees to secure its obligations under this Agreement by either (i) the payment to an escrow agent acceptable to the Town of the amount of $1,100,000 or (ii) the furnishing of an irrevocable letter of credit in such amount. Upon completion of portions of the improvements, upon payment of the cost of such improvements, as evidenced by proof satisfactory to the Town, and upon inspection and approval thereof, the Town shall authorize reduction of the amount of such collateral, provided the amount thereof shall not be reduced below the amount provided in paragraph 5 hereof.

5. Upon completion of the Improvements and upon payment of the cost of such Improvements, as evidenced by proof satisfactory to the Town, and further upon either (i) the payment to the Escrow Agent of the amount set forth on Exhibit D to the Amended Agreement and incorporated herein, or (ii) the furnishing of an irrevocable letter of credit in the appropriate amount set forth on said Exhibit D, which letter of credit or escrow, as the case may be, shall secure the continuing obligations of Subdivider under this Agreement, the Town agrees to release the security provided for in paragraph 4 hereof.

6. Subdivider shall at all times prior to acceptance of any publicly dedicated roadways within the Subdivision, and including Buck Creek Road, by the Town give good and adequate warning to the traveling public of each and every dangerous condition existent in said roads and shall protect the traveling public from such defective or dangerous conditions. Until the completion of all the Improvements herein agreed to be constructed, roads not accepted as improved shall be under the charge and control of Subdivider for the purpose of this agreement; and Subdivider may close all or a portion of any street or road within the Subdivision whenever it is necessary to protect the traveling public during the construction or installation of the Improvements herein agreed to be made.

7. Upon completion of portions of the Improvements, Subdivider will cause its engineers (who shall be registered in the State of Colorado) to certify to the Town in writing that the installation of the Improvements, as portions thereof may be completed from time to time, have been completed in conformance with all standards, drawings, and specifications as submitted to and previously approved by the Town Inspection reports, test results, and other supporting documentation shall be submitted weekly during construction with the certification. The Town may provide periodic inspections as it deems necessary to ensure conformance with the approved plans and specifications.

8. a) Fees in accordance with the Town's Subdivision Regulations for the review of Preliminary Plans and Final Plats have been paid in full.
b) Additional fees shall be paid to the Town by Subdivider, within twenty (20) days after delivery of written invoice for such fees, to cover the cost of inspections by the Town. The fees will be based on direct (out-of-pocket) costs of the Town, but in no event will the total amount of such additional fees exceed two percent of construction costs.

9. Subdivider agrees that in the event it shall fail to perform its obligations as set forth herein, the Town shall be under no obligation to complete or perform any of the said Improvements. No one, individually or otherwise, other than the parties hereto, shall acquire, as a result of this Agreement, any rights, claims, or obligations from or against the Town, its agents, employees, or officers. Actions by the Town against Subdivider to enforce any provision of this Agreement shall be at the sole discretion of the Town. No third parties shall have any rights to require any action by the Town pursuant to this Agreement; and this Agreement shall not create a liability on the part of or be a cause of action against the Town, for any personal or property damage that may result to any third parties from the failure of the Subdivider to complete the improvements herein specified.

10. The Town shall not, nor shall any officer, agent, or employee thereof, be liable or responsible for any accident, loss or damage related to the work specified in this Agreement, nor liable for any persons or property injured by reason of the nature of said work. Subdivider hereby agrees to indemnify and hold harmless the Town, and any of its officers, agents, and employees against any losses, claims, damages, or liabilities to which the town or any of its officers, agents, or employees may become subject to, because of any losses, claims, damages, or liabilities (or actions in respect thereof) that arises out of, or are based upon, any obligation of Subdivider as hereinbefore stated, which arise prior to the expiration of all warranty periods set forth in Section 11 below. Furthermore, Subdivider shall reimburse the Town for any and all legal or other expenses reasonably incurred by the Town in connection with investigating or defending any such loss or claim.

11. The Improvements shall be warranted to be free from defect in workmanship or quality for a period of one (1) year after acceptance of all work by the Town. In the event of any such defect, the Town may require Subdivider to correct the defect in material or workmanship. The amounts discussed under paragraph 5 above for completion of all Improvements shall be retained in escrow in a separate interest bearing account or accounts during such one (1) year period as a guaranty of performance of any work required pursuant to the above-described warranty or, alternatively, Subdivider shall, at its option, provide an irrevocable letter of credit to the Town in a form approved by the Town, which approval shall not be unreasonably withheld. In the event an escrow is used, an escrow agreement satisfactory to the Town shall be entered into. In the event any corrective work is performed during the one-year warranty period the warranty on said corrected work shall be extended for one year from the date on which it is completed. Subdivider agrees to allow 110% of the cost of any significant corrective work, as estimated and approved by the Town, to be retained in escrow, or alternatively, at Subdivider's option, to remain subject to the above-mentioned letter of credit, for a period of one year from the date of completion of the corrected work. Interest on the balance in said escrow account shall accrue to the benefit of the Subdivider, provided that the obligations set forth in this Agreement are satisfied by Subdivider.

12. In the event that Subdivider defaults in whole or in part in the performance of this Agreement, and after the expiration of thirty (30) days after having given written notice to Subdivider of such default during which period of time the Subdivider failed to correct said default, the Town may, at its sole discretion, proceed with the construction or completion of the Improvements. All such costs paid by Town for the Improvements, together with all costs of personnel, equipment and other matters expended by Town in furtherance of the construction responsibilities of Subdivider, shall be paid by Subdivider. Any such costs which have not been reimbursed by Subdivider shall be paid out of the escrow or the proceeds of the letter of credit hereinabove provided for. Without limiting the foregoing, Town may bring a mandatory injunction action against Subdivider to require installation and construction of the improvements, if not constructed within the time limits described in this Agreement. If any such action is brought by Town, Town shall be awarded its court costs and attorneys' fees.

13.   In addition to the other Improvements described in this Agreement, Subdivider hereby agrees as follows:

    (a)   Subdivider agrees to pay all costs, up to a maximum of $300,000, for certain asphalting and related work to Nottingham, Metcalf and Wildridge Roads as outlined on Exhibit E attached hereto and incorporated herein by reference. All work related to such roads will be managed and implemented by the Town, and Subdivider's obligation under this Section is limited solely to the one-time payment of costs as discussed herein. The Town agrees to employ a competitive bidding process in awarding the work. The project budget based on successful bid amount plus other estimated costs, or $300,000, whichever is less, shall be paid to the Town by Subdivider within ten (10) days following notice from the Town of the receipt of a successful bid.

    (b)   Subdivider agrees to pay to the Town certain sums related to a proposed public works facility, vehicle garage, and material storage (the "Facility"). Prior to or contemporaneously with final plat approval of the Subdivision by the Town, Subdivider agrees to pay to the Town $25,000 to be applied toward initial costs of developing the Facility. All work related to the Facility will be managed and implemented by the Town, and Subdivider's obligation under this Section is limited solely to the one-time payment of costs as discussed herein. The Town agrees to employ a competitive bidding process in awarding the work. Within ten (10) days following notice from the Town of the receipt of a successful bid, Subdivider agrees to pay to the Town the lesser of the sum of $150,000.00 or the project budget based on successful bid amount plus other estimated costs, in addition to the $25,000.00 discussed above.

    14.   It is understood that the construction of Buck Creek Road as access to the Subdivision is conditioned upon the Subdivider's effecting a land trade with the United States Forest Service, obtaining an easement for Buck Creek Road, or maintaining in effect a special use permit for Buck Creek Road. Buck Creek Road accordingly shall be constructed in accordance with any requirements of the Forest Service pertaining thereto. In the event of the failure of all of the aforesaid conditions, this Agreement shall be deemed to be of no further force and effect, and an amended agreement shall be entered into by the parties acknowledging that Wildwood Road shall be the sole access to the Subdivision.

    15.   Subdivider agrees that, upon completion of the construction of the hiking trail provided for in Tract C of the Subdivision, it will grant an easement therefor to the Town.

    16.   The first priority lien on real property within the Subdivision provided for in the Amended Agreement shall be released and discharged upon the providing of the collateral hereinabove described. Upon request, the Town will surrender the promissory note and execute a release of the deed of trust securing the performance of the Amended Agreement.

    17.   This Agreement may be amended from time to time, provided that such amendment be in writing and signed by all parties hereto.

    18.   In the event of a lawsuit arising out of the terms of this Agreement, the prevailing party shall be entitled to court costs and reasonable attorney fees.

    19.   This Agreement and the obligations hereof shall be deemed to be covenants running with the land and shall be binding on the successors and assigns of the parties hereto.

    The parties have executed this Agreement as of the date first above written.

[Signatures and Acknowledgements]

Design Review

In some communities, design review regulations have been adopted. The purpose of *design review regulations* is to provide harmony of architectural design in a particular community. For example, the architecture of Santa Fe, New Mexico, has been strictly controlled through design regulation. Historic communities have similar architectural controls. Newer communities, such as Vail, Colorado, have design guidelines calculated to cause similar architectural style throughout the community. The latter type of regulations, lacking a historic theme, tend to create a process that is more negotiation than regulation.

Design review may occur by the governing body, the planning commission, or a special design review board. The process is quasi-judicial, appeal is provided, and judicial review is allowed. Design review requirements sometimes are found in a subdivision's protective covenants. When this is so, the design requirements also are private and are not subject to the appeal process required of public agencies.

Building Codes and Boards of Building Appeals

The adoption of building codes is widespread, if not universal. With the adoption of building codes, local governments established building departments and building inspectors; and they require that buildings not be constructed or improved without the issuance of a building permit. Thereafter, new buildings cannot be occupied without issuance of a certificate of occupancy.

The building codes generally in use are promulgated by the International Conference of Building Officials. They are the *uniform codes*: the Uniform Building Code, the Uniform Fire Code, the Uniform Plumbing Code, the Uniform Electrical Code, the Uniform Mechanical Code, and so forth. These codes come in a variety of editions and are updated every few years. Before referring to any of the codes, the builder's attorney or legal assistant must be certain that he or she is using the current edition.

The uniform codes challenge the Internal Revenue Code for complexity. They deal with such matters as size and placement of handrailings, height of stair risers, ventilation, fire protection, and all aspects of the construction process. Each local government enacts amendments to the uniform codes in the process of adopting them. These amendments must be consulted as well. Fortunately, most reputable builders are more familiar with the code provisions than their attorneys are.

The Uniform Building Code also deals with the process of issuing building permits. Anyone who wants to build a residence, for example, must submit detailed plans to the building department of the municipality and must pay a fee based on the value of the building proposed to be built. Once the plans are reviewed by the building department and (usually) by the fire department and once any errors discovered during the process are corrected, a building permit is issued.

In the course of construction, a building inspector examines the work being done to ensure that it conforms to the plans and to the building codes. After the work is complete and after a final inspection is made to determine that all construction meets the code requirements, a certificate of occupancy is issued. Temporary certificates of occupancy may be issued as well. For example, a temporary certificate would permit the occupancy of one business in a shopping center, with the final certificate of occupancy reserved until completion of all building within the shopping center.

As a part of this process, a building board of appeals exists by ordinance or by statute in each local government. The purpose of the building board of appeals is to hear appeals from decisions of the building inspector and to render opinions upon the interpretation of the building codes. Usually, members of the building trades serve on these boards. The hearing before a building board of appeals is quasi-judicial, and appeals may be heard by the courts.

Building departments now have responsibility for enforcement of federal building regulations as well, including in particular the Americans With Disabilities Act (the ADA). That Act generally requires that all new buildings be fully accessible by persons with disabilities.

The administrative regulations discussed in this chapter place far more restrictions on the use of land than the common law judges ever dreamed of. The fact that the growth of those regulations has occurred within the past sixty years makes them even more remarkable. The fact that they are limited only by constitutional principles causes each set of land use regulations to be unique in many ways. The legal assistant can be particularly helpful to the attorney by being familiar with those regulations.

Chapter 7 Quiz

Fill in each blank with the most correct word or phrase.

1. Types of variances, which provide flexibility for zoning ordinances, are _____ variances and _____ variances.

2. To amend a zoning ordinance, a determination must be made that the amendment is consistent with _____.

3. Rezoning of individual lots may be done by the process of negotiation between the landowner and the municipality and is known as _____ zoning.

4. The process of dividing single, large lots into several smaller ones is governed by _____.

5. The certificate of approval issued by the Building Department, determining that all construction complies with the applicable codes, is _____ _____.

Circle the most correct answer.

6. True or False. Placing restrictions on the use of private property raised constitutional issues.

7. True or False. Valid zoning regulations must be supported by and relate to a comprehensive plan adopted by the governing body of the community.

8. True or False. The U.S. Supreme Court holds that restrictions on the use of property by zoning regulations are an improper exercise of police power.

9. True or False. Zoning regulations regulate the density of geographic areas.

10. True or False. Zoning regulations govern only those areas with residential or commercial buildings.

11. True or False. Each zoning district has some uses by right as well as conditional uses.

12. True or False. Building under a permitted use within a district requires a building permit.

13. True or False. Granting a conditional use permit requires a public hearing before a public body.

14. True or False. A conditional use typically may not be continued by successive owners.

15. True or False. The procedure for conditional use permits is discretionary with the public body and is valid if the public body complies with notice provisions.

16. True or False. Steep topography requires that for zoning purposes, the height of the building is measured from its mid-point.

17. True or False. A planned unit development is a customized zone district which eliminates commercial uses.

18. True or False. The U.S. Supreme Court cases which established the two-step test in determining (a) whether a particular exaction is sustainable under the zoning power or (b) whether the condition of approval is a taking under the Fifth Amendment are Village of Euclid v. Ambler Realty Co., 272 U.S. 365 (1926) and Nollan v. California Coastal Comm'n, 483 U.S. 825 (1987).

19. True or False. Subdivision improvement agreements require the completion of subdivision improvements and require the developer to maintain all roads after completion.

20. True or False. The design review process is quasi-judicial and allows appeals and judicial review.

21. True or False. The uniform building codes generally in use are promulgated by the International Conference of Local Governments.

22. True or False. A member of the building trade would be prohibited from serving on a building board of appeals.

23. The statutory system of private property regulation is known as:

   1. Master Plan
   2. Euclidean zoning
   3. Planning and zoning
   4. Land use law
   5. b and d
   6. c and d
   7. none of the above

24. The Master Plan establishes:

   1. long-range goals and maintenance for the community.
   2. exaction is sustainable under zoning power and provides architectural harmony with the community.
   3. requirements for completion of subdivision improvements.
   4. all of the above.

25. Traditional zoning is sometimes referred to as:

   1. Euclidian zoning
   2. spot zoning
   3. planned unit developments
   4. contract zoning

26. Zoning restrictions designed to reduce density and to prevent the crowding of buildings are:

   1. use restrictions
   2. area restrictions
   3. topography restrictions
   4. conditional restrictions

27. Uses that preexisted the adoption of zoning ordinances are:

   1. conditional uses
   2. PUD uses
   3. nonconforming uses
   4. Grandfather uses

28.   An owner applying for a use variance must show that she will suffer:

   1.   financial hardship
   2.   practical difficulty
   3.   physical hardship
   4.   no grant of special privileges
   5.   a and d
   6.   c and d

29.   An owner applying for an area variance usually must show only:

   1.   financial hardship
   2.   practical difficulty
   3.   physical hardship
   4.   no grant of special privilege
   5.   c and d
   6.   a and d

Essay Question:

30.   Review the subdivision agreement in Figure 7-3 (supra). According to that agreement, who is entitled to the interest earned on the escrow accounts provided for in the agreement?

   Cite the appropriate provision(s) to support your answer.

Chapter 8
SOURCES AND CONVEYANCE OF TITLE

All things have a beginning, and this is true of the title to real property as well. In ancient times, title often was acquired by conquest. Thus, when William the Conqueror won the Battle of Hastings in 1066, he acquired title to England. Thereafter, title descended from him and his successors. The government remains the usual source of title today and, from time to time, causes a rebirth of title. However, title still can be acquired by adverse possession, a method reminiscent of ancient conquest.

Land Patents

If one tracks the title back far enough, the government usually will turn out to be the original owner of any parcel of land. In the eastern United States, some lands were conveyed to their initial owners by royal grant. As the United States moved westward, a *land patent* was used by the United States government to convey land to its initial title owners, who usually were its occupants.

Similarly, *virgin title* is conveyed by the government when property is sold for unpaid taxes. If real property taxes are not paid, all states have enacted a statutory procedure that authorizes the treasurer or other taxing entity to convey the property in exchange for payment of taxes. The title thus conferred is virgin in the sense that a prospective purchaser need not inquire into the quality of title prior to the date of the tax deed. What the purchaser at tax sale receives is as good as a government patent, although it may be subject to claims of persons under disability (minors and incompetent persons). A treasurer's deed, sometimes called a tax deed, is shown at Figure 8-1.

Figure 8-1
Tax Deed

TREASURER'S DEED

KNOW ALL MEN BY THESE PRESENTS, that, whereas, the following described real property, viz: Lot 1, Block 1, Oro City, situate in the county of Carbon and state of Colorado, was subject to taxation for the years A.D. 1991 and 1992; and

Whereas, the taxes assessed upon said property for the years aforesaid remained due and unpaid at the date of the sale hereinafter named, and, whereas, the treasurer of said county did, on the 2nd day of January, 1993, by virtue of the authority vested in her by law, at the sale begun and publicly held on the 2nd day of January, 1993, expose to public sale at the office of the treasurer, in the county aforesaid, in substantial conformity with the requirements of the statute in such case made and provided, the tax lien on the real property above described for the payment of taxes, penalty interest, and costs then due and remaining unpaid on said property; and

Whereas, at the time and place aforesaid, John Doe of the county of Carbon and state of Colorado bid on the tax lien on all of the above described property the sum of One Hundred Dollars and No Cents, being the whole amount of taxes, penalty interest, and costs then due and remaining unpaid on said property, and the said John Doe having offered in his said bid to pay the sum of One Hundred Dollars and No Cents in excess of said taxes, penalty interest, and costs, and said bid being the largest amount which any person offered to pay in excess of said taxes, penalty interest, and costs so due upon said property for those years, and payment on such property was stricken off to him at that price; and

Whereas, the said John Doe has paid subsequent taxes on said property in the amount of One Hundred Twenty Dollars and No Cents; and

Whereas, the said property was valued for assessment for those years at One Hundred Dollars and No Cents; and

Whereas, all provisions of the statutes prescribing prerequisites to obtaining tax deeds have been fully complied with and are now of record and filed in the office of the treasurer of said county;

Now, therefore, I, May Linn, treasurer of the county aforesaid, for and in consideration of the sum to the treasurer paid as aforesaid, and by virtue of the statute in such case made and provided, have granted, bargained, and sold, and by these presents do grant, bargain, and sell the above and foregoing described real estate unto the said John Doe, his heirs and assigns, forever, subject to all the rights of redemption by minors or incompetent persons as provided by law.

In Witness Whereof, I, May Linn, treasurer as aforesaid, by virtue of the authority aforesaid, have hereunto set my hand and seal of this office this 2nd day of January, 1996.

(SEAL)

_____
May Linn, Treasurer

STATE OF COLORADO   ]
                                       ]ss.
COUNTY OF CARBON   ]

The foregoing instrument was acknowledged before me this 2nd day of January, 1996, by May Linn as Treasurer of said county.

Witness my hand and official seal.

My Commission expires: _____

_____
Notary Public

Adverse Possession

Throughout history, acquiring property simply by possessing it has been recognized. The reason for this is not entirely clear but may relate to early difficulties in tracing paper title. In any event, all jurisdictions today recognize *adverse possession* as a way to acquire title merely by possessing it for a specified period of time. The specified time ranges anywhere from five to thirty years, depending on the particular jurisdiction and depending on such factors as *color of title* (conveyance by a defective deed) and payment of taxes.

In most states, the particular period of time for adverse possession is determined by the state's statute of limitations for real property. That statute establishes a period of time after which an action in ejectment may not be brought to recover possession of real property. Once that period passes, title automatically vests in the possessor. This type of title is known as a *prescriptive title* (title by adverse possession).

Since a prescriptive title depends on possession and not on record title, it is important that anyone purchasing real property go upon the property and satisfy himself that no one is in possession. In fact, any policy of title insurance or attorney's opinion of title will except the rights of parties in possession. It is also important that improvements to real estate be surveyed to be certain there is no encroachment by neighboring buildings or other structures.

Prescriptive title or title by adverse possession can arise in a number of ways. It may arise when the improvements on one parcel encroach upon a neighboring parcel. If the improvements remain in place for the statutory period, title by adverse possession will result. Title by adverse possession also may arise when the fence between two parcels is located improperly. In hilly or mountainous country, for example, fence lines often follow hillcrests rather than property lines. This is done as a matter of convenience in the usual case. If the fence remains in place for the statutory period and if the property is farmed or otherwise used up to the fence line, the fence itself will set the boundary line. The diagram in Figure 8-2 shows how a fence built along a hill for convenience ultimately may establish the boundary line for the property.

Figure 8-2
Fence Line

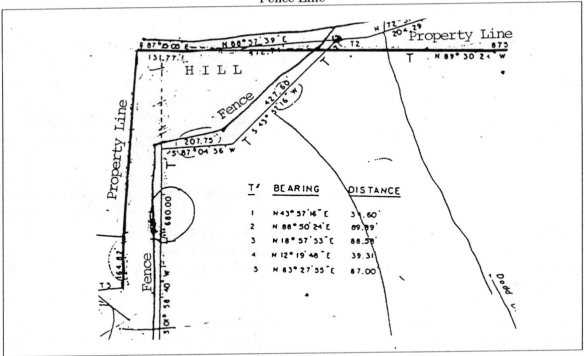

Adverse possession also may originate from a mistake concerning the location of property conveyed. A particular parcel of land may be conveyed to a grantee, who thereafter occupies another parcel by mistake. Or adverse possession may be relied upon where a deed is defective. For example, if a deed is not signed, it nevertheless provides color of title; and on that basis, the grantee's possession can ripen into legal ownership. Or a trespasser may build a cabin or other structure on a remote portion of someone else's land. If the cabin remains in use for the period of the statute, without acknowledgment of the superior title, adverse possession will result. If the cabin is surrounded by a fence or if the area surrounding the cabin is used in some way along with the cabin, the entire area may become adversely possessed.

Cabin → ⌂

(80 acres)

Regardless of the way in which the adverse possession arises, certain elements of ownership must be established; otherwise, the possession is not adverse. By statute in some states, a person qualifies as an adverse possessor only by performing certain acts, such as cultivating, enclosing, or residing on the property. In most states, however, there are no such requirements; and any act of possession of the necessary quality can support a finding of adverse possession.

First, the possession must be *open and notorious*. In other words, the land must be occupied in such a way that the true owner has notice *(open)*; or the occupancy must be of a type that would be obvious to the owner if she were attentive to her land holdings *(notorious)*. Building a cabin on someone else's property certainly is open and notorious possession, as is encroaching on the land of one's neighbor. Whether possession of the area surrounding the cabin is open and notorious may be more difficult to determine.

Second, the possession must be *hostile and under claim of right*. Adverse possession does not arise if a person moves into possession with the permission of the true owner (a tenant, for example). A hostile possession under claim of right essentially means an occupancy without permission of the true owner. This requirement is easily shown when the possession comes about because of an error concerning the property's boundary line. Examples may include a fence that does not follow the true boundary line or a building that encroaches because the true boundary line was not known. In those circumstances, the state of mind of the possessor is that he occupies his own land. It generally is not material that the possession is unintentional or mistaken.

Third, the possession must be *exclusive*. This means that the possessor must act alone and not as a member of the public, for example. Thus, adverse possession does not result in the favor of any particular person if everyone in the community picnics on Farmer Brown's land. Nor is possession of one cotenant adverse to the other in relation to land they own together.

Finally, the possession must be *continuous and uninterrupted* for the statutory period. If the cabin built by the trespasser in the earlier example is abandoned before the statutory period elapses, the statute stops running. If the trespasser later returns, the period of the statute begins to run anew. A question frequently arises concerning whether an intermittent type of possession meets the elements of adverse possession. For example, one might occupy the cabin only during those months when the cabin is accessible and not during winter months when the cabin is snowed in. The general rule is that whatever possession ordinarily and reasonably would occur is sufficient. In a mountainous area, it might be ordinary and reasonable for a cabin to be unoccupied during winter months.

Tacking occurs when more than one person is the possessor over a period of time. Using the example of an encroachment, if land with encroaching improvements is owned initially by Anna Marie and then is conveyed to Billy Bob before the period of the statute expires, Billy Bob's ownership is *tacked* to Anna Marie's ownership to establish the necessary statutory period.

A shorter statutory period may apply if the possession is under *color of title* (based on paper title). For example, Bernadette may enter into possession of High Country Estates, thinking she purchased it from Abel when, in fact, Abel did not own High Country Estates. If it is recorded, the deed from Abel to Bernadette constitutes color of title and, in some jurisdictions, shortens the time required to create title by adverse possession. Further, the extent of the title acquired this way is the parcel of land described in the deed and not a lesser part of the land actually occupied.

By statute in some states, no one can become an owner by adverse possession unless he pays taxes on the property being adversely possessed. In other states, the time required for adverse possession may be shortened by payment of taxes, particularly when the payment is coupled with color of title. Where adverse possession is based on a fence line that is different from the true boundary line, both the adverse possessor and the true owner may pay the taxes since the tax records will not make any distinction as to the disputed area. The requirement of payment of taxes nevertheless is met, although under the laws of some states, the issue will turn on who was the first to pay.

Title vested by adverse possession is automatic. Once vesting occurs, the resulting title is as good as any other. Thus, using the example of the cabin, if the cabin is abandoned by the adverse possessor after the statutory period has expired, title is not lost any more than if the title had been conveyed by land patent. On the other hand, the title obtained is a legal title and not a record title. For the title to be record title, one must file a *quiet title action* in a court of competent jurisdiction to obtain a decree that establishes title ownership, which will be effective as of the date of the original entry.

Title by adverse possession generally cannot be acquired against the federal or state government. Thus, one who encroaches onto a state highway right-of-way never acquires title to the premises encroached upon, no matter how long the encroachment continues. The same rule also may apply to counties and municipalities, depending on the particular jurisdiction.

Statute of Frauds

The Statute of Frauds, 29 Car. II. c. 3, originally was enacted by the English Parliament in 1677 to deter the "perpetuation of frauds." The Statute is part of either the common law or the statutory law of every state in the United States. It requires that certain agreements be in writing to be enforceable. As it relates to real estate, the Statute requires that any contract for the sale of land (or for any interest in land) is void unless the contract or some memorandum thereof states the consideration in writing and is signed by the party to be bound, that is, the seller of the real estate. *Contracts for sale of land are discussed in detail in Chapter 9.*

Not every detail of the agreement must be in writing. As long as the consideration is stated and as long as there are enough other details to permit a court to enforce the agreement, the agreement is given effect.

An oral contract for the sale of land nevertheless may be enforced if it has been partially performed. For example, if Adam agrees to sell Adam's Acres to Bridget and if Adam accepts all or part of the purchase price, he may not repudiate the contract later by claiming that it was not in writing. Other types of partial performance that may take the agreement *out of the statute* are delivery of possession, making improvements, and combinations of those acts.

In general, then, the first rule of conveyancing is that any agreement relating to an interest in land must be in writing to be enforceable. Once the agreement is written and is signed by the parties, it is enforceable between them. The second rule of conveyancing is that the document must be recorded to be enforceable against third parties who do not have actual notice of the contract or other instrument. Once the document is recorded, it is enforceable *against the world*.

Recording Acts

Documents relating to real estate are recorded in an office established for that purpose, usually at the county seat. The office may be that of the county recorder, the recorder of deeds, or some similar title. Not only deeds are recorded, however. To be enforceable against third parties, any document related to real property must be recorded. Therefore, all types of documents affecting title to land are found in the public records.

Anyone engaged in any aspect of real property law should visit the office where instruments are recorded and should take a tour to understand the concept of recording. Methods of recording have changed dramatically as technology has advanced. For many years, recording consisted of hand-copying the particular document into a record book. With the advent of the haloid copier, recording came to mean copying by copy machine, with the copies inserted into the record book. Today, microfilm or microfiche has replaced the original record book in many states. Whatever method is used, the practice is for the recorder to place the date, book number, and page number of the recording on the instrument. Once recorded, the original document is returned to the person who delivered it for recording.

In addition, every recorder's office contains various indices that are critical to the process of title examination. Among them are a *grantor-grantee index* and a *grantee-grantor index*. One is the reverse of the other, allowing the title examiner to locate a particular title record if she knows the name of either the grantor or the grantee.

Determining who is the grantor and who is the grantee is easy when the instrument involved is a deed. In other instruments, the determination is less simple. For instance, the lessor in a lease becomes the grantor for purpose of the index. If the instrument is an encumbrance of some sort, such as an easement or a lien, the owner of the property encumbered is considered the grantor; the person or entity holding the encumbrance is considered the grantee.

A few jurisdictions maintain official *tract indices*, although not necessarily in the recorder's office. In some jurisdictions, the county assessor or similar official maintains maps from which ownership of property can be determined. Also, each county typically has an abstract company where duplicate records as well as grantor-grantee, grantee-grantor, and tract indices are maintained. These are not official records, but they can be important in determining interests in real property.

When a document is recorded, the recording provides **constructive notice** to third parties or, as it often is phrased, *to the world*. Anyone acquiring an interest in a particular parcel of real estate acquires that interest subject to all interests shown *of record*, whether or not those interests actually are known. When one records a deed or other instrument that affects title to real property, he provides constructive notice to third parties. This protects his recorded interest in the property against subsequent purchasers.

The protection given by recording assumes three things. First, it assumes that the interest acquired is valid. Recording a void instrument does not make it valid, either as to the instrument or as to the interest it purports to convey. Second, it assumes that the grantee or other beneficiary of the instrument is a bona fide purchaser for value. Third, it assumes that the recorded interest was acquired without actual or constructive knowledge of prior, unrecorded interests. Constructive knowledge of prior, unrecorded interests occurs when there are circumstances that create a duty to inquire about such interests. For example, if there is a cabin occupied by strangers on the land being purchased, the purchaser has a duty to inquire further. This circumstance is called *inquiry notice*.

When inquiry notice exists, the prospective purchaser must make a reasonable effort to determine whether an unrecorded interest may exist in the property. Using the example of the cabin occupied by strangers, a prospective purchaser has a duty to inquire if the strangers claim a right to the property, whether by an unrecorded lease, by some other grant of interest, or by mere possession of the property over time. Any prospective purchaser with inquiry notice takes the property subject to any interest that the strangers may have, regardless of whether inquiry is made or not. Thus, if the occupants of the cabin have obtained title by adverse possession and if that fact could have been determined by reasonable inquiry, the strangers' title will be good against the prospective purchaser.

The common law rule was, "first in time, first in right" in relation to conveyance of title by deed. The first person to accept delivery of a deed prevailed over any person who subsequently received a deed to the same land. That system proved unworkable because there was no way to know whether the owner already had delivered a deed to someone else. Bona fide purchasers for value without actual notice of a prior sale were not protected.

For that reason, recording statutes were adopted in the American colonies. They borrowed from and expanded the personal property concept of the bona fide purchaser for value. Under that equitable doctrine, a purchaser of stolen goods could acquire valid title to those goods if she purchased them for full value without notice that they were stolen, usually from a dealer in the type of goods purchased. Under the recording acts, a subsequent bona fide purchaser of land similarly is protected against prior, unrecorded interests.

Recording statutes are of three types: pure race, pure notice, and race notice. The distinctions among the three types ordinarily do not matter. However, the distinctions become important when a property owner conveys her interest more or less simultaneously to more than one person. This may be intentional (part of a fraudulent scheme, for example) or unintentional (such as by allowing a lien to attach to the property). The distinctions, then, are important only between the time an instrument is delivered and the time the instrument is recorded.

Pure Race Statute   In a *pure race* jurisdiction, the one who wins the race to the courthouse is the one who prevails.

> Ada sells Ada's Acres to Bernard and gives him a deed. She later
> sells the same property to Carlos, gives him a deed, and leaves for
> Tahiti with the money.

If Bernard's deed is recorded first, Bernard becomes the owner of Ada's Acres. In that event, Carlos owns nothing except a claim for fraud against Ada. It makes no difference whether Bernard or Carlos (or both of them) knew the other also had received a deed.

Pure Notice Statute   In a *pure notice* jurisdiction, a later purchaser for value who has no actual notice of a prior, unrecorded conveyance takes free and clear of the prior conveyance. In states where this type of statute exists, it makes no difference who records his deed first or whether the deed is recorded at all. About half the states are pure notice jurisdictions, including Florida, Illinois, Massachusetts, and Texas.

If Carlos in the above example were in a pure notice state and if he knew about the deed to Bernard, Carlos would not prevail even if he had recorded his deed before Bernard recorded. If Carlos did not know about the deed to Bernard, however, Carlos would prevail even if Bernard had recorded his deed first. The bona fide purchaser without notice always prevails in a pure notice jurisdiction. Notice of a prior conveyance, however, always defeats a later conveyance.

Race Notice Statute   Race notice statutes are a compromise between pure race statutes and pure notice statutes. In a *race notice* jurisdiction, a later purchaser for value who has no actual notice of a prior, unrecorded conveyance takes free and clear of that conveyance *only if* he records his deed first. About half of the states are race notice jurisdictions, including California, Michigan, New Jersey, and New York.

In this type of jurisdiction, the first person to record his deed (whether Bernard or Carlos in the example) would prevail unless he had notice of the other's deed. Here, the bona fide purchaser for value prevails only if he records first. Notice of a prior conveyance always defeats a later conveyance, however.

Most pure race jurisdictions have become race notice jurisdictions by judicial interpretation. Courts in those jurisdictions concluded it was unfair to permit a person with notice of a prior interest to prevail simply because she was the first to record. Accordingly, they determined that the first person to record an instrument could prevail only if she had no notice of any prior, unrecorded interests.

The risk that another interest will be asserted or will be recorded between the time of closing and the time of recording the deed (commonly referred to as the *gap period*) varies somewhat, depending on the jurisdiction. As a practical matter, the only person concerned with this issue is the one who insures title or delivers a title opinion.

Property Description

The most important part of the deed (or of any other instrument that affects property) is the property's description, sometimes called the *legal description*. Any error in the description can raise questions about the validity of the deed. Generally, the property description takes one of two forms: it is either a description by reference to a plat (map) or a metes-and-bounds description prepared by a surveyor.

The essence of any real property description is that it must identify the particular parcel in such a way that it cannot be confused with any other parcel in the world. Every description should include the city, county, and state in which the parcel is located. Beyond that, the contents of the description depend on whether the parcel is identified as part of a recorded plat or map of a subdivision (including a condominium plat) or must be described by metes and bounds (based on a survey).

Subdivision Maps   Under the Uniform Common Interest Ownership Act, which has been enacted only in a limited number of jurisdictions, a *plat* gives both horizontal and vertical descriptions; a *map* gives only a vertical description. Therefore, a subdivision is shown on a map. Only a condominium is shown on a plat. As a practical matter, however, the two terms are used interchangeably even in those jurisdictions that have adopted the Act.

A subdivision map subdivides the land comprising the subdivision into blocks and further divides the blocks into lots. A description that refers to a subdivision map might describe a particular parcel, for example, as "Lot 1, Block A, State Street Subdivision, City of Chicago, County of Cook, and State of Illinois."

One frequently sees more in legal descriptions, but more than this is not necessary. Language such as "according to the subdivision plat for State Street Subdivision, recorded in plat book A, page 20, as amended by the amended subdivision plat recorded in plat book A at page 100," is surplusage and increases the possibility of error. However, the more common practice is to use the surplus language. The rule to follow is to copy any description verbatim from the title policy or other document relied upon and to proofread the description very, very carefully after it is copied.

If the property is not described by reference to a plat or map, it likely will be described by metes and bounds. The exception is when the particular parcel is a section of land (or some portion of a section of land). Before turning to the metes-and-bounds description, and to understand the metes-and-bounds description better, it is helpful to review the phrases *section, township, range,* and *principal meridian.*

United States Government Survey   Thomas Jefferson gave us not only the Declaration of Independence but also the rectangular survey system. This system was initiated by the Continental Congress in 1785, in part to survey lands that were to be given to soldiers who had served in the Continental Army. The same rectangular survey system, now known as the United States Government Survey, is used in thirty states: Alabama, Florida, Mississippi, all states north of the Ohio River, and all states west of the Mississippi River except Texas.

The area now comprising those states was surveyed into a rectangular grid, first divided by 34 north-south lines (called *principal meridians* or prime meridians) and then by east-west lines (called *principal base lines*) to form rectangles. Between meridians are *range* lines, each one six miles from the next. Between the base lines are township lines, each one six miles from the next. Each six-mile-by-six-mile square forms a *township*. No township is a perfect square, however. All lines in the survey are run with respect to meridians and parallels of latitude, and all meridians converge as they run north from the equator. This convergence makes the north side of all townships slightly shorter than the south side. Figure 8-3 shows the layout of a township.

Figure 8-3
Township Map and Numbering Diagram

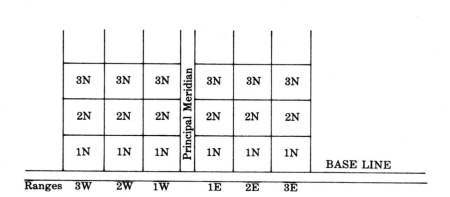

Townships are numbered consecutively. The first tier of townships north of the base line all are part of Township 1 North; the second tier, Township 2 North, and so on. The first tier of townships south of the base line all are part of Township 1 South; the second tier, Township 2 South, and so on. The layout and scheme of numbering within each township is shown in the next figure.

Each township is divided into 36 sections. Each *section* is approximately one square mile in size (about 640 acres). To keep the range lines six miles apart as they converge on the North Pole, they are laid out for a distance of sixty miles. Then they are stopped and moved over to make them six miles apart again. As a result, sections often are slightly larger or slightly smaller than 640 acres, particularly those located on the west side of a township.

The sections in a township are numbered from 1 to 36, starting in the northeast corner and moving west from 1 to 6, then moving east from 7 to 12 (immediately beneath sections 1 through 6), then moving back west from 13 to 18 (immediately beneath sections 7 through 12), and so on to section 36 in the southeast corner of the township. Figure 8-4 illustrates the way in which sections are numbered within each township.

Figure 8-4
Section Layout in each Township

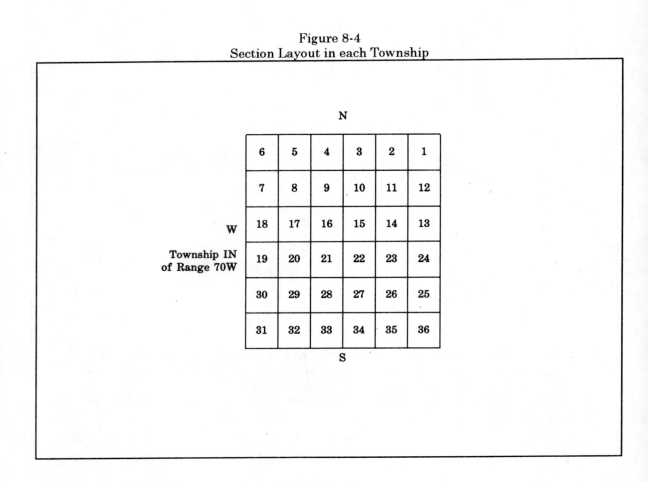

To describe smaller parcels, a section is divided into half sections, quarter sections, half-quarter sections, and quarter-quarter sections. Figure 8-5 illustrates the way a section is divided for purposes of property description.

Figure 8-5
Description of Parcels within a Section

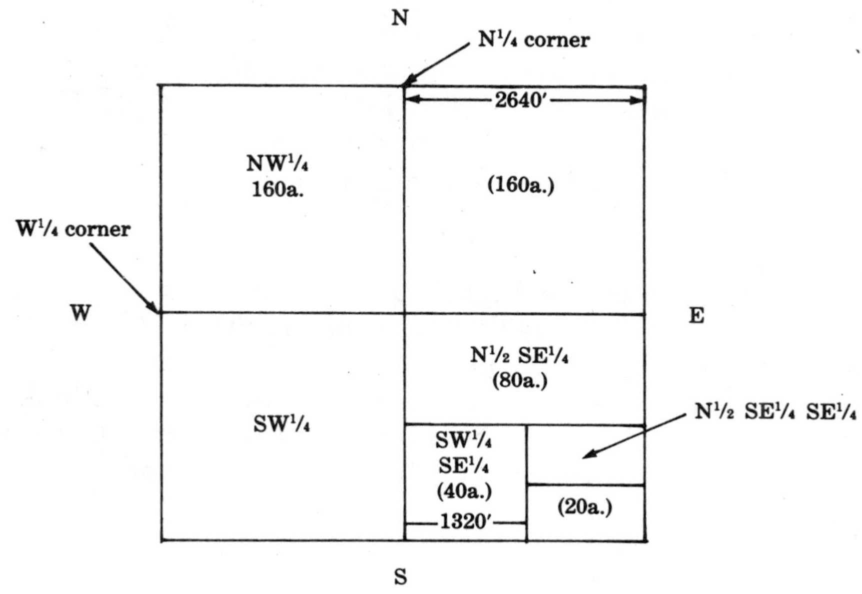

Over the years since 1785, government surveyors have moved across the United States, placing a monument at each *section corner* so created. Each section corner monument marks the corner of four sections. Where the corner cannot be monumented for some reason (where it is under water, for example), a *witness corner* nearby is used. The task of placing monuments continues today.

Metes and Bounds   In the remaining states, if a parcel of land is not described in reference to a plat or map, it is described by metes and bounds. Even in the thirty states included in the United States Government Survey, if the parcel to be described is smaller than or different from a quarter-quarter section or some combination of quarter-quarter sections, a metes-and-bounds description is used. In those states included in the United States Government Survey, however, the description *ties to* (is related to) a section corner. In the other states, the description ties to some other recognized monument, such as a building or a tree.

A description by ***metes*** (distances) and ***bounds*** (directions) traces the perimeter of the parcel described. It starts from a fixed point (the tie) and proceeds either clockwise or counterclockwise (it makes no difference which way) along straight lines and arcs of curves that end at the starting point (the point of beginning). The metes, of course, are stated in inches and feet. The bounds are stated in the directions of the compass or in degree variation from the directions of the compass. Thus, a simple metes-and-bounds description might be stated:

Beginning at a point from within the north quarter corner of Section 4, Township 1 North, Range 70 West of the 6th P.M., County of Boulder and State of Colorado bears N 45° W 1320 feet, which point of beginning an iron stake has been placed; thence South 600 feet to a point also marked by a stake; thence N 45° West 700 feet to a large oak tree; thence Northeasterly 700 feet, more or less, to the point of beginning.

This legal description is diagrammed on the next page in Figure 8-6.

Figure 8-6
Diagram of Metes-and-Bounds Description

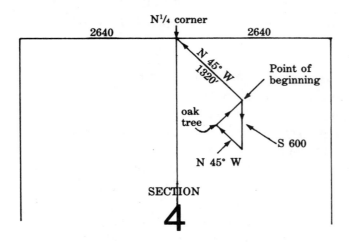

Notice that on course N 45 ° W to the oak tree, the distance obviously is less than the 700 feet specified in the legal description. The distance in the description would yield to the natural monument (the large oak tree).

To be valid, a metes-and-bounds description must *close*. In other words, when it is plotted, the description must return to the point of beginning. Using the phrase "more or less" in the final mete saves a description that otherwise might be off by a few feet. In addition, the location of a monument controls over distance. If the distance (described in feet) passes by a monument, for example, the monument location prevails to shorten the distance described.

Errors in descriptions frequently are resolved through these rules. Less serious errors, such as a misspelled word, can be ignored. Some errors are obvious and can be ignored on that basis. For example, a description that proceeds north and then west and then south and then west again to the point of beginning is an obvious error. It is apparent that *east* was intended when *west* was used. Obvious errors such as these are best corrected; but when they appear in older documents, they frequently are ignored.

Errors that cannot be resolved this way must be corrected (reformed). If the original parties to the instrument are available, a *corrective deed* or other instrument is prepared and recorded. If the original parties are not available or if there is some dispute over the error, a suit for *reformation* of the deed or other instrument must be filed.

In the absence of any clear indication of what the parties intended, the court may apply canons of construction to give effect to what the parties most likely intended. Canons of construction establish the following order: **original survey monuments** prevail over **natural monuments**, which prevail over **artificial monuments**, which prevail over **maps**, which prevail over **courses**, which prevail over **distances**, which prevail over a **name**, which prevails over **quantity.**

An *original survey monument* is a surveyor's stake, brass monument, or some natural object used in marking the lines and corners of a survey. Trees and rivers are examples of *natural monuments*. Because natural monuments are less easily moved, they are considered more reliable than *artificial monuments* such as a fence. Thus, a call of "West 700 feet to a large spruce tree" prevails over a call of "West 700 feet." One theory for this rationale is that property ordinarily is bought in reliance on what can be seen rather than in reliance on paper calculations, and distances cannot be measured accurately with the naked eye.

A survey map of the property giving courses and distances can be used to establish boundaries even if the original survey marks no longer can be found. Descriptions by courses and distances give a starting point and the direction and length of the lines, for example, "Commencing at the Southeast Corner of Section 4, thence West 700 feet. . . ." Courses (angles), such as S66°07'24"E prevail over distances (700 feet). Sometimes the parcel does not close as described but does close by following the courses and adjusting the distances. In such a case, the description that uses the courses prevails, it being assumed that an angle, which describes the shape of the lot, is more obvious to the parties than the length. A name (Spencer's Mountain, for example) may be used, but is unreliable because it is difficult to know exactly what land is included in such a description; and preference is given to any other description except a description by quantity. Descriptions by quantity (for instance, 5200 acres) are considered the least reliable.

When descriptions refer to streets, rivers, or streams, it generally is presumed that the middle of the stream or the centerline of the street is intended. When a stream changes course gradually over time, the party on one side gains land (*accretion*), while the party on the other side loses land (*reliction*), depending on which way the stream moves. On the other hand, when the stream moves violently (*avulsion*), the boundaries do not change.

Legal assistants are not expected to be land surveyors. However, a legal assistant who can use a ruler and a protractor to read (to plot) a simple metes-and-bounds description can provide a valuable service by identifying errors that may appear in the description.

The Deed

This section reviews the various forms of deeds and their provisions. From the time of the Norman Conquest (1066) until passage of the Statute of Uses (1535), conveyancing of real property was called *feoffment*. In a ceremony known as *livery of seisin*, the parties went on the property; and the grantor literally handed soil to the grantee. This ceremony then was memorialized by a *charter of feoffment*, which was the earliest form of deed at common law. After the Statute of Uses, the charter of feoffment was replaced by the *bargain and sale deed*, which has evolved into the warranty deed of today.

The modern warranty deed as well as other types of deeds continue to be modeled on the charter of feoffment and the bargain and sale deed. For instance, the typical deed might begin as follows:

KNOW ALL MEN BY THESE PRESENTS, that Doe Corporation, a corporation, hereinafter known as the Grantor, in consideration of the sum of TEN DOLLARS and other good and valuable consideration, does hereby grant, bargain, sell, and convey to Roe Corporation, a corporation, hereinafter known as the Grantee, the following described property located in the County of Cook and State of Illinois:

Lot 1, Block 4, State Street Subdivision, City of Chicago, County of Cook and State of Illinois;

TOGETHER with all hereditaments and appurtenances thereunto belonging, or in anywise appertaining, and the reversion and reversions, remainder and remainders, rents, issues, and profits thereof; and all the estate, right, title, interest, claim, and demand whatsoever of the grantor, either in law or equity, of, in, and to the above bargained premises, with the hereditaments and appurtenances.

The language in this example is known as the *premises* or **grant** of the deed. Although it contains a recitation of consideration, no consideration is required. This is because a deed is not a contract and need not be supported by consideration, which is different from the contract for sale. As a matter of record, however, it is important to establish that the deed is given for value. This allows the purchaser, as a bona fide purchaser for value, to qualify for protection under the recording acts. The consideration or value does not have to take the form of money; often, it takes the form of love and affection.

TEN DOLLARS and other good and valuable consideration is a typical recitation of consideration, which reflects the reluctance of a lawyer to place on record any information that she considers confidential, such as the exact amount of money paid. Many jurisdictions require disclosure of the exact purchase price to taxing authorities (often by a separate document). This makes it possible to establish property values for the purpose of setting tax valuations.

The language *grant, bargain, sell, and convey* varies from state to state. It may be limited to the single word *grant* or it may be expanded to the traditional, formalistic language of the bargain and sale deed in the example.

The language that follows the description of the property is ancient rhetoric and has little significance today. The term **hereditaments** indicates the inheritable nature of the estate being conveyed, and the term **appurtenances** describes improvements upon the property, conveying them as well. Taken together, this ancient scrivener's language describes and redescribes an estate in fee simple absolute. The plain and simple phrase *hereby grants* does just as well to convey the fee, together with all improvements.

The next language found in the typical deed is the **habendum** (Latin for *holding*) clause:

TO HAVE AND TO HOLD the said premises above bargained and described, with the appurtenances, unto the grantee, its successors, and assigns forever.

The original purpose of the habendum was to identify the lord under whom the land was held. That purpose, of course, is long gone; and the habendum clause now serves only to reemphasize the fee simple nature of the estate conveyed and inclusion of the improvements. The habendum clause is unnecessary today, and its omission would not invalidate the deed.

If the deed is a *warranty deed* (so called because it contains *warranties* or *covenants* of title), the following language of warranty will follow the habendum clause:

> And the grantor for itself, its successors, and assigns, does covenant, grant, bargain, and agree to and with the grantee, its successors, and assigns, that at the time of the ensealing and delivery of these presents, it is well seized of the premises above conveyed, has good, sure, perfect, absolute, and indefeasible estate of inheritance, in law, in fee simple, and has good right, full power, and lawful authority to grant, bargain, sell, and convey the same in manner and form aforesaid, and that the same are free and clear from all former and other grants, bargains, sales, liens, taxes, assessments, encumbrances, and restrictions of whatever kind or nature soever, except
>
> *[stating exceptions to title]*
>
> The grantor shall and will WARRANT AND FOREVER DEFEND the above bargained premises in the quiet and peaceable possession of the grantee, its successors, and assigns, against all and every person or persons lawfully claiming or to claim the whole or any part thereof.

The *testimonium* clause, sometimes called the execution clause, follows the warranty clause:

> IN WITNESS WHEREOF, the grantor has caused its corporate name to be hereunto subscribed by its president and its corporate seal affixed by its secretary the . . . *[date]*.

The testimonium clause is followed by signature blanks and often by blanks for witnesses to sign as well. Of course, a deed must be signed by all grantors to comply with the Statute of Frauds. Approximately ten states require that the signatures be *attested* (witnessed). In many states that do not have an attestation requirement, blanks for witnesses to sign nevertheless appear on the deed.

A forged deed is absolutely void and conveys no title. When the signature is induced fraudulently, however, the deed is voidable only; and if it is not set aside, it will convey title. If title is conveyed thereafter to a bona fide purchaser for value, the intervening rights of that purchaser prevent the fraudulently induced conveyance from being set aside.

Excluding corporate seals, reference in deeds to seals is another throwback to ancient times when seals were used routinely in place of signatures by those who were unable to write. Originally, the seal was a wax impression of the name or initials of its owner. If it appears today at all, it takes the form of the word *SEAL* or the letters *L.S.* A few states still require a seal; in other states, its use is entirely customary and without legal effect. Corporate seals, on the other hand, still serve to prove corporate authority in many states.

The final part of the deed is the *acknowledgment*. One who signs a deed is expected to sign it before an officer empowered to administer oaths, usually a notary public. When a deed is signed (but not before an officer empowered to administer oaths), one nevertheless must acknowledge the signature as his own. The form of the acknowledgment frequently is set by statute. Ordinarily, it must contain 1) the name of the person signing; 2) the capacity in which the person signs if she signs other than on her own behalf (for example, as trustee or as a corporate officer); and 3) the date of the signing.

Omission of any of these requirements results in a defective acknowledgment. If a defective acknowledgment exists or if the acknowledgment is omitted entirely, the deed still may be valid. The purpose of the acknowledgment is to give *prima facie* validity to the information contained in it. In other words, when the title examiner sees the acknowledgment, he or she safely may assume the signature is that of the person whose name appears. However, a defective or omitted acknowledgment is a title defect, to which objection to title should be made. This defect may be cured by the passage of time (twenty years, for example), after which the defect may be ignored because of the applicable statute of limitations *(see discussion above)*.

The deed under discussion throughout the last few pages is a warranty deed because of the warranties of title that it contains.

Excluded from those warranties of title are any exceptions from title to which the grantee agreed as part of the contract for sale. Exceptions typically include restrictive covenants, rights-of-way in existence or of record, and taxes for current and future years. If the purchasers are to assume either a deed of trust or a mortgage, it should be described by its date, its recorded book and page numbers, and language such as *which parties of the second part* (the purchasers) *assume and agree to pay*.

The warranties of title, sometimes called covenants of title, are 1) the covenant of seisin, 2) the covenant of the right to convey, 3) the covenant against encumbrances, 4) the covenant of warranty, 5) the covenant of further assurances, and 6) the covenant of quiet enjoyment.

Covenant of Seisin   The grantor represents that he has *seisin* (that he owns the property at the time of its conveyance).

Covenant of the Right to Convey The grantor represents that he has full power to convey the property interest he purports to convey and that he is not subject to any lack of capacity.

Covenant Against Encumbrances The grantor represents that the property conveyed is free of the following three types of encumbrances: 1) those of a pecuniary nature, such as liens, mortgages, judgments, assessments, and the like; 2) an estate which is less than the fee, such as an estate burdened by the right of dower; and 3) easements or other equitable servitudes not excepted from the title.

Covenant of Warranty The grantor warrants that he will defend the grantee's title against any adverse claims existing at the time of the conveyance and that he will compensate the grantee for any losses resulting from the assertion of a superior adverse interest.

Covenant of Quiet Enjoyment   The grantor warrants that the grantee will not be ousted from possession because of any adverse claim existing at the time of the conveyance. This covenant is essentially the same as the covenant of warranty and may be omitted without adverse effect.

Covenant of Further Assurances   The grantor warrants that he will "forever defend" the title conveyed to the grantee and will execute any documents necessary to perfect title in the grantee. From the point of view of the title examiner, this is the most important covenant because it supports the doctrine of *after-acquired title*. Assume, for example, that Austin enters into a contract with Belle on April 1 to convey Another's Acres to Belle. Then he delivers and records the deed conveying Another's Acres on April 10. Assume, further, that on April 1 and April 10, Austin did not own Another's Acres, but Austin acquired ownership of Another's Acres on April 15. The chain would look like this:

Austin
|
WD—4/10/95—4/10/95—book 530, page 82
|
Belle

```
        Prior Owner
        |
        WD—4/15/95—4/15/95—book 531, page 3
        |
        Austin
```

As of April 15, 1995, title is vested in Belle. Because of the covenant of further assurances, Austin's after-acquired title automatically is conveyed to Belle on April 15. No further delivery or recording of any deed or other instrument is required. Although this example may be unusual, it is not unusual for deeds to be recorded in the wrong order. So long as they are either warranty deeds or special warranty deeds that contain the covenant of further assurances, their delivery or recording in the wrong order can be ignored.

Breach of Covenants   If a breach of the covenants of seisin, of the right to convey, or against encumbrances occurs, it occurs at the time of the conveyance. These covenants are *present covenants*. If the outstanding interest exists, it is sufficient to cause the breach; eviction of the grantee is not required. However, any breach of the covenants of warranty, quiet enjoyment, or further assurances occurs only upon an attempt to evict the grantee. They are *future covenants*. The point is important when calculating the statute of limitations. In the case of present covenants, the statute runs from the time of the conveyance and not from the time the outstanding interest becomes known.

The damages that may be recovered for breach of a covenant depend on the covenant breached, although they cannot exceed the value of the property. When the covenant of seisin or the covenant of right to convey has been breached, the grantee may recover the purchase price and probably will be required to convey the property back to the grantor. When the covenant against encumbrances is breached and when the encumbrance is a monetary one, the cost of removing it is the measure of damages, not to exceed the value of the property. When the encumbrance is a nonmonetary one, the measure of damages is the extent to which the market value of the property has been reduced.

When the covenants of warranty, quiet enjoyment, or further assurances have been breached, the measure of damages is the purchase price of the property. If the grantee is evicted from less than the entire property (partial eviction), the measure of damages is a prorated portion of the purchase price equal to that part of the property from which the grantee is evicted. In some states, the value of the land at the time the covenant is violated is used as the measure, rather than the purchase price.

A general warranty deed contains all of the warranties described above. A *special warranty deed* is limited in its warranties to acts of the grantor only, as opposed to acts of third parties ("the entire world," as it is sometimes said). In other words, when a special warranty deed is given, the grantor warrants only that she has not encumbered the property; that she has not conveyed an interest to a third party; and that neither she nor persons claiming under her will oust the grantee. The grantor under a special warranty deed makes no warranties concerning the acts or omissions of her predecessors in title.

Compare the language shown earlier from the general warranty deed with the typical language of a special warranty deed shown here:

> And grantor, for himself and his heirs, executors, and assigns, does hereby covenant with the grantee, his heirs, and assigns, that he has not made, done, executed, or suffered any act or thing whereby the above described premises or any part thereof now are or at any time hereafter shall or may be imperiled, charged, or encumbered in any manner whatsoever; and the title to the above granted premises against all persons lawfully claiming the same from, through or under him the grantor forever will warrant and defend.

A *quitclaim deed* omits the warranties of title altogether. Instead of the grant language used above, a quitclaim deed often contains the language *remise, release, and quitclaim* or merely *quitclaim*. The effect of a quitclaim deed is to convey to the grantee only that interest, if any, that the grantor possesses. In conveying whatever interest he has, the grantor makes no representation that he has any interest at all to convey.

Quitclaim deeds are used for a number of reasons. One who is clearing title defects may ask that persons convey their interest in the property by quitclaim deed. Or a purchaser may be willing to waive title defects, in which case a quitclaim deed may be used. Quitclaim deeds also are used to release the interests of tenants, to terminate easements, and for similar purposes.

Legislatures often enact *statutory deed* forms, which set out a standard form and define the warranties of title that attach to the form, making the express inclusion of the warranties unnecessary. For example, California law provides a *grant deed,* which carries the statutory warranties that the grantor has not previously encumbered nor conveyed the same interest to someone else. These warranties do not warrant that the grantor owns the land or that title is free of all encumbrances. Statutory forms do not preclude the use of other forms; however, they usually are shorter, omitting unnecessary historical language.

Ordinarily, deeds are signed only by the grantor. The grantee's acceptance of the deed binds her to any affirmative obligations of the deed, such as assumption of outstanding debt that is secured by the land conveyed. Although the terms are no longer in general use, a deed signed only by the grantor is a *deed poll*; a deed signed by both grantor and grantee is an *indenture*.

When parties are married, some states require both spouses to sign the deed because of the marital interest of each spouse. In addition, both spouses may need to sign the deed when the property has been homesteaded. A *homestead* is a principal residence occupied by the head of a household and is exempt from execution up to a certain dollar amount, depending on the state where the property is located. For example, if the amount of a homestead in a particular state is $25,000 and if the property is foreclosed against by a judgment creditor, the first $25,000 is paid to the owner of the property. Only the excess is paid to the judgment creditor. Most mortgages and deeds of trust require waiver of the homestead exemption.

Methods of homesteading differ. In some states, a notation of homestead is required in the deed. In other states, homesteading is automatic when the property is occupied by the head of a household as a primary residence.

If the name of the grantor has changed since he or she took title, that fact should be explained in the deed. If a woman marries and takes the name of her husband, both of her names should be used in the body of the deed; in the signature blank; and in the acknowledgment (for example, *Jane P. Jones, formerly Jane P. Brown*).

From time to time, special forms of deed may be needed. For instance, a *conservator's deed* must be used in transferring property from the estate of a minor or an incompetent. A *personal representative's deed* must be used in transferring property from the estate of a decedent. A sheriff's deed must be used in transferring property following foreclosure and sale.

Transfer of title does not occur without delivery of the deed. A full discussion of the concept of delivery is contained in Chapter 9 of this text. The next few pages contain examples of various types of deeds, including a general warranty deed, a special warranty deed, a quitclaim deed, and a sheriff's deed. Compare them to see the similarities and the differences in their provisions.

Figure 8-7
General Warranty Deed

WARRANTY DEED

THIS DEED, made this   day of   , 19 , between
 , whose address is
                                                          (herein Grantor), and
                         , whose address is
                                                          (herein Grantee).
WITNESSETH, that the Grantor for and in consideration of the sum of   Dollars, the receipt and sufficiency of which
is hereby acknowledged, has(ve) granted, bargained, sold and conveyed, and by these presents do(es) grant, bargain, sell,
convey and confirm unto the Grantee, his(their) heirs and assigns forever, all of the real property together with
improvements, if any, lying and being in the County of   and State of Colorado, described as follows:

also known by the following address:

TOGETHER with all and singular the hereditaments and appurtenances thereto belonging, or in anywise appertaining,
and the reversion and reversions, remainder and remainders, rents, issues and profits thereof, and all the estate, right,
title, claim, and demand whatsoever of the Grantor, either in law or equity, of, in and to the above bargained premises,
with the hereditaments and appurtenances.
TO HAVE AND TO HOLD the said premises above bargained and described, with the appurtenances, unto the Grantee,
his(their) heirs and assigns forever. And the Grantor, for himself(themselves), his(their) heirs, and personal
representatives, do(es) covenant, grant, bargain, and agree to and with the Grantee, his(their) heirs and assigns, that
at the time of the ensealing and delivery of these presents, he(they) is(are) well seized of the premises above conveyed,
has(ve) good, sure, perfect, absolute and indefeasible estate of inheritance, in law, in fee simple, and has(ve) good right,
full power and lawful authority to grant, bargain, sell and convey the same in manner and form as aforesaid, and that
the same are free and clear from all former and other grants, bargains, sales, liens, taxes, assessments, encumbrances
and restrictions of whatever kind or nature soever, except

THE GRANTOR shall and will WARRANT AND FOREVER DEFEND the above bargained premises in the quiet and
peaceable possession of the Grantee, his(their) heirs and assigns, against all and every person or persons lawfully
claiming the whole or any part thereof. The singular number shall include the plural, the plural the singular, and the
use of any gender shall be applicable to all genders.

IN WITNESS WHEREOF, the Grantor has executed this WARRANTY DEED on the date set forth above.

_____

_____

STATE OF COLORADO   )
) SS.
COUNTY OF _____)

The foregoing Warranty Deed was acknowledged and affirmed before me this   day of   19 , by

Witness my hand and official seal.

My Commission expires:_____

_____
                              Notary Public

Figure 8-8
Special Warranty Deed

SPECIAL WARRANTY DEED

KNOW ALL MEN BY THESE PRESENTS THAT ACME CORPORATION, INC., a corporation duly organized under the laws of the State of Anystate (herein Grantor), for and in consideration of TEN DOLLARS and other good and valuable consideration, to the said party of the first part, in hand paid by the party of the second part, the receipt of which is hereby acknowledged, has granted, bargained, sold and conveyed, and by these presents does grant, bargain, sell, convey and confirm unto RICHARD ROE and JANE ROE, as joint tenants, (herein Grantees), whose address is: 123 County Road 1, Anycity, Anystate 0000, their heirs and assigns forever, all of the following real property in the County of Anycounty, and State of Anywhere, to-wit:

        Lot 1, Block 1, Strayhorse Addition to the City of Anycity, County of Anycounty
        and State of Anywhere

Also known and numbered as: 0059 East 7th Street, Anycity, Anywhere 00000

TOGETHER WITH all and singular the hereditaments and appurtenances thereunto belonging or in anywise appertaining, and the reversion and reversions, remainder and remainders, rents, issues, and profits thereof; and all the estate, right, title, interest, claim and demand whatsoever of the Grantor, either in law or equity, of, in and to the above bargained premises, with the hereditaments and appurtenances; TO HAVE AND TO HOLD the said premises above bargained and described, with the appurtenances unto the said party of the second part, their heirs and assigns forever.

AND THE SAID Grantor for itself, its successors and assigns, does covenant, grant, bargain and agree to and with the said party of the second part, their heirs and assigns, the above bargained premises in the quiet and peaceable possession of said party of the second part, their heirs and assigns, against all and every person or persons lawfully claiming or to claim the whole or any part thereof, by, through or under the said Grantor to warrant and forever defend.

IN WITNESS WHEREOF, the Grantor has caused its corporate name to be hereunto subscribed by its _____ President, and its corporate seal to be hereunto affixed, attested by its _____Secretary, the 21st day of August, 1996.

                                    ACME CORPORATION, INC.
                                    By_____
                                    Juan L. Garcia
ATTEST: Its _____President

_____
_____ Secretary   [Acknowledgement]

Note: This special Warranty Deed agrees to "warrant and defend" the title only as to those claiming under the Grantor, not "all and every person or persons lawfully claiming . . ." as in a general warranty deed. Note also there are no warranties as to the real property's being free and clear from all encumbrances or the like.

Figure 8-9
Quitclaim Deed

QUITCLAIM DEED

JOHN W. DOE, also known as JOHN DOE, and JANE DOE, husband and wife, as joint tenants, for Ten Dollars and other good and valuable consideration, in hand paid, hereby quit-claim to RICHARD ROE, Post Office Box 123, Any City, Anystate 00000, the following real property in the County of Anywhere, and State of Anystate, to-wit:

Condominium Units F-1 and F-2, ANY CONDOMINIUMS, according to the Condominium Map recorded November 17, 1996, in Book 452 at Page 438 and the supplemental map thereto recorded September 8, 1997, in Book 469 at Page 376, and as described in the Condominium Declaration thereof recorded November 17, 1996, in Book 452 at Page 439, and the Supplemental Condominium Declaration thereof recorded September 8, 1997, in Book 469 at Page 375, County of Anywhere, State of Anystate, with all its appurtenances.

Also known by street and number as Units F-1 and F-2, 24 Condominium Court, Any Subdivision, Anywhere County, Anystate.

Signed and delivered this 18th day of December. 1997.

_____
John W. Doe, also known as
John Doe

_____
John Doe

_____
Jane Doe

STATE OF ANYSTATE   )
)ss.
COUNTY OF ANYWHERE)

The foregoing instrument was acknowledged before me, the undersigned Notary Public, this 18th day of December, 1997, by John W. Doe, also known as John Doe and Jane Doe, husband and wife, as joint tenants.

My commission expires:_____

Witness my hand and official seal.

_____ _____
Notary Public

Figure 8-10
Sheriff's Deed

SHERIFF'S DEED

THIS DEED is made February _____, 1999, between A. J. JOHNSON as Sheriff of Eagle County, State of Colorado, and SEVENTY-FIFTH NATIONAL BANK, N. A., a National Banking Association, the holder of the Certificate of Purchase, whose address is: 1399 S.W. First Avenue, Anytown, Anystate 00000, herein described as "GRANTEE".

WHEREAS, GRANTEE did in the District Court for the County of Eagle, State of Colorado, on October 9, 1995 in Civil Action No. 98 CV 000, obtain a Judgment and Decree of Foreclosure, in the amount of $58,803.39 and costs of suit and which Judgment and Decree was directed to the Sheriff of Eagle County, Colorado; and

WHEREAS, by virtue of said Judgment and Decree, the Sheriff levied upon the property hereinafter described and, after public notice had been given of the time and place of sale as required by law, said property was offered for sale and sold according to said notice, and a Certificate of Purchase was made to GRANTEE, as purchaser thereat, and recorded in the Office of the Eagle County Clerk and Recorder; and

WHEREAS, all periods of redemption have expired and no redemption has been made.

NOW THEREFORE, I, A.J. Johnson, Sheriff of the County of Eagle, State of Colorado, in consideration of the premises and the sum of $14,500.00 paid by said GRANTEE, confirm the sale and do hereby sell and convey to the Grantee above described the following described property, located in Eagle County, Colorado:

As described on Exhibit A attached hereto and incorporated herein by reference.

TO HAVE AND TO HOLD the same, with all appurtenances thereunto, forever.

Witness my hand this _____ day of February, 1996.

                                         _____

                                         A.J. Johnson, Sheriff of Eagle
                                         County, Colorado

STATE OF COLORADO   )
) SS.
COUNTY OF EAGLE   )

The foregoing Sheriff's Deed was acknowledged before me this _____ day of February, 1996, by A.J. Johnson, Sheriff of Eagle County, Colorado.

Witness my hand and official seal.

My commission expires:_____

                                         _____
                                                  Notary Public

Chapter 8 Quiz

Fill in each blank with the most correct word or phrase.

1. Acquiring property by occupying it for a period of time is known as _____ title or title by _____ _____.

2. Adverse possession must be (1)_____, (2) _____, (3) _____, (4) _____ (5)_____,(6)_____, and (7)_____.

3. _____ may occur when more than one person is the possessor during the statutory period for adverse possession.

4. An action to _____ is necessary to establish that title has been acquired by adverse possession.

5. Title by adverse possession generally may not be acquired against _____.

6. The three types of recording statutes are: _____, _____, and _____.

7. When government surveyors cannot place a monument at a corner, a(n) _____ corner is used.

8. Metes are stated in _____, and bounds are stated in _____.

9. The gaining of land by a change in the course of a stream is _____, while losing land in the same manner is _____.

Circle the most correct answer.

10. True or False. Title to lands were conveyed to initial owners by royal grant from England or by land patents from the United States.

11. True or False. A purchaser at a tax sale need not inquire into the quality of title prior to the tax deed.

12. True or False. The general rule is that no action in ejectment can be maintained for recovery of possession of real property after 15 years.

13. True or False. Title by adverse possession vests automatically.

14. True or False. A tenant never may acquire title by prescription.

15. True or False. A person acting as a member of the public, such as one of many who uses a pond for fishing, may acquire title by adverse possession.

16. True or False. Every state has statutes prohibiting one from becoming an owner by adverse possession unless she pays taxes on the property being adversely possessed.

17. True or False. Possession under a defective deed may shorten the time required for acquiring title by adverse possession.

18. True or False. The Statute of Frauds requires that certain contracts be in writing to be enforceable.

19. True or False. Oral contracts for the sale of land cannot be enforced by the courts.

20. True or False. Any contract for the sale of land or any interest in land is void unless it or a memorandum thereof, expressing the consideration, is in writing and is subscribed by the party to be bound.

21. True or False. Grantee-grantor and grantor-grantee indices reflect conveyances; encumbrances are indexed by tract.

22. True or False. An instrument that otherwise would be void is deemed to be valid if it is recorded.

23. True or False. Recording statutes are important in matters involving intentional, simultaneous conveyances of the same interest in real property.

24. True or False. Any description of a parcel of real property must identify the parcel to the exclusion of any other parcel in the world.

25. True or False. The terms map and plat are interchangeable under the Uniform Common Interest Ownership Act.

26. True or False. Under the rectangular survey system, east-west lines are prime meridians; and north-south lines are principal base meridians.

27. True or False. A township is a square that is ten miles by ten miles.

28. True or False. A section consists of 640 acres.

29. True or False. Metes and bounds descriptions are used only in the 22 states that do not have the rectangular survey system.

30. True or False. Valid descriptions must close, but a description that is off by a few feet may be valid by using the term "more or less" in the final mete.

31. True or False. When descriptions refer to streets, rivers, or streams, the general presumption is that the edge of the street or stream is intended.

32. True or False. In a pure notice state, a subsequent purchase for value without actual notice of a prior, unrecorded conveyance takes free and clear of that conveyance.

33. True or False. Acceptance of delivery of a deed by the grantee is presumed any time title is beneficial.

34. True or False. Delivery of a deed is effective even if it is made to an agent under the control of neither party.

35. True or False. The covenants of seisin, right to convey, and against encumbrances are present covenants; and the statute of limitations will run from the time of conveyance rather than from the time a breach is discovered.

36. True or False. The covenant of seisin supports the doctrine of after-acquired title.

37. Randy believed he owned the south half of the south half of Blackacre, which was located in a remote, unimproved area and was used mainly for hunting and fishing. He fenced part of the area and built a hunting cabin on it. For six years, he used the cabin during the two-week hunting season. Randy's health failed, and he stopped going to the cabin. As a result, Randy decided to sell his interest in Blackacre. A title examination

disclosed that Randy's deed was defective. The statute of limitations in that jurisdiction required an adverse possessor under color of title to occupy the property for five years. Does Randy own the property?

1. Yes, by adverse possession.
2. Yes, by adverse possession, but only the portion of the property he fenced and built upon.
3. No, because adverse possession requires that possession be continuous and uninterrupted.
4. No. He has a claim for adverse possession but must maintain a quiet title action before title vests.

38. R.C. occupied Homestead Ranch openly, continuously, exclusively, under claim of right, and hostilely to Marsha, the real owner, from January 1970 to December 1975, when he conveyed the property to Mac by quitclaim deed. Mac occupied Homestead Ranch from December 1975 until December 1988. Mac left Homestead Ranch in 1988 and moved to California. On the day of his departure, Elaine moved in and occupied the premises openly, continuously, exclusively, and hostilely for four years. Assuming the statutory time for adverse possession is 20 years, is title to Homestead Ranch vested in Elaine?

1. Yes. By tacking onto R.C.'s possession, Mac and Elaine have possessed the premises for the statutory period.
2. No. Elaine must file a quiet title action to have the premises vest in her.
3. No. Elaine's possession cannot be tacked onto Mac's because privity of estate is not present between Elaine and R.C.
4. No. Elaine's possession cannot be tacked onto Mac's because privity of estate is not present between Elaine and Mac.

39. Courts may apply the following canon(s) of construction to determine the boundaries of real property:

1. Original survey monuments prevail over natural monuments, which prevail over artificial monuments, which prevail over maps, which prevail over courses, which prevail over distances, which prevail over a name, which prevails over quantity.
2. Original survey monuments prevail over artificial monuments, which prevail over maps, which prevail over courses, which prevail over distances, which prevail over a name, which prevails over quantity.

3. Original survey monuments prevail over natural monuments, which prevail over artificial monuments, which prevail over maps, which prevail over distances, which prevail over courses, which prevail over a name, which prevails over quantity.

4. Surveyor's stakes prevail over trees, which prevail over subdivision plats, which prevail over fences, which prevail over angles, which prevail over feet, which prevail over a name, which prevails over acreage.

5. None of the above.

6. (a) and (d) only.

40. The covenants of title contained in a general warranty deed are:

1. Seisin, quiet enjoyment, against encumbrances, warranty, right to convey, and assurance of delivery.

2. Premises, words of purchase, habendum clause, signature, and acknowledgment.

3. Fee simple determinable, fee simple absolute, fee simple subject to condition subsequent.

4. Warranty, right to convey, further assurances, against encumbrances, quiet enjoyment, seisin.

41. A deed that is limited in its warranties to acts of the grantor rather than to acts of third parties is a:

1. Bargain and sale deed
2. Warranty deed
3. Grant deed
4. Special warranty deed

Chapter 9
SALE AND FINANCING OF REAL ESTATE

The subjects sale and financing of land deal with how title is transferred from one owner to another. This chapter includes the contract for sale of land; how titles are searched; the types of deeds that may be used to convey land; and mortgage financing. After environmental issues are reviewed, the chapter moves to the real estate closing itself. Installment sale contracts also are covered.

Contract for Sale of Land

The first step in any real estate transaction is to prepare what is described in this section as the *contract for sale of land*, which is an offer and acceptance for the sale of real estate. In some jurisdictions, this contract is called an *earnest money agreement* or a *purchase and sale agreement*.

In a few jurisdictions, the term *installment sales contract* is used to refer to a contract for sale. The difference between them is that a contract for sale is an offer and acceptance to sell land (see above), while an *installment sales contract* is a seller-financed purchase contract. Seller financing has nothing to do with the contract for sale as that term is used in this section.

A contract for sale of land must be in writing to satisfy the Statute of Frauds; and, at a minimum, it must contain a description of the parties, a description of the land to be conveyed, and the purchase price to be paid. As a general rule, the contract contains a great deal more; and it frequently takes the form of a standardized document promulgated by the state real estate commission or similar body.

More than land may be included in a contract for sale, and the contract must be complete in that regard. Water rights and mineral rights may or may not be included. Unless mineral rights are expressly excluded, both the surface and subsurface estates are included with the conveyance. In a *riparian right* jurisdiction, water rights are included without specific reference to them. In a *prior appropriation* jurisdiction, water rights usually are treated separately. In addition, the contract may specify that fixtures or improvements are included. Even without this language, however, a deed to the land also conveys fixtures or improvements that exist on the land. Finally, the contract may provide for conveyance of designated items of personal property by separate bill of sale, sometimes listed on an attached inventory.

The purchase price should be expressed in U.S. Dollars and usually is divided into two installments: 1) a down payment or deposit and 2) the balance, which is the amount paid at the closing.

This division of the purchase price has aspects of an option, although a contract for sale is not an option. An *option* is a unilateral contract in which the optionee, in consideration of the payment of option money, has the right (but not the obligation) to buy the property under option. A purchase contract, on the other hand, is a bilateral contract in which both parties are obligated to perform. The use of the deposit apparently is a matter of custom and provides protection for the seller. If the purchaser fails to perform, the seller is entitled to retain the deposit as *liquidated damages*. Between the time the contract for sale is signed and the time of closing, it is customary for the deposit to be held in escrow by a title company or some other, third party.

The contract also may deal with the subject of the financing for the purchase. It might provide that the seller will accept a promissory note as a part of the purchase price. Or the sale may be made contingent on the purchaser's arranging outside financing; and the details of acceptable financing, including interest rate and term, may be set forth in the contract. If the parameters of financing are included, the contract usually provides that if financing is not obtained, the contract is invalidated; and the earnest deposit (earnest money) is returned to the purchaser.

Alternatively, the contract may provide for the *assumption* of (taking title subject to) outstanding debt in the form of a mortgage or deed of trust. If the mortgage or deed of trust contains a *due-on-sale clause* that requires the lender to consent to the assumption, the contract will be conditioned upon obtaining consent on reasonable terms concerning interest and any assumption fee. When assumption of the debt occurs, it usually does not release the seller as the original debtor. Rather, most lenders insist that the seller remains secondarily liable on the note, with the purchaser becoming primarily liable. On the other hand, if consent of the lender is not required (and, therefore, not obtained), the seller remains primarily liable even though the purchaser assumes and agrees to pay the promissory note. In either case, the property continues as security for the debt and will be foreclosed upon if the note is not paid.

The contract also deals with title to the real estate and generally provides that marketable title in fee simple must be conveyed. A *marketable title* is one that a title company is willing to insure or one that is free from defect in the opinion of an attorney.

The contract for sale typically requires *evidence of title* either in the form of an abstract of title or a commitment for title insurance. Evidence of title must be provided by a specified date after the contract is signed, after which the purchaser has a limited time to deliver any objections to the title's marketability. When evidence of title is first received, it is crucial that the person representing the purchaser note the deadline to deliver any objections.

Closely related to the provisions dealing with title are provisions excepting specific liens and encumbrances from the interest to be conveyed. For example, the seller may be aware of protective covenants that affect the property and, therefore, excepts (excludes) those covenants from the property interest that she intends to convey. Other than this type of exception, if the title search discloses any lien or encumbrance recorded against the property, an objection to the title must be made. If an objection is not made, it is waived. As a general rule, the contract also excepts current real property taxes and provides that they will be prorated to the date of closing.

If the title search discloses a lien, encumbrance, or other defect in the seller's title that is not excepted by the contract and if timely objection is made, the contract ordinarily entitles the seller to adjourn or to extend the closing. During this time, efforts are made to cure (correct) the title defect. If those efforts are fruitless, the contract ordinarily gives the purchaser the choice of 1) accepting the title "as is" or of 2) terminating the contract and having the earnest money returned.

If the contract provides for delivery of a title insurance commitment, it also may provide for deletion of standard exceptions. These might include exceptions for mechanic's liens or any state of facts that would be disclosed by an accurate survey. An additional amount may be charged to obtain such a deletion.

The contract for sale also states the time and place of closing. At *closing*, the deed of conveyance is exchanged for the balance of the purchase price. Ordinarily, the contract provides for delivery of possession at the time of closing unless the property is subject to an outstanding lease. In that case, the current rent payment is prorated to the date of closing. The contract should provide that taxes, assessments, and other charges be prorated to the time of closing. Since the purchaser is obligated to pay real property taxes after the closing, she should receive a credit for any portion of those taxes which were accrued during the seller's ownership. The most recent tax statement is used to make the calculation. Other prorated items might include interest payments on assumed loans, liability insurance premiums, water and sewer use charges, and so forth.

The contract likely covers risk of loss should the property be damaged or destroyed before the closing. Under the common law rule of equitable conversion, all risk of loss was placed on the purchaser as the equitable owner. When a prospective purchaser contracted for purchase of land, she immediately became the equitable owner. This gave her the right to enforce the contract in equity. Under that doctrine, however, risk of loss shifted immediately to the prospective purchaser. As a result, if the property were destroyed before closing, the purchaser would be liable for the purchase price.

To modify the common law rule, a contract for sale may obligate the seller to repair any intervening damage of less than ten percent of the property's value and may allow the purchaser to terminate the contract in the event of greater intervening damage, including destruction of the property. Otherwise, the contract usually provides that the property is sold "as is."

To protect the purchaser from unknown risks or hazards, she may go upon the land and into any building to make an inspection for a certain period of time. This is called a *due diligence period*. The inspection may include an environmental assessment to determine whether hazardous substances such as radon, asbestos, or soil pollution are present. If an older building is involved, a structural engineering evaluation may be called for. Inspection for termites also may be included; in some states, it is required.

The contract may permit the purchaser to have the land surveyed at his or her expense and may provide for abatement of the purchase price if the survey discloses that the property area is less than was believed. The contract also may allow termination of the contract if the survey discloses matters unacceptable to the purchaser, such as an encroachment on neighboring property or a violation of setback requirements.

If financing is involved, an appraisal is required; and the contract may be conditioned upon the appraisal's establishing a specified, minimum value for the property.

Any contract for sale likely contains a *time of the essence provision*. Simply by stating that time is of the essence, parties are obligated to tender performance of any condition of the contract on the date stated. Without this type of provision, the date of closing might come and go with both parties remaining bound to the agreement unless, on that date, one party demands performance of the other.

Finally, the contract establishes remedies for breach of the contract. The contract may grant to both parties a right of specific performance if the other defaults. For instance, if the seller fails to tender the deed, the purchaser may go to court to enforce conveyance of the property. Or, if the purchaser fails to tender the purchase price, the seller may go to court to obtain a judgment in the amount of the purchase price in exchange for tender of the deed. On the other hand, the remedy of specific performance by the seller may be expressly eliminated by the contract's terms; or the purchaser may be limited to forfeiture of the deposit as liquidated damages. Without an express provision in the contract, however, the common law provides the remedy of specific performance to both parties.

As an alternative to specific performance, both the seller and the buyer may recover damages for breach by the other party. If a damages remedy is pursued, the party can recover *benefit of the bargain* damages. For example, the seller may recover the carrying charges for the property that are incurred while finding another purchaser. Or, the purchaser may recover his expected profits from the resale of the property.

Real estate contracts usually are negotiated in a different way than are other contracts, and real estate brokers often are involved in the process. When a prospective purchaser decides she wants to buy a particular piece of property, she submits an offer in the form of the complete contract discussed above. The owner of the property may accept the offer by signing it, which creates a binding contract. Frequently, however, the owner submits a counteroffer to establish different terms. The purchaser may accept the counteroffer, or she may submit yet another counteroffer. This process continues until the parties arrive at mutually satisfactory terms for the purchase and sale of the property. The contract between the parties then consists of a compilation of the original offer and all of the counteroffers.

Finally, undertakings contained in the contract for purchase *merge in the deed*. For example, if title is accepted even though it is unmarketable, the purchaser cannot file suit after closing to recover damages that result from unmarketability of the title. This is so not only because the purchaser waived the requirement of marketability but also because the requirement merged in the deed, causing it to be extinguished.

An exception to the rule of merger exists when a particular provision does not relate either to title or to possession. For instance, real estate contracts frequently provide that in the event of litigation arising out of the contract, the prevailing party will be awarded attorney's fees. This type of provision continues after the closing because it relates neither to title nor to possession. Notwithstanding the general rule and its exception, it always is good practice to state specifically that a particular provision will survive closing if that is the parties' intent.

Figure 9-1 shows a standard residential contract to buy and sell real estate, completed according to the facts of the following example:

John Doe looked at many residential properties advertised for sale by listing companies. Doug at Real Estate Associates showed John a home in Mountain Valley Subdivision owned by Jane Roe. John liked the house immediately and decided to buy the property to use as his residence. He wanted to use his present home as rental property. At the urging of Doug, John decided to offer $174,500 for the new home. He offered it as a cash deal and was willing do deposit $10,000 with the broker to show good faith. John wanted to make sure that things such as storm windows, garage door openers, and the like were being included in the purchase. He need to have the closing occur on June 15, 1996, because he anticipated leasing his present residence on June 16, 1996. He was agreeable to dividing the closing costs equally with the seller, but he would not agree to pay any transfer fees. He wanted to pay for his own appraisal because he thought he would get a more unbiased opinion.

Preprinted contracts for sale are available in nearly every state and may vary slightly from one state to another.

Figure 9-1
Contract for Sale of Residential Real Estate

The printed portions of this form have been approved by
the Colorado Real Estate Commission. (CBS 5A-9-95)

THIS FORM HAS IMPORTANT LEGAL CONSEQUENCES AND THE PARTIES SHOULD CONSULT LEGAL AND TAX OR OTHER COUNSEL BEFORE SIGNING.

RESIDENTIAL
CONTRACT TO BUY AND SELL REAL ESTATE
(FINANCING SECTIONS OMITTED)

May 1 , 19 96

1. PARTIES AND PROPERTY. JOHN W. DOE
, buyer(s) [Buyer] (as joint tenants/tenants in common)
agrees to buy, and the undersigned seller(s) [Seller], agrees to sell, on the terms and conditions set forth in this contract, the following described real
estate in the County of Carbon , Colorado, to wit:

UNIT A, a resubdivision of Lot 66, Block 1, Mountain Valley Subdivision,
Filing No. 1, County of Carbon, State of Colorado

known as No. 55-W Coyote Circle, Mountain Valley Subdivision, Colorado 80001 ,
Street Address   City   State   Zip

together with all interest of Seller in vacated streets and alleys adjacent thereto, all easements and other appurtenances thereto, all improvements
thereon and all attached fixtures thereon, except as herein excluded (collectively the Property).

2. INCLUSIONS/EXCLUSIONS. The purchase price includes the following items (a) if attached to the Property on the date of this contract: lighting, heating, plumbing, ventilating, and air conditioning fixtures, TV antennas, water softeners, smoke/fire/burglar alarms, security
devices, inside telephone wiring and connecting blocks/jacks, plants, mirrors, floor coverings, intercom systems, built-in kitchen appliances, sprinkler
systems and controls, built-in vacuum systems (including accessories), and garage door openers including NO remote controls; (b) if on the
Property whether attached or not on the date of this contract: storm windows, storm doors, window and porch shades, awnings, blinds, screens,
curtain rods, drapery rods, fireplace inserts, fireplace screens, fireplace grates, heating stoves, storage sheds, all keys and (c)

The above-described included items (Inclusions) are to be conveyed to Buyer by Seller by bill of sale at the closing, free and clear of all taxes, liens and
encumbrances, except as provided in Section 12. The following attached fixtures are excluded from this sale: None

3. PURCHASE PRICE AND TERMS. The purchase price shall be $ 174,500.00 , payable in U.S. dollars by Buyer as
follows: (Complete the applicable terms below.)
(a) Earnest Money.
$ 10,000 in the form of cash , as earnest money deposit and part payment of the purchase
price, payable to and held by Real Estate Associates , broker, in its trust
account on behalf of both Seller and Buyer. Broker is authorized to deliver the earnest money deposit to the closing agent, if any, at or before closing.
The balance of $ 164,500.00 (purchase price less earnest money) shall be paid as follows:
(b) Cash at Closing.
$ 164,500.00 , plus closing costs, to be paid by Buyer at closing in funds which comply with all applicable Colorado laws, which
include cash, electronic transfer funds, certified check, savings and loan teller's check, and cashier's check (Good Funds). Subject to the provisions of
Section 4, if the existing loan balance at the time of closing shall be different from the loan balance in Section 3, the adjustment shall be made in
Good Funds at closing or prior to closing.

4. FINANCING CONDITIONS AND OBLIGATIONS.

FINANCING TERMS, CONDITIONS AND OBLIGATIONS, PERTAINING TO SECTIONS 3 AND 4,
ARE ATTACHED BY REAL ESTATE COMMISSION APPROVED ADDENDUM AS FOLLOWS: (check as applicable)
☐ New Loan
☐ Assumption
☐ Seller or Private Third-Party Financing

5. APPRAISAL PROVISION. This Section 5 shall not apply if the Buyer is to obtain a new FHA or VA loan. (Check only one box.)
This Section 5 ☒ shall ☐ shall not apply. If this Section 5 applies, as indicated above, Buyer shall have the sole option and election to terminate
this contract if the purchase price exceeds the Property's valuation determined by an appraiser engaged by Buyer .
The contract shall terminate by the Buyer causing the Seller to receive written notice of termination and a copy of such appraisal or written notice
from lender which confirms the Property's valuation is less than the purchase price, on or before May 25, 1996
(Appraisal Deadline). If Seller does not receive such written notice of termination on or before the appraisal deadline, Buyer waives any right to
terminate under this section.
6. COST OF APPRAISAL. Cost of any appraisal to be obtained after the date of this contract shall be timely paid by
Buyer .
7. NOT ASSIGNABLE. This contract shall not be assignable by Buyer without Seller's prior written consent. Except as so restricted, this
contract shall inure to the benefit of and be binding upon the heirs, personal representatives, successors and assigns of the parties.
8. EVIDENCE OF TITLE. Seller shall furnish to Buyer, at Seller's expense, either a current commitment for owner's title insurance policy in
an amount equal to the purchase price or at Seller's choice, an abstract of title certified to a current date, on or before
May 10, 1996 (Title Deadline). If a title insurance commitment is furnished, Buyer may require of Seller that copies
of instruments (or abstracts of instruments) listed in the schedule of exceptions (Exceptions) in the title insurance commitment also be furnished to
Buyer at Seller's expense. This requirement shall pertain only to instruments shown of record in the office of the clerk and recorder of the designated

county or counties. The title insurance commitment, together with any copies or abstracts of instruments furnished pursuant to this Section 8, constitute the title documents (Title Documents). Buyer, or Buyer's designee, must request Seller, in writing, to furnish copies or abstracts of instruments listed in the schedule of exceptions no later than ___2___ calendar days after Title Deadline. If Seller furnishes a title insurance commitment, Seller will pay the premium at closing and have the title insurance policy delivered to Buyer as soon as practicable after closing.

9. TITLE.

(a) Title Review. Buyer shall have the right to inspect the Title Documents or abstract. Written notice by Buyer of unmerchantability of title or of any other unsatisfactory title condition shown by the Title Documents or abstract shall be signed by or on behalf of Buyer and given to Seller on or before ___15___ calendar days after Title Deadline, or within five (5) calendar days after receipt by Buyer of any Title Document(s) or endorsement(s) adding new Exception(s) to the title commitment together with a copy of the Title Document adding new Exception(s) to title. If Seller does not receive Buyer's notice by the date(s) specified above, Buyer accepts the condition of title as disclosed by the Title Documents as satisfactory.

(b) Matters Not Shown by the Public Records. Seller shall deliver to Buyer, on or before the Title Deadline set forth in Section 8, true copies of all lease(s) and survey(s) in Seller's possession pertaining to the Property and shall disclose to Buyer all easements, liens or other title matters not shown by the public records of which Seller has actual knowledge. Buyer shall have the right to inspect the Property to determine if any third party(s) has any right in the Property not shown by the public records (such as an unrecorded easement, unrecorded lease, or boundary line discrepancy). Written notice of any unsatisfactory condition(s) disclosed by Seller or revealed by such inspection shall be signed by or on behalf of Buyer and given to Seller on or before ___May 30___ , 19 __96__ . If Seller does not receive Buyer's notice by said date, Buyer accepts title subject to such rights, if any, of third parties of which Buyer has actual knowledge.

(c) Special Taxing Districts. SPECIAL TAXING DISTRICTS MAY BE SUBJECT TO GENERAL OBLIGATION INDEBTEDNESS THAT IS PAID BY REVENUES PRODUCED FROM ANNUAL TAX LEVIES ON THE TAXABLE PROPERTY WITHIN SUCH DISTRICTS. PROPERTY OWNERS IN SUCH DISTRICTS MAY BE PLACED AT RISK FOR INCREASED MILL LEVIES AND EXCESSIVE TAX BURDENS TO SUPPORT THE SERVICING OF SUCH DEBT WHERE CIRCUMSTANCES ARISE RESULTING IN THE INABILITY OF SUCH A DISTRICT TO DISCHARGE SUCH INDEBTEDNESS WITHOUT SUCH AN INCREASE IN MILL LEVIES. BUYER SHOULD INVESTIGATE THE DEBT FINANCING REQUIREMENTS OF THE AUTHORIZED GENERAL OBLIGATION INDEBTEDNESS OF SUCH DISTRICTS, EXISTING MILL LEVIES OF SUCH DISTRICT SERVICING SUCH INDEBTEDNESS, AND THE POTENTIAL FOR AN INCREASE IN SUCH MILL LEVIES.

In the event the Property is located within a special taxing district and Buyer desires to terminate this contract as a result, if written notice is given to Seller on or before the date set forth in subsection 9 (b), this contract shall then terminate. If Seller does not receive Buyer's notice by the date specified above, Buyer accepts the effect of the Property's inclusion in such special taxing district(s) and waives the right to so terminate.

(d) Right to Cure. If Seller receives notice of unmerchantability of title or any other unsatisfactory title condition(s) as provided in subsection (a) or (b) above, Seller shall use reasonable effort to correct said unsatisfactory title condition(s) prior to the date of closing. If Seller fails to correct said unsatisfactory title condition(s) on or before the date of closing, this contract shall then terminate; provided, however, Buyer may, by written notice received by Seller, on or before closing, waive objection to said unsatisfactory title condition(s).

10. INSPECTION. Seller agrees to provide Buyer on or before ___May 25, 1996___ , with a Seller's Property Disclosure form completed by Seller to the best of Seller's current actual knowledge. Buyer or any designee, shall have the right to have inspection(s) of the physical condition of the Property and Inclusions, at Buyer's expense. If written notice of any unsatisfactory condition, signed by or on behalf of Buyer, is not received by Seller on or before ___May 30___ , 19 __96__ (Objection Deadline), the physical condition of the Property and Inclusions shall be deemed to be satisfactory to Buyer. If such notice is received by Seller as set forth above, and if Buyer and Seller have not agreed, in writing, to a settlement thereof on or before ___June 3___ , 19 __96__ (Resolution Deadline), this contract shall terminate three calendar days following the Resolution Deadline; unless, within the three calendar days, Seller receives written notice from Buyer waiving objection to any unsatisfactory condition. Buyer is responsible for and shall pay for any damage which occurs to the Property and Inclusions as a result of such inspection.

11. DATE OF CLOSING. The date of closing shall be ___June 15___ , 19 __96__ , or by mutual agreement at an earlier date. The hour and place of closing shall be as designated by ___Buyer___

12. TRANSFER OF TITLE. Subject to tender or payment at closing as required herein and compliance by Buyer with the other terms and provisions hereof, Seller shall execute and deliver a good and sufficient ___general warranty___ deed to Buyer, on closing, conveying the Property free and clear of all taxes except the general taxes for the year of closing, and except ___None___ . Title shall be conveyed free and clear of all liens for special improvements installed as of the date of Buyer's signature hereon, whether assessed or not; except (i) distribution utility easements (including cable TV), (ii) those matters reflected by the Title Documents accepted by Buyer in accordance with subsection 9(a), (iii) those rights, if any, of third parties in the Property not shown by the public records in accordance with subsection 9(b), (iv) inclusion of the Property within any special taxing district, and (v) subject to building and zoning regulations.

13. PAYMENT OF ENCUMBRANCES. Any encumbrance required to be paid shall be paid at or before closing from the proceeds of this transaction or from any other source.

14. CLOSING COSTS, DOCUMENTS AND SERVICES. Buyer and Seller shall pay, in Good Funds, their respective closing costs and all other items required to be paid at closing, except as otherwise provided herein. Buyer and Seller shall sign and complete all customary or required documents at or before closing. Fees for real estate closing services shall not exceed $ ___400.00___ and shall be paid at closing by ___Buyer and Seller in equal amounts___ . The local transfer tax of ___3___ % of the purchase price shall be paid at closing by ___Seller___ . Any sales and use tax that may accrue because of this transaction shall be paid when due by ___Seller___

15. PRORATIONS. General taxes for the year of closing, based on the taxes for the calendar year immediately preceding closing, rents, water and sewer charges, homeowner's association dues, and interest on continuing loan(s), if any, /nd/ _____ shall be prorated to date of closing. FHA or private mortgage insurance premium ☒shall ☒ shall not be apportioned to date of closing. Any such amount shall be apportioned as follows: ___N/A___

16. POSSESSION. Possession of the Property shall be delivered to Buyer as follows: ___on June 15, 1996, immediately after closing___ , subject to the following lease(s) or tenancy(s): ___None___ . If Seller, after closing, fails to deliver possession on the date herein specified, Seller shall be subject to eviction and shall be additionally liable to Buyer for payment of $ ___125.00___ per day from the date of agreed possession until possession is delivered. Buyer ☒ does ☐ does not represent that Buyer will occupy the Property as Buyer's principal residence.

17. CONDITION OF AND DAMAGE TO PROPERTY. Except as otherwise provided in this contract, the Property and Inclusions shall be delivered in the condition existing as of the date of this contract, ordinary wear and tear excepted. In the event the Property shall be damaged by fire or other casualty prior to time of closing, in an amount of not more than ten percent of the total purchase price, Seller shall be obligated to repair the same before the date of closing. In the event such damage is not repaired within said time or if the damages exceed such sum, this contract may be terminated at the option of Buyer. Should Buyer elect to carry out this contract despite such damage, Buyer shall be entitled to credit for all the insurance proceeds resulting from such damage to the Property and Inclusions, not exceeding, however, the total purchase price. Should any Inclusion(s) or service(s) fail or be damaged between the date of this contract and the date of closing or the date of possession, whichever shall be earlier, then Seller shall be liable for the repair or replacement of such Inclusion(s) or service(s) with a unit of similar size, age and quality, or an equivalent credit, less any insurance proceeds received by Buyer covering such repair or replacement.

18. TIME OF ESSENCE/REMEDIES. Time is of the essence hereof. If any note or check received as earnest money hereunder or any other payment due hereunder is not paid, honored or tendered when due, or if any other obligation hereunder is not performed or waived as herein provided, there shall be the following remedies:

(a) IF BUYER IS IN DEFAULT:

(Check one box only.)

☐ **(1) Specific Performance.**

Seller may elect to treat this contract as cancelled, in which case all payments and things of value received hereunder shall be forfeited and retained on behalf of Seller, and Seller may recover such damages as may be proper, or Seller may elect to treat this contract as being in full force and effect and Seller shall have the right to specific performance or damages, or both.

☒ **(2) Liquidated Damages.**

All payments and things of value received hereunder shall be forfeited by Buyer and retained on behalf of Seller and both parties shall thereafter be released from all obligations hereunder. It is agreed that such payments and things of value are LIQUIDATED DAMAGES and (except as provided in subsection (c)) are SELLER'S SOLE AND ONLY REMEDY for Buyer's failure to perform the obligations of this contract. Seller expressly waives the remedies of specific performance and additional damages.

(b) IF SELLER IS IN DEFAULT:

Buyer may elect to treat this contract as cancelled, in which case all payments and things of value received hereunder shall be returned and Buyer may recover such damages as may be proper, or Buyer may elect to treat this contract as being in full force and effect and Buyer shall have the right to specific performance or damages, or both.

(c) COSTS AND EXPENSES.

Anything to the contrary herein notwithstanding, in the event of any arbitration or litigation arising out of this contract, the arbitrator or court shall award to the prevailing party all reasonable costs and expenses, including attorney fees.

19. EARNEST MONEY DISPUTE. Notwithstanding any termination of this contract, Buyer and Seller agree that, in the event of any controversy regarding the earnest money and things of value held by broker or closing agent, unless mutual written instructions are received by the holder of the earnest money and things of value, broker or closing agent shall not be required to take any action but may await any proceeding, or at broker's or closing agent's option and sole discretion, may interplead all parties and deposit any moneys or things of value into a court of competent jurisdiction and shall recover court costs and reasonable attorney fees.

20. ALTERNATIVE DISPUTE RESOLUTION: MEDIATION. If a dispute arises relating to this contract, and is not resolved, the parties and broker(s) involved in such dispute (Disputants) shall first proceed in good faith to submit the matter to mediation. The Disputants will jointly appoint an acceptable mediator and will share equally in the cost of such mediation. In the event the entire dispute is not resolved within thirty (30) calendar days from the date written notice requesting mediation is sent by one Disputant to the other(s), the mediation, unless otherwise agreed, shall terminate. This section shall not alter any date in this contract, unless otherwise agreed.

21. ADDITIONAL PROVISIONS: (The language of these additional provisions has not been approved by the Colorado Real Estate Commission.)

None

22. RECOMMENDATION OF LEGAL COUNSEL. By signing this document, Buyer and Seller acknowledge that the Selling Company or the Listing Company has advised that this document has important legal consequences and has recommended the examination of title and consultation with legal and tax or other counsel before signing this contract.

23. TERMINATION. In the event this contract is terminated, all payments and things of value received hereunder shall be returned and the parties shall be relieved of all obligations hereunder, subject to Section 19.

24. SELLING COMPANY BROKER RELATIONSHIP. The selling broker, _Real Estate Associates_
_____ , and its salespersons have been engaged as _____ agent for the seller _____ .
Selling Company has previously disclosed in writing to the Buyer that different relationships are available which include buyer agency, seller agency, subagency, or transaction-broker.

25. NOTICE TO BUYER. Any notice to Buyer shall be effective when received by Buyer, or, if this box is checked ☐ when received by Selling Company.

26. NOTICE TO SELLER. Any notice to Seller shall be effective when received by Seller or Listing Company.

27. MODIFICATION OF THIS CONTRACT. No subsequent modification of any of the terms of this contract shall be valid, binding upon the parties, or enforceable unless made in writing and signed by the parties.

28. ENTIRE AGREEMENT. This contract constitutes the entire contract between the parties relating to the subject hereof, and any prior agreements pertaining thereto, whether oral or written, have been merged and integrated into this contract.

29. NOTICE OF ACCEPTANCE: COUNTERPARTS. This proposal shall expire unless accepted in writing, by Buyer and Seller, as evidenced by their signatures below, and the offering party receives notice of such acceptance on or before _____ May 4, _____ ,
19 _96_ (Acceptance Deadline). If accepted, this document shall become a contract between Seller and Buyer. A copy of this document may be executed by each party, separately, and when each party has executed a copy thereof, such copies taken together shall be deemed to be a full and complete contract between the parties.

Buyer John W. Doe
Date of Buyer's signature ___ May 1 ___ , 19 _96_   Buyer
Date of Buyer's signature _____ , 19 ___

Buyer's Address P. O. Box 1, Eagle-Vail, Colorado 81620

Seller Jane Roe
Date of Seller's signature ___ May 1 ___ , 19 _96_   Seller
Date of Seller's signature _____ , 19 ___

Seller's Address 123 County Line Road, Eagle-Vail, Colorado 80000

The undersigned Broker(s) acknowledges receipt of the earnest money deposit specified in Section 3, and Selling Company confirms its Broker Relationship as set forth in Section 24.

Selling Company REAL ESTATE ASSOCIATES, 1 Main Street, Eagle-Vail, Colorado 80000
                                        Name and Address

By: _____   _____ , 19 ___
    Signature   Date

Listing Company REAL ESTATE ASSOCIATES, 1 Main Street, Eagle-Vail, Colorado 80000
                                        Name and Address

By: _____   _____ , 19 ___
    Signature   Date

NOTE: Closing Instructions should be signed at the time this contract is signed.

No. CBS5A-9-95.   Page 4 of 4

Once the title search is complete, closing documents are prepared. These documents include a deed and may include a promissory note with either a mortgage or a deed of trust. Chapter 8 reviews the various forms of deeds and their provisions.

The Title Search

Once the contract for sale of land is accepted by both parties and is signed, evidence of title must be furnished to the purchaser. Before the advent of title insurance, an abstract of title was ordered from an abstract company. Abstracts remain in use today, but the preferred form of title evidence is a title commitment or a title binder from a title insurance company. When title insurance is used, the title company normally performs the title search and issues the policy of insurance once the transaction is closed, insuring the purchaser's title.

An *abstract of title* merely is a compilation of all the instruments related to a particular parcel of land. It affords no guarantee of the quality of the title. *Title insurance*, on the other hand, is a guarantee. If title is questioned after the policy is issued, the title company is obligated to defend the title that it has insured. If the title turns out to be invalid, the title company is obligated to pay the value of the property.

In either case, someone must conduct a title search concerning the property described in the contract. In the case of the abstract of title, a document bearing that name is delivered to the purchaser. An abstract of title contains a copy or summary of every recorded instrument affecting the property and is certified by the abstract company as true and complete. Before the advent of title insurance, the abstract of title was updated each time the property was transferred. Someone, most often an attorney, then was employed to examine the abstract of title and to provide a title opinion on the basis of that examination. The *title opinion* expressed the conclusion of the title examiner as to whether title was marketable in the seller and described any exceptions to title.

Obtaining a title commitment or a title binder follows much the same process. Rather than delivering an abstract of title to the purchaser, the purchaser receives a short document (title commitment) that identifies the current owner; identifies the proposed owner; and states the requirements that must be fulfilled to transfer title to the new owner.

Although the final title policy provides insurance protection, the policy generally contains conditions and exceptions that are stated initially in the commitment. These should be reviewed carefully. A typical condition of insurance coverage might be that if the purchaser has or acquires actual knowledge of any defect, lien, or encumbrance not described in the commitment and fails to disclose it to the insurance company in writing, the insurance company has no liability concerning that defect, lien, or encumbrance.

The commitment also contains *standard exceptions*, which may be removed upon production of certain documentation. In some areas, an additional premium may be charged as well. The standard exceptions typically include 1) rights or claims of parties in possession that are not shown by the public records; 2) easements or claims of easements not shown by the public records; 3) any state of facts, including boundary conflicts, area shortages, and encroachments that would be disclosed by an accurate survey; 4) any lien or right to a lien for services, labor, or materials furnished (based on *mechanic's lien* statutes) but not shown by the public records; and 5) defects, liens, encumbrances, adverse claims, or other matters first appearing in the public records after the date of the commitment.

The exceptions for rights of parties in possession and for defects arising after the date of the commitment sometimes may be deleted if appropriate affidavits are furnished. The commitment is updated continuously until the time of closing to disclose matters that might arise from the recording of additional documents, and *gap coverage* also may be obtained. The exception for any state of facts disclosed by an accurate survey is deleted without charge when a current survey is provided. Mechanic's lien protection is provided when the title insurance company receives affidavits of the seller (and sometimes of the purchaser as well as any contractor), representing that any work done on the premises has been paid for. In some areas of the country, this requires payment of an additional premium. Statutes in some states require that these types of standard exceptions be deleted where possible. A well-drafted real estate contract requires that these standard exceptions be deleted from the final policy.

Two schedules are attached to the title commitment, one containing requirements and the other containing exceptions. The *schedule of requirements* establishes the steps that must be taken to insure title. Typically, those requirements include 1) payment of full value, since recording statutes protect only bona fide purchasers for value; 2) recording the deed; and 3) release or partial release of any mortgages or other liens against the property. If mortgagee coverage is included, a separate policy is issued to the purchaser's lender; and a requirement to record the mortgage or deed of trust also is shown.

The schedule of exceptions states those items that are excluded from coverage. Exceptions usually include taxes, special assessments, or other charges for improvements against the property; any exceptions contained in the patent by which title initially was conveyed by the government; any exceptions for a reserved mineral interest; rights-of-way; easements; and protective covenants. Again, the title insurance company may be willing to delete some of those exceptions by having the buyer or the seller pay an additional premium or by providing documentation to establish that the particular exception does not pertain to the property being insured. In some areas, patent exceptions may be removed by payment of an additional premium as well.

Figure 9-2
Title Insurance Commitment

COMMITMENT FOR TITLE INSURANCE
Issued by
ACME TITLE INSURANCE COMPANY

    Acme Title Insurance Company, a corporation, herein called the Company, for a valuable consideration, hereby commits to issue its policy or policies of title insurance, as identified in Schedule A, in favor of the proposed insured named in Schedule A, as owner or mortgagee of the estate or interest covered hereby in the land described or referred to in Schedule A, upon payment of the premiums and charges therefor; all subject to the provisions of Schedules A and B and to the Conditions and Stipulations hereof.

    This Commitment shall be effective only when the identity of the proposed Insured and the amount of the policy or policies committed for have been inserted in Schedule A hereof by the Company, either at the time of the issuance of this Commitment or by subsequent endorsement.

    This Commitment is preliminary to the issuance of such policy or policies of title insurance and all liability and obligations hereunder shall cease and terminate within ninety (90) days after the effective date hereof or when the policy or policies committed for shall issue, whichever first occurs, provided that the failure to issue such policy or policies is not the fault of the Company.

    This Commitment shall not be valid or binding until countersigned by either an officer or authorized agent of this Company.

    IN WITNESS WHEREOF, Acme Title Insurance Company has caused its corporate name and seal to be hereunto affixed and these presents to be signed in facsimile under authority of its by-laws on the date shown in Schedule A.

        ACME TITLE INSURANCE COMPANY

            By:_____
            President
                ATTEST:

            _____
            Secretary

Countersigned:

_____
Authorized Signatory

CONDITIONS AND STIPULATIONS

1.   The term "mortgage," when used herein, shall include deed of trust, trust deed or other security instrument.

2.   If the proposed Insured has or acquires actual knowledge of any defect, lien, encumbrance, adverse claim or other matter affecting the estate or interest or mortgage thereon covered by this Commitment other than those shown in Schedule B hereof and shall fail to disclose such knowledge to the Company in writing, the Company shall be relieved from liability for any loss or damage resulting from any act of reliance hereon to the extent the Company is prejudiced by failure to so disclose such knowledge. If the proposed Insured shall disclose such knowledge to the Company or if the Company otherwise acquires actual knowledge of any such defect, lien, encumbrance, adverse claim or other matter, the Company at its option may amend Schedule B of this Commitment accordingly, but such amendment shall not relieve the Company from liability previously incurred pursuant to paragraph 3 of these Conditions and Stipulations.

ACME TITLE INSURANCE COMPANY
SCHEDULE A

1.   Effective date: May 9, 1996 at 8:00 A.M.
2.   Policy or Policies to be issued: Amount
          _____Owner's Policy Form A-1990 $174,500.00
          _____Owner's Policy Form B-1990
Proposed Insured: **JOHN W. DOE**
3.   The estate or interest in the land described or referred to in this Commitment and covered herein is **FEE SIMPLE**
4.   Title to the Fee Simple estate or interest in said land is at the effective date hereof vested in: **JANE ROE**
5.   The land referred to in this Commitment is described as:

Unit A, a resubdivision of Lot 66, Block 1, Mountain Valley Subdivision, Filing No. 1, County of Carbon, State of Colorado.

ACME TITLE INSURANCE COMPANY

SCHEDULE B-1
(Requirements)

The following are the requirements to be complied with:

1.   Payment to, or for the account of, the sellers or mortgagors of the full consideration for the estate or interest to be insured.

2.   Instruments in insurable form which must be executed, delivered and duly filed for record:
   (a)   Recordation of properly executed and approved plat of subject property.
   (b)   Recordation of properly executed party wall agreement for subject property.
   (c)   Deed from Jane Roe to John W. Doe conveying subject property described in plat and party wall agreement to be provided in items 3 and 4.
   (d)   Partial Release of Deed of Trust from Jane Roe to the Public Trustee of Carbon County for the use of Bank of Carbon to secure $350,000, dated December 12, 1994, recorded December 30, 1994, in Book 351 at Page 229.

AMERICAN TITLE INSURANCE COMPANY

SCHEDULE B-2
(Exceptions)

Schedule B of the policy or policies to be issued will contain exceptions to the following matters unless the same are disposed of to the satisfaction of the Company:

1.   Defects, liens, encumbrances, adverse claims or other matters, if any, created, first appearing in the public records or attaching subsequent to the effective date hereof but prior to the date the proposed Insured acquires for value of record the estate or interest or mortgage thereon covered by this Commitment.

2.   All assessments and taxes for the year 1995 and all subsequent years.

3.   Any lien, or right to a lien, for services, labor or material heretofore or hereafter furnished, imposed by law and not shown by the public records.

4.   Any encroachments, easements, measurements, variations in area or content, party walls or other facts which a correct survey of the premises would show.

5.   Rights or claims of parties in possession not shown by the public records.

6.   Roads, ways, streams or easements, if any, not shown by the public records, riparian rights and the title to any filled-in lands.

7.   Any and all unpaid taxes and assessments and unredeemed tax sales.

8.   Right of proprietor of a vein or lode to extract and remove his ore therefrom should the same be found to penetrate or intersect the premises hereby granted, and right of way for ditches and canals as constructed by the authority of the United States, as reserved in United States Patents of record.

9.   Utility and drainage easements as shown on Plat of Mountain Valley Subdivision, Filing 1, said easements being 7.5 feet in width along each side of every side not fronting on a dedicated street or road.

10.   Restrictions as contained in instrument recorded September 6, 1972 in Book 225 at Page 302.

Regardless of whether an abstract of title is provided or a title commitment is provided, someone (either an attorney or a title examiner) must form an opinion of the marketability (insurability) of the title. The concepts are the same. The primary issue is whether the current title will be accepted by the purchaser without challenge or whether the seller lacks some part of the title that she claims to have. The secondary issue is whether any exceptions to the title should be included, even though the title is complete and may be accepted without challenge. The exceptions to the title may present defects in the title. Or, if they were exceptions contained in the contract for the sale of the land, they may have no effect.

Title defects usually are obvious. For example, the deed by which the seller acquired title may not have been signed, or the grantor's signature may not have been acknowledged (notarized). Possibly, the description of the property contained errors. Or perhaps there is an unreleased mortgage recorded against the property. Unless the contract for sale of the property listed the unreleased mortgage as an exception from the title, the unreleased mortgage is grounds to object to the title.

Title to property is not required to be perfect, however, as United States Supreme Court Justice Benjamin Cordozo once observed while he was serving on the New York Court of Appeals:

> The law assures to a buyer a title free from reasonable
> doubt, but not free from every doubt. . . . If the only
> defect in the title is a very remote and improbable
> contingency, a slender possibility only, a conveyance
> will be decreed. . . .

Norwegian Evangelical Free Church v. Milhauser, 252 N.Y. 186, 169 N.E. 134, 135 (1929).

A purchaser does not need to prove that the title is unmarketable; she needs to prove only that there is a reasonable doubt about its marketability. Defects unrelated to the title do not count. For instance, the fact that the property is termite infested or subject to flooding, bad soil conditions, or undesirable zoning does not make the title unmarketable.

What makes the title search so complex is that the title examiner must examine not only the deed by which the seller acquired title, but also every other deed in the seller's *chain of ownership*, from the beginning of time to the present.   Furthermore, the title examiner must examine each and every instrument that might affect title to the property and must determine whether it affects the title or not.   When any mortgage or other lien appears, the title examiner must assure herself that each encumbrance subsequently was released.

To accomplish her purpose, the title examiner prepares a chain of title, which might look something like this:

U.S.A.
|
Patent—1/4/1889 *[date of instrument]*—4/6/1890 *[date of recording]*—book 4, page 36
|
John Smith and Mary Smith
|
WD *[warranty deed]*—6/2/02—6/3/02—book 22, page 4
|
Fred Palmer and Betty Palmer (JT *[joint tenants]*)
    |
        Mortgage—6/2/02—6/3/02—book 22, page 5
          |
           John Smith and Jane Smith
           |
           Rel *[release]*—9/10/22—9/12/22—book 43, page 28
|
QCD *[quitclaim deed]*—4/22/39—5/18/40—book 67, page 109 (BY FRED PALMER ONLY)
|
Fred Palmer Jr.
    |
    DC *[death certificate]*—10/5/45—2/3/46—book 72, page 87
    |
____   Order Admitting—2/6/47—2/6/47—book 78, page 2
|
Ex's D *[executor's deed]*—2/7/47—2/8/47—book 78, page 92
|
William Williams and Joan Williams (JT)

In the chain of title outlined here, one title defect exists: Betty Palmer failed to join in the conveyance to Fred Palmer Jr. Possibly, Betty had died at the time the conveyance was made; and if so, the defect can be cured easily by ordering and recording her death certificate. Once that is done, the title examiner will be able to conclude that the title is vested in William Williams and Joan Williams as joint tenants and that the title is marketable (insurable).

Title examiners are helped by statutes that allow minor defects in title to be *passed*. This means a minor title defect can be ignored after a specified number of years have passed. An example of this type of statute is one that allows a deed with no acknowledgment (or a defective acknowledgment) to be treated as valid after it has been of record for ten years. Another statute may permit recitals contained in a recorded instrument to be relied upon as proof of what they recite when the instrument has been of record for twenty years (using the above chain, for example, a statement in the quitclaim deed that Fred Palmer was the surviving joint tenant of Betty Palmer). A statute also may permit an unreleased mortgage or deed of trust to be ignored after a period of time, such as fifteen years. In addition, statutes usually provide that variations concerning names (such as a missing middle name or middle initial) may be ignored after a period of only a few years. In some states, *marketable title acts* have been enacted. These statutes extinguish all claims and defects after a particular period of time, typically thirty or forty years.

State bar associations also have adopted title standards, which are used to determine whether or not a title is marketable. For example, a title standard may provide that signing a deed with a mark is valid so long as the mark is acknowledged. Other title standards might provide that a deed can be ignored if it is signed by a stranger to title (a person not in the chain of title) or that variations in corporate names can be ignored (*company* rather than *co.*, for example).

Fewer than one-fourth of the states have adopted an alternative method of title registration, called the *Torrens System*, which co-exists with the record system. Imported from Australia, this method of title registration is somewhat similar to the type of title registration used for automobiles. The owner of property is issued a title certificate upon which liens and other matters affecting title are noted. This system has not been popular because initial registration involves a court proceeding similar to a quiet title proceeding. Even in those states where the Torrens system exists, it seldom is used.

Land Financing

When a purchaser pays the entire purchase price in cash at the closing, no financing documents are necessary. On the other hand, if any portion of the purchase price is to be financed, one must prepare a promissory note and security instruments, including a mortgage or deed of trust. Where appropriate, an assignment of rents also must be prepared.

Land financing is provided either by the seller or by some third party. Seller financing is straightforward and requires no more than the documents mentioned above. Third party financing typically is provided by a bank or other lending institution.   If the institution is *federally related* (if the lender is chartered by the federal government or if it maintains deposits guaranteed by the federal government), it must comply with the Real Estate Settlement Procedures Act of 1974, 12 U.S.C. § 2601, et seq. (RESPA) when it lends money to finance real estate.

Mortgage   The primary security instrument is the mortgage or deed of trust. A mortgage is used predominantly and has a far longer history than the deed of trust. When a *mortgage* is used, the owner of the property conveys the property to the lender. The owner of the property is the mortgagor, and the lender is the *mortgagee*.

Because it conveys property as security for the loan, the mortgage itself contains the language of a deed. At one time, the legal effect of a mortgage was an actual conveyance of the property in fee simple subject to the condition subsequent that upon repayment of the loan on time, the conveyance was void. Or it was a conveyance of the fee simple estate with a covenant of the mortgagee to reconvey the property upon payment of the loan on time.   If the borrower-mortgagor failed to pay the loan on time, the condition subsequent (or covenant) was discharged; and fee simple title vested absolutely in the lender-mortgagee.

Figure 9-3, which begins on the following page, illustrates a mortgage that was prepared on a preprinted form.

Figure 9-3
Mortgage

Recorded at ______________ o'clock ________ M., ______________________________

Reception No. ______________ ______________________________ Recorder

MORTGAGE DEED

THIS INDENTURE, Made this 1st day of August ,
1996 , between JOHN W. DOE

of the *County of Carbon and
State of Colorado , Mortgagor, and

JANET W. DOE

Mortgagee, whose legal address is 55-E Coyote Circle, Mountain Valley Subdivision, Colorado 80001

WITNESSETH: That the Mortgagor, for and in consideration of the sum of------------------------
ONE HUNDRED THOUSAND -- Dollars,
to him in hand paid by the Mortgagee, the receipt whereof is hereby acknowledged, does hereby grant, bargain, sell and convey unto the Mortgagee, the following described real estate, situate in the County of Carbon , and State of Colorado, to wit:

Unit A, a resubdivision of Lot 66, Block 1, Mountain Valley Subdivision, Filing No. 1, County of Carbon, State of Colorado

also known by street and number as: 55-W Coyote Circle, Mountain Valley Subdivision, Colorado 80001

TO HAVE AND TO HOLD the above described premises, together with all and singular the appurtenances and privileges thereunto belonging unto the Mortgagee, forever.

*If in Denver, insert "City and".

No. 11. Rev. 12-85. MORTGAGE DEED Bradford Publishing, 5825 W. 6th Ave., Lakewood, CO 80214 — (303) 233-6900 12-85

PROVIDED, ALWAYS, and these presents are upon this express condition, that if the Mortgagor shall pay or cause to be paid to the Mortgagee the said sum of -
ONE HUNDRED THOUSAND - Dollars
according to the terms, tenor and effect of that promissory note for the sum of - - - - - - - - - - - - - - - - - -
ONE HUNDRED THOUSAND - Dollars.
bearing even date herewith, made and delivered by the Mortgagor, and payable to the order of the Mortgagee
after the date thereof, together with interest thereon at the rate
of five   per cent per annum from the date thereof until paid, principal and interest payable as follows:

in two equal payments of Fifty-Three Thousand Five Hundred Forty-One Dollars
and Sixty-Eight Cents, on the first day of each January, beginning on January 1,
1997, and continuing until the entire indebtedness is fully paid; provided,
however, the entire principal amount outstanding and accrued interest thereon,
shall be due and payable on January 1, 1998.

AND PROVIDED FURTHER, That if the Mortgagor shall well and truly perform all and singular the several covenants, conditions, agreements and promises contained in the said note, and in these presents, and shall pay all sums of money for taxes, assessments and insurance as hereinafter provided, then these presents shall be null and void, otherwise to remain in full force.

And the Mortgagor covenants and agrees to and with the Mortgagee that he holds the said premises by title in fee simple; that he has good right and lawful authority to sell and convey the same; that said premises are free and clear of all liens and encumbrances whatsoever except None

And the Mortgagor shall and will WARRANT AND DEFEND said premises against the lawful claims of all persons whomever, except as aforesaid. Until payment in full of the indebtedness, the Mortgagor shall timely pay all taxes and assessments levied on the property; and any and all amounts due on account of principal or interest or other sums on any senior encumbrances, if any; and will keep the improvements on said lands in good repair and insured against casualty loss, including extended coverage, by a company or companies meeting the net worth requirements of the Mortgagee hereof, in an amount not less than the total indebtedness, including senior encumbrances. Each policy shall contain a loss payable clause for the benefit of the Mortgagee and shall further provide that the insurance may not be cancelled upon less than ten (10) days written notice to the Mortgagee. At the option of the Mortgagee, the original policy or policies of insurance shall be delivered to the Mortgagee as further security for the indebtedness. Should the Mortgagor fail to insure and deliver the policies or to pay taxes or assessments as the same may fall due, or to keep the property in good repair, or to pay any amount payable upon senior encumbrances, if any, the Mortgagee may make such repairs or any such payments or procure any such insurance, without being required to do so, and all monies so paid with interest thereon at the rate of five   per cent per annum shall be added to and become a part of the indebtedness secured by this Mortgage Deed and may be paid out of the proceeds of the sale of the property, if not paid by the Mortgagor. In addition, at its option, the Mortgagee may declare the indebtedness secured hereby and this Mortgage Deed to be in default for failure to procure insurance or make any payments or repairs required by this paragraph.

And it is expressly convenanted and agreed that if default shall be made in the payment of said note, or any of them, or of any part thereof, or in the payment of any interest thereon, according to the tenor and effect of said note, or if the Mortgagor shall allow the taxes or assessments upon the above described premises, or any part thereof, to become delinquent, or shall do or suffer any act to be done, whereby the value of the said premises shall be impaired as a security for the said note and interest, or shall fail to insure the said buildings as hereinbefore provided, or if the Mortgagor, shall fail to perform or keep any of the agreements, covenants or promises contained in said note, or in these presents, then, upon the violation or breach of any of said covenants, promises or agreements, the whole amount represented by said note shall, at the election of the lawful holder thereof, become due and collectible at once, notice of such election being hereby waived, and the Mortgagee may proceed to foreclose this mortgage for the purpose of satisfying and paying the entire indebtedness secured hereby, together with interest, and all taxes, assessments and insurance premiums which may have been paid by the Mortgagee as aforesaid, together with interest on the same at the rate of eight   per cent per annum from the dates of such payments, all of which are to be included in the judgment or decree in such foreclosure suit or action.

And in case suit is brought to foreclose this mortgage, the Mortgagor agrees to pay a reasonable attorney's fee therefor, which is to be included in such judgment or decree.

And in case any action or suit shall be commenced, and the Mortgagee be made a party plaintiff or defendant, by reason of this mortgage, he shall be allowed a reasonable attorney's fee and all costs therein, and the same shall be a further lien upon said premises, and, in case of the foreclosure of this mortgage, shall be included in such judgment or decree.

All the covenants and conditions contained herein shall extend to and be binding upon the heirs, personal representatives, successors and assigns of the parties. Whenever used, the singular number shall include the plural, the plural the singular, and the use of any gender shall be applicable to all genders.

IN WITNESS WHEREOF, The Mortgagor executed this deed on the date set forth above.

_____

John W. Doe

_____

STATE OF COLORADO,

County of   Carbon   } ss.

The foregoing instrument was acknowledged before me this 1st   day of August   , 19 96 ,

by   John W. Doe.

My commission expires   . Witness my hand and official seal.

_____
Notary Public

After reciting the borrower's indebtedness to the lender, today's standard mortgage contains the following language or language similar to it:

> To secure to Lender the repayment of the indebtedness, together with interest thereon, and the covenants and agreements of Borrower herein contained, Borrower does hereby mortgage, grant, and convey to Lender the following described property: . . .

Once the debt is paid in full, a *release of mortgage* is delivered and recorded to reconvey title to the mortgagor (owner/borrower). If the debt is not paid, the mortgagee (lender) must use judicial proceedings to *foreclose* the mortgage. In a foreclosure proceeding, the court authorizes sale of the mortgaged property in full or partial satisfaction of the debt secured by the mortgage.

The mortgage typically contains further covenants, including the agreements of the mortgagor to keep the property fully insured; to pay all taxes assessed against the property; and to keep the property in good repair. Beyond nonpayment of the mortgage debt, a default in the performance of any of these covenants also constitutes a breach of the mortgage and permits foreclosure.

Deed of Trust   In approximately one-third of the states, a *deed of trust* or *trust deed* is used as an alternative to the mortgage. When a deed of trust is used, the owner of the property conveys the property *in trust* to some person or entity other than the lender. That person or entity is the trustee. The lender is the beneficiary of the trust created. The deed of trust contains the same provisions and covenants as does the mortgage. Once the underlying debt is paid, a release is provided.

Because of the nature and the specific provisions of the deed of trust, the trustee is empowered to sell the property in full or partial satisfaction of the debt if a default occurs. No judicial proceeding is necessary. The only substantive difference between a mortgage and deed of trust, therefore, is the method of its enforcement. Avoiding a judicial proceeding—and its possible delays—is easier, faster, and usually less expensive.

Enforcement of deeds of trust usually is subject to detailed statutes that direct the manner in which the sale must occur, including specific notice requirements. Although default in a single payment of principal gives rise to the right of sale, a statute may give the debtor a one-time right to cure the default and to reinstate the deed of trust. Figure 9-4 shows a sample deed of trust.

Figure 9-4
Deed of Trust

The printed portions of this form approved by
the Colorado Real Estate Commission (TD 73-11-83)

IF THIS FORM IS USED IN A CONSUMER CREDIT TRANSACTION, CONSULT LEGAL COUNSEL.

THIS IS A LEGAL INSTRUMENT. IF NOT UNDERSTOOD, LEGAL, TAX OR OTHER COUNSEL SHOULD BE CONSULTED BEFORE SIGNING.

DEED OF TRUST
(Due on Transfer — Creditworthy Restriction)

THIS DEED OF TRUST is made this __1st__ day of __August__, 19 __96__, between _____
__John W. Doe__ (Borrower),
whose address is __55-W Coyote Circle, Mountain Valley Subdivision, Colorado 80001__ ;
and the Public Trustee of the County in which the Property (see paragraph 1) is situated (Trustee); for the benefit of
__Janet W. Doe__

(Lender), whose address is
__55-E Coyote Circle, Mountain Valleu Subdivision, Colorado   80001__
Borrower and Lender covenant and agree as follows:

1. Property in Trust.   Borrower, in consideration of the indebtedness herein recited and the trust herein created, hereby grants and conveys to Trustee in trust, with power of sale, the following described property located in the _____
County of __Carbon__, State of Colorado:

Unit A, a resubdivision of Lot 66, Block 1, Mountain Valley
Subdivision, Filing No. 1, County of Carbon, State of Colorado

, which has the address of __55-W Coyote Circle, Mountain Valley Subdivision,__ ,
(Street)
_____, Colorado __80001__
(City)   (Zip Code)

(Property Address), together with all its appurtenances (Property).

2. Note; Other Obligations Secured.   This Deed of Trust is given to secure to Lender:
A. the repayment of the indebtedness evidenced by Borrower's note (Note) dated __August 1__, 19 __96__, in the principal sum of __ONE HUNDRED THOUSAND__ -------------------------------------
U.S. Dollars, with interest on the unpaid principal balance from __August 1__, 19 __96__, until paid, at the rate of __five__ percent per annum, with principal and interest payable at
__55-E Coyote Circle, Mountain Valley Subdivison, Colorado   80001__
or such other place as the Lender may designate, in __two__ payments of
__Fifty-Three Thousand Five Hundred Forty-One and 68/100__
Dollars (U.S. $__53,541.68__) due on the __1__ day of each __January__
beginning __January 1__, 19 __97__; such payments to continue until the entire indebtedness evidenced by said Note is fully paid; however, if not sooner paid, the entire principal amount outstanding and accrued interest thereon, shall be due and payable on __January 1__, 19 __98__;

and Borrower is to pay to Lender a late charge of __one__ % of any payment not received by the Lender within __ten__ days after payment is due; and Borrower has the right to prepay the principal amount outstanding under said Note, in whole or in part, at any time without penalty ~~except~~ ;

B. the payment of all other sums, with interest thereon at __five__ % per annum, disbursed by Lender in accordance with this Deed of Trust to protect the security of this Deed of Trust; and
C. the performance of the covenants and agreements of Borrower herein contained.

3. Title.   Borrower covenants that Borrower owns and has the right to grant and convey the Property, and warrants title to the same, subject to general real estate taxes for the current year, easements of record or in existence, and recorded declarations, restrictions, reservations and covenants, if any, as of this date ~~except:~~

4. Payment of Principal and Interest.   Borrower shall promptly pay when due the principal of and interest on the indebtedness evidenced by the Note, and late charges as provided in the Note and shall perform all of Borrower's other covenants contained in the Note.

5. Application of Payments.   All payments received by Lender under the terms hereof shall be applied by Lender first in payment of amounts due pursuant to paragraph 23 (Escrow Funds for Taxes and Insurance), then to amounts disbursed by Lender pursuant to paragraph 9 (Protection of Lender's Security), and the balance in accordance with the terms and conditions of the Note.

6. **Prior Mortgages and Deeds of Trust; Charges; Liens.** Borrower shall perform all of Borrower's obligations under any prior deed of trust and any other prior liens. Borrower shall pay all taxes, assessments and other charges, fines and impositions attributable to the Property which may have or attain a priority over this Deed of Trust, and leasehold payments or ground rents, if any, in the manner set out in paragraph 23 (Escrow Funds for Taxes and Insurance) or, if not required to be paid in such manner, by Borrower making payment when due, directly to the payee thereof. Despite the foregoing, Borrower shall not be required to make payments otherwise required by this paragraph if Borrower, after notice to Lender, shall in good faith contest such obligation by, or defend enforcement of such obligation in, legal proceedings which operate to prevent the enforcement of the obligation or forfeiture of the Property or any part thereof, only upon Borrower making all such contested payments and other payments as ordered by the court to the registry of the court in which such proceedings are filed.

7. **Property Insurance.** Borrower shall keep the improvements now existing or hereafter erected on the Property insured against loss by fire or hazards included within the term "extended coverage" in an amount at least equal to the lesser of (1) the insurable value of the Property or (2) an amount sufficient to pay the sums secured by this Deed of Trust as well as any prior encumbrances on the Property. All of the foregoing shall be known as "Property Insurance".

The insurance carrier providing the insurance shall be qualified to write Property Insurance in Colorado and shall be chosen by Borrower subject to Lender's right to reject the chosen carrier for reasonable cause. All insurance policies and renewals thereof shall include a standard mortgage clause in favor of Lender, and shall provide that the insurance carrier shall notify Lender at least ten (10) days before cancellation, termination or any material change of coverage. Insurance policies shall be furnished to Lender at or before closing. Lender shall have the right to hold the policies and renewals thereof.

In the event of loss, Borrower shall give prompt notice to the insurance carrier and Lender. Lender may make proof of loss if not made promptly by Borrower.

Insurance proceeds shall be applied to restoration or repair of the Property damaged, provided such restoration or repair is economically feasible and the security of this Deed of Trust is not thereby impaired. If such restoration or repair is not economically feasible or if the security of this Deed of Trust would be impaired, the insurance proceeds shall be applied to the sums secured by this Deed of Trust, with the excess, if any, paid to Borrower. If the Property is abandoned by Borrower, or if Borrower fails to respond to Lender within 30 days from the date notice is given in accordance with paragraph 16 (Notice) by Lender to Borrower that the insurance carrier offers to settle a claim for insurance benefits, Lender is authorized to collect and apply the insurance proceeds, at Lender's option, either to restoration or repair of the Property or to the sums secured by this Deed of Trust.

Any such application of proceeds to principal shall not extend or postpone the due date of the installments referred to in paragraphs 4 (Payment of Principal and Interest) and 23 (Escrow Funds for Taxes and Insurance) or change the amount of such installments. Notwithstanding anything herein to the contrary, if under paragraph 18 (Acceleration; Foreclosure; Other Remedies) the Property is acquired by Lender, all right, title and interest of Borrower in and to any insurance policies and in and to the proceeds thereof resulting from damage to the Property prior to the sale or acquisition shall pass to Lender to the extent of the sums secured by this Deed of Trust immediately prior to such sale or acquisition.

All of the rights of Borrower and Lender hereunder with respect to insurance carriers, insurance policies and insurance proceeds are subject to the rights of any holder of a prior deed of trust with respect to said insurance carriers, policies and proceeds.

8. **Preservation and Maintenance of Property.** Borrower shall keep the Property in good repair and shall not commit waste or permit impairment or deterioration of the Property and shall comply with the provisions of any lease if this Deed of Trust is on a leasehold. Borrower shall perform all of Borrower's obligations under any declarations, covenants, by-laws, rules, or other documents governing the use, ownership or occupancy of the Property.

9. **Protection of Lender's Security.** Except when Borrower has exercised Borrower's rights under paragraph 6 above, if the Borrower fails to perform the covenants and agreements contained in this Deed of Trust, or if a default occurs in a prior lien, or if any action or proceeding is commenced which materially affects Lender's interest in the Property, then Lender, at Lender's option, with notice to Borrower if required by law, may make such appearances, disburse such sums and take such action as is necessary to protect Lender's interest, including, but not limited to, disbursement of reasonable attorney's fees and entry upon the Property to make repairs. Borrower hereby assigns to Lender any right Borrower may have by reason of any prior encumbrance on the Property or by law or otherwise to cure any default under said prior encumbrance.

Any amounts disbursed by Lender pursuant to this paragraph 9, with interest thereon, shall become additional indebtedness of Borrower secured by this Deed of Trust. Such amounts shall be payable upon notice from Lender to Borrower requesting payment thereof, and Lender may bring suit to collect any amounts so disbursed plus interest specified in paragraph 2B (Note; Other Obligations Secured). Nothing contained in this paragraph 9 shall require Lender to incur any expense or take any action hereunder.

10. **Inspection.** Lender may make or cause to be made reasonable entries upon and inspection of the Property, provided that Lender shall give Borrower notice prior to any such inspection specifying reasonable cause therefor related to Lender's interest in the Property.

11. **Condemnation.** The proceeds of any award or claim for damages, direct or consequential, in connection with any condemnation or other taking of the Property, or part thereof, or for conveyance in lieu of condemnation, are hereby assigned and shall be paid to Lender as herein provided. However, all of the rights of Borrower and Lender hereunder with respect to such proceeds are subject to the rights of any holder of a prior deed of trust.

In the event of a total taking of the Property, the proceeds shall be applied to the sums secured by this Deed of Trust, with the excess, if any, paid to Borrower. In the event of a partial taking of the Property, the proceeds remaining after taking out any part of the award due any prior lien holder (net award) shall be divided between Lender and Borrower, in the same ratio as the amount of the sums secured by this Deed of Trust immediately prior to the date of taking bears to Borrower's equity in the Property immediately prior to the date of taking. Borrower's equity in the Property means the fair market value of the Property less the amount of sums secured by both this Deed of Trust and all prior liens (except taxes) that are to receive any of the award, all at the value immediately prior to the date of taking.

If the Property is abandoned by Borrower, or if, after notice by Lender to Borrower that the condemnor offers to make an award or settle a claim for damages, Borrower fails to respond to Lender within 30 days after the date such notice is given, Lender is authorized to collect and apply the proceeds, at Lender's option, either to restoration or repair of the Property or to the sums secured by this Deed of Trust.

Any such application of proceeds to principal shall not extend or postpone the due date of the installments referred to in paragraphs 4 (Payment of Principal and Interest) and 23 (Escrow Funds for Taxes and Insurance) nor change the amount of such installments.

12. **Borrower Not Released.** Extension of the time for payment or modification of amortization of the sums secured by this Deed of Trust granted by Lender to any successor in interest of Borrower shall not operate to release, in any manner, the liability of the original Borrower, nor Borrower's successors in interest, from the original terms of this Deed of Trust. Lender shall not be required to commence proceedings against such successor or refuse to extend time for payment or otherwise modify amortization of the sums secured by this Deed of Trust by reason of any demand made by the original Borrower nor Borrower's successors in interest.

13. **Forbearance by Lender Not a Waiver.** Any forbearance by Lender in exercising any right or remedy hereunder, or otherwise afforded by law, shall not be a waiver or preclude the exercise of any such right or remedy.

14. **Remedies Cumulative.** Each remedy provided in the Note and this Deed of Trust is distinct from and cumulative to all other rights or remedies under the Note and this Deed of Trust or afforded by law or equity, and may be exercised concurrently, independently or successively.

15. **Successors and Assigns Bound; Joint and Several Liability; Captions.** The covenants and agreements herein contained shall bind, and the rights hereunder shall inure to, the respective successors and assigns of Lender and Borrower, subject to the provisions of paragraph 24 (Transfer of the Property; Assumption). All covenants and agreements of Borrower shall be joint and several. The captions and headings of the paragraphs in this Deed of Trust are for convenience only and are not to be used to interpret or define the provisions hereof.

16. **Notice.** Except for any notice required by law to be given in another manner, (a) any notice to Borrower provided for in this Deed of Trust shall be in writing and shall be given and be effective upon (1) delivery to Borrower or (2) mailing such notice by first-class U.S. mail, addressed to Borrower at Borrower's address stated herein or at such other address as Borrower may designate by notice to Lender as provided herein, and (b) any notice to Lender shall be in writing and shall be given and be effective upon (1) delivery to Lender or (2) mailing such notice by first-class U.S. mail, to Lender's address stated herein or to such other address as Lender may designate by notice to Borrower as provided herein. Any notice provided for in this Deed of Trust shall be deemed to have been given to Borrower or Lender when given in any manner designated herein.

17. **Governing Law; Severability.** The Note and this Deed of Trust shall be governed by the law of Colorado. In the event that any provision or clause of this Deed of Trust or the Note conflicts with the law, such conflict shall not affect other provisions of this Deed of Trust or the Note which can be given effect without the conflicting provision, and to this end the provisions of the Deed of Trust and Note are declared to be severable.

18. **Acceleration; Foreclosure; Other Remedies.** Except as provided in paragraph 24 (Transfer of the Property; Assumption), upon Borrower's breach of any covenant or agreement of Borrower in this Deed of Trust, or upon any default in a prior lien upon the Property, (unless Borrower has exercised Borrower's rights under paragraph 6 above), at Lender's option, all of the sums secured by this Deed of Trust shall be immediately due and payable (Acceleration). To exercise this option, Lender may invoke the power of sale and any other remedies permitted by law. Lender shall be entitled to collect all reasonable costs and expenses incurred in pursuing the remedies provided in this Deed of Trust, including, but not limited to, reasonable attorney's fees.

If Lender invokes the power of sale, Lender shall give written notice to Trustee of such election. Trustee shall give such notice to Borrower of Borrower's rights as is provided by law. Trustee shall record a copy of such notice as required by law. Trustee shall advertise the time and place of the sale of the Property, for not less than four weeks in a newspaper of general circulation in each county in which the Property is situated, and shall mail copies of such notice of sale to Borrower and other persons as prescribed by law. After the lapse of such time as may be required by law, Trustee, without demand on Borrower, shall sell the Property at public auction to the highest bidder for cash at the time and place (which may be on the Property or any part thereof as permitted by law) in one or more parcels as Trustee may think best and in such order as Trustee may determine. Lender or Lender's designee may purchase the Property at any sale. It shall not be obligatory upon the purchaser at any such sale to see to the application of the purchase money.

Trustee shall apply the proceeds of the sale in the following order: (a) to all reasonable costs and expenses of the sale, including, but not limited to, reasonable Trustee's and attorney's fees and costs of title evidence; (b) to all sums secured by this Deed of Trust; and (c) the excess, if any, to the person or persons legally entitled thereto.

19. **Borrower's Right to Cure Default.** Whenever foreclosure is commenced for nonpayment of any sums due hereunder, the owners of the Property or parties liable hereon shall be entitled to cure said defaults by paying all delinquent principal and interest payments due as of the date of cure, costs, expenses, late charges, attorney's fees and other fees all in the manner provided by law. Upon such payment, this Deed of Trust and the obligations secured hereby shall remain in full force and effect as though no Acceleration had occurred, and the foreclosure proceedings shall be discontinued.

20. **Assignment of Rents; Appointment of Receiver; Lender in Possession.** As additional security hereunder, Borrower hereby assigns to Lender the rents of the Property; however, Borrower shall, prior to Acceleration under paragraph 18 (Acceleration; Foreclosure; Other Remedies) or abandonment of the Property, have the right to collect and retain such rents as they become due and payable.

Lender or the holder of the Trustee's certificate of purchase shall be entitled to a receiver for the Property after Acceleration under paragraph 18 (Acceleration; Foreclosure; Other Remedies), and shall also be so entitled during the time covered by foreclosure proceedings and the period of redemption, if any; and shall be entitled thereto as a matter of right without regard to the solvency or insolvency of Borrower or of the then owner of the Property, and without regard to the value thereof. Such receiver may be appointed by any Court of competent jurisdiction upon ex parte application and without notice — notice being hereby expressly waived.

Upon Acceleration under paragraph 18 (Acceleration; Foreclosure; Other Remedies) or abandonment of the Property, Lender, in person, by agent or by judicially-appointed receiver, shall be entitled to enter upon, take possession of and manage the Property and to collect the rents of the Property including those past due. All rents collected by Lender or the receiver shall be applied, first, to payment of the costs of preservation and management of the Property, second, to payments due upon prior liens, and then to the sums secured by this Deed of Trust. Lender and the receiver shall be liable to account only for those rents actually received.

21. **Release.** Upon payment of all sums secured by this Deed of Trust, Lender shall cause Trustee to release this Deed of Trust and shall produce for Trustee the Note. Borrower shall pay all costs of recordation and shall pay the statutory Trustee's fees. If Lender shall not produce the Note as aforesaid, then Lender, upon notice in accordance with paragraph 16 (Notice) from Borrower to Lender, shall obtain, at Lender's expense, and file any lost instrument bond required by Trustee or pay the cost thereof to effect the release of this Deed of Trust.

22. **Waiver of Exemptions.** Borrower hereby waives all right of homestead and any other exemption in the Property under state or federal law presently existing or hereafter enacted.

23. **Escrow Funds for Taxes and Insurance.** This paragraph 23 is not applicable if Funds as defined below are being paid pursuant to a prior encumbrance. Subject to applicable law, Borrower shall pay to Lender, on each day installments of principal and interest are payable under the Note, until the Note is paid in full, a sum (herein referred to as "Funds") equal to ____N/A____ of the yearly taxes and assessments which may attain priority over this Deed of Trust, plus ____N/A____ of yearly premium installments for Property Insurance, all as reasonably estimated initially and from time to time by Lender on the basis of assessments and bills and reasonable estimates thereof, taking into account any excess Funds not used or shortages.

The principal of the Funds shall be held in a separate account by the Lender in trust for the benefit of the Borrower and deposited in an institution the deposits or accounts of which are insured or guaranteed by a federal or state agency. Lender shall apply the Funds to pay said taxes, assessments and insurance premiums. Lender may not charge for so holding and applying the Funds, analyzing said account or verifying and compiling said assessments and bills. Lender shall not be required to pay Borrower any interest or earnings on the Funds. Lender shall give to Borrower, without charge, an annual accounting of the Funds showing credits and debits to the Funds and the purpose for which each debit to the Funds was made. The Funds are pledged as additional security for the sums secured by this Deed of Trust.

If the amount of the Funds held by Lender shall not be sufficient to pay taxes, assessments and insurance premiums as they fall due, Borrower shall pay to Lender any amount necessary to make up the deficiency within 30 days from the date notice is given in accordance with paragraph 16 (Notice) by Lender to Borrower requesting payment thereof.

Upon payment in full of all sums secured by this Deed of Trust, Lender shall simultaneously refund to Borrower any Funds held by Lender. If under paragraph 18 (Acceleration; Foreclosure; Other Remedies) the Property is sold or the Property is otherwise acquired by Lender, Lender shall apply, no later than immediately prior to the sale of the Property or its acquisition by Lender, whichever occurs first, any Funds held by Lender at the time of application as a credit against the sums secured by this Deed of Trust.

24. **Transfer of the Property; Assumption.** The following events shall be referred to herein as a "Transfer": (i) a transfer or conveyance of title (or any portion thereof, legal or equitable) of the Property (or any part thereof or interest therein), (ii) the execution of a contract or agreement creating a right to title (or any portion thereof, legal or equitable) in the Property (or any part thereof or interest therein), (iii) or an agreement granting a possessory right in the Property (or any portion thereof), in excess of three (3) years, (iv) a sale or transfer of, or the execution of a contract or agreement creating a right to acquire or receive, more than fifty percent (50%) of the controlling interest or more than fifty percent (50%) of the beneficial interest in the Borrower, (v) the reorganization, liquidation or dissolution of the Borrower. Not to be included as a Transfer are (i) the creation of a lien or encumbrance subordinate to this Deed of Trust, (ii) the creation of a purchase money security interest for household appliances, or (iii) a transfer by devise, descent or by operation of the law upon the death of a joint tenant. At the election of Lender, in the event of each and every Transfer:

(a) Borrower shall, upon Lender's request, submit information required to enable Lender to evaluate the creditworthiness of the person ("Transferee") who is, or is to be, the recipient of a Transfer, as if a new loan were being made to Transferee. If Transferee is reasonably determined by the Lender to be financially incapable of retiring the indebtedness according to its terms, based upon standards normally used by persons in the business of making loans on real estate in the same or similar circumstances, then all sums secured by this Deed of Trust, at Lender's option, may become immediately due and payable ("Acceleration").

(b) If Lender exercises such option to Accelerate, Lender shall give Borrower notice of Acceleration in accordance with paragraph 16 (Notice). The notice shall inform Borrower of the right to assert in the foreclosure proceeding the nonexistence of a default or any other defense of Borrower to Acceleration and sale. Such notice shall also provide a period of not less than 10 days from the date the notice is given within which Borrower may pay the sums delcared due. If Borrower fails to pay such sums prior to the expiration of such period, Lender may, without further notice or demand on Borrower, invoke any remedies permitted by paragraph 18 (Acceleration; Foreclosure; Other Remedies). Lender shall give notice of such Acceleration, within thirty (30) days after notice of any Transfer is given to Lender by Borrower or Transferee in accordance with paragraph 16 (Notice). If Lender shall not give notice of such Acceleration within such thirty (30) days, then Lender will have no further right to such Acceleration.

(c) If a Transfer occurs and should Lender not exercise Lender's option pursuant to this paragraph 24 to Accelerate, Transferee shall be deemed to have assumed all of the obligations of Borrower under this Deed of Trust including all sums secured hereby whether or not the instrument evidencing such conveyance, contract or grant expressly so provides. This covenant shall run with the Property and remain in full force and effect until said sums are paid in full. The Lender may without notice to the Borrower deal with Transferee in the same manner as with the Borrower with reference to said sums including the payment or credit to Transferee of undisbursed reserve Funds on payment in full of said sums, without in any way altering or discharging the Borrower's liability hereunder for the obligations hereby secured.

(d) Should Lender not elect to Accelerate upon the occurrence of such Transfer then, subject to (b) above, the mere fact of a lapse of time or the acceptance of payment subsequent to any of such events, whether or not Lender had actual or constructive notice of such Transfer, shall not be deemed a waiver of Lender's right to make such election nor shall Lender be estopped therefrom by virtue thereof. The issuance on behalf of the Lender of a routine statement showing the status of the loan, whether or not Lender had actual or constructive notice of such Transfer, shall not be a waiver or estoppel of Lender's said rights.

25. **Borrower's Copy.** Borrower acknowledges receipt of a copy of the Note and of this Deed of Trust.

Continued on reverse side.

EXECUTED BY BORROWER.

IF BORROWER IS NATURAL PERSON(s):

John W. Doe

doing business as _____

IF BORROWER IS CORPORATION:

ATTEST:

_____
Name of Corporation

_____
Secretary

by _____
President

(SEAL)

IF BORROWER IS PARTNERSHIP:

_____
Name of Partnership

by _____
A General Partner

STATE OF COLORADO

_____ COUNTY OF ___ Carbon ___ } ss.

The foregoing instrument was acknowledged before me this ___ 1st ___ day of ___ August ___,

19 _96_ , by* ___ John W. Doe ___

Witness my hand and official seal.
My commission expires: _____ .

_____
Notary Public

_____
Address

*If a natural person or persons. insert the name(s) of such person(s). If a corporation. insert. for example. "John Doe as President and Jane Doe as Secretary of Doe & Co., a Colorado corporation." If a partnership. insert. for example. "Sam Smith as general partner in and for Smith & Smith. a general partnership."

No. _____

DEED OF TRUST

FROM

TO

THE PUBLIC TRUSTEE
FOR THE USE OF

STATE OF COLORADO,
County of _____ } ss.

I hereby certify that this instrument was filed for record in my office at _____ o'clock _____ M., _____ . 19 _____ . and is duly recorded in book _____ . page _____

Film No. _____ Reception No. _____

_____
Clerk and Recorder

By _____
Deputy

Fees, $ _____

BRADFORD PUBLISHING CO

Among those states that use the mortgage, the majority of jurisdictions subscribe to the lien theory of the mortgage, as opposed to the title theory. *Lien theory* jurisdictions disregard the form of the mortgage and describe the interest of the mortgagee as only a lien and not as fee title to the property. *Title theory* jurisdictions observe the form of the mortgage, finding actual fee title to be in the mortgagee.

Default   When a default occurs and the mortgage is foreclosed in a title theory jurisdiction, the mortgagee retains the property without regard to any discrepancy between the value of the property and the amount of the debt. In other words, it does not matter whether the mortgagor-owner has equity in the property. Conversely, the mortgagor is entitled to retain the equity in a lien theory jurisdiction, and the mortgagee receives only an amount of money equal to the debt. As a practical matter, the distinction has disappeared almost entirely; and the instrument recites that the mortgagor *mortgages* the property to the mortgagee.

If foreclosure occurs and if the value of the property is less than the amount of the debt, the debtor risks having a deficiency judgment entered against her for the difference between the value of the property and the amount of the debt. There are a variety of ways in which debtors are protected against mortgagees that intentionally underbid at the foreclosure sale as a way to receive both the property and a deficiency judgment.

Some states require or permit a hearing on the property's value, either before or shortly after the sale. The purpose of the hearing is to limit the deficiency to the difference between the debt and the actual value of the property, regardless of how much was bid at the sale. Other states require mortgagees to elect between recovery of the property and recovery of judgment for the amount owed. Still other states prohibit deficiencies entirely for certain types of property, such as single family residences and farms.

In addition, many states protect the borrower through a statutory right of redemption. Those states provide by statute that a *right of redemption* exists in favor of the debtor after foreclosure of the mortgage or deed of trust. For a specified period, the borrower can pay to the foreclosure sale purchaser the amount secured by the mortgage at the time of the sale plus costs of the foreclosure. By making this payment within the time frame allowed under the statute, the property is redeemed; and the borrower is restored to title.

The mortgage or deed of trust must be reviewed carefully and its provisions explained to the borrower. It is important for the borrower to know whether or not she may sell the property to third parties and have those third parties assume (take over) the debt secured by the mortgage. Unless specifically restricted in the mortgage, it is presumed to be assumable. The question often arises whether, when the property is sold "subject to" the mortgage, the original borrower will be relieved from liability to her lender. The answer is no unless the lender agrees, and that rarely happens. As a result, the original debtor remains liable on the mortgage even though the property may be resold a number of times. The mortgagor's right of redemption, however, may permit her to regain title if some subsequent buyer defaults on the mortgage.

Usually, the mortgage contains an *acceleration clause* or a *due-on-sale clause* that gives the mortgagee the right to declare the entire indebtedness due and payable immediately if the property is sold or transferred without the mortgagee's consent. As a practical matter, the effect of this type of provision is to permit the mortgagee to approve the purchaser and possibly to negotiate new terms of the loan.

Most mortgages also contain a *receivership clause*, particularly when the property generates income. When any event of default occurs, this type of clause allows the mortgagee to apply to a court to have a receiver appointed for the property. If the application is approved, the receiver takes control of the property during the pendency of the foreclosure as well as any period of redemption.

Finally, if the property generates income, the mortgage may contain an *assignment of rents* (or a separate assignment of rents can be made). This provision assigns the rentals or other income of the property to the mortgagee if a default occurs. Because of the assignment, the mortgagee may demand immediately upon default that all income be paid directly to it in partial satisfaction of the indebtedness secured by the mortgage. An assignment of rents, together with a receivership clause, gives the mortgagee maximum protection by allowing it to take possession and to collect the rents in the event of default.

Mortgages frequently are referred to as first mortgages, second mortgages, and so on. The reference to *first* and *second* merely indicates the priority of the mortgages in relation to each other. Mortgages generally are governed by the same rules as are deeds in relation to priority. If the first mortgage is released of record, the second mortgage becomes the first mortgage in terms of priority without any further action by either the mortgagor or the mortgagee.

When a second mortgage is foreclosed, the first mortgage continues in place. It is unaffected by the foreclosure of a second mortgage. When a first mortgage is foreclosed and if the sale generates more money than is owed to the first mortgagee, the excess is paid to the second mortgagee. When a statutory right of redemption exists, the second mortgage has a right of redemption if the first mortgagee forecloses the mortgage. The second mortgagee can pay the same amount bid at the foreclosure sale and obtain the property. If the second mortgagee fails to exercise its right of redemption, the second mortgage is extinguished by the foreclosure of the first; and the purchaser at the foreclosure sale takes the property free and clear of the second mortgage.

A mortgage or deed of trust may contain a *partial release provision* if the parties anticipate that the promissory note will be paid down by the sale of portions of the property securing it. If the acquisition and development of a parcel of subdivided real estate is financed by using a mortgage or deed of trust, the developer usually wants to be able to sell individual lots free of the lien. In this situation, the mortgage or deed of trust can provide for partial releases as each lot is sold and payment of a certain sum is made to the lender.

The mortgage does not evidence the debt; it only secures it. The debt itself is evidenced by a promissory note. The promissory note may be payable either on demand or in equal, amortized installments of both principal and interest that are spread over the term of the loan. When the loan is to become due earlier than would be the case if equal, amortized installments were used, a balloon payment is required on the note's due date. To the extent that the value of the property exceeds the amount owed under the promissory note, one is said to have *equity* in the property.

Figure 9-5 on the following page gives an example of a type of promissory note that might be used in financing the purchase of real estate.

Figure 9-5
Promissory Note

IF THIS FORM IS USED IN A CONSUMER CREDIT TRANSACTION, CONSULT LEGAL COUNSEL.

THIS IS A LEGAL INSTRUMENT. IF NOT UNDERSTOOD, LEGAL, TAX OR OTHER COUNSEL SHOULD BE CONSULTED BEFORE SIGNING.

PROMISSORY NOTE
(Right to Cure)

U.S. $ __100,000.00__   Mountain Valley , Colorado
    August 1 , 19 96

1. FOR VALUE RECEIVED, the undersigned (Borrower) promise(s) to pay   JANET W. DOE

or order, (Note Holder) the principal sum of ---ONE HUNDRED THOUSAND DOLLARS ------------------

U.S. Dollars, with interest on the unpaid principal balance from __August 1__ , 19 96 until paid, at the rate of __five__ percent per annum. Principal and interest shall be payable at __55-E Coyote Circle,__ __Mountain Valley Subdivision, Colorado 80001__ , or such other place as the Note Holder may designate, in __two__ payments of FIFTY-THREE THOUSAND FIVE HUNDRED FORTY-ONE and 68/100------------------------------------ Dollars (U.S. $ __53,541.68__), due on the __first__ day of each __January__ , beginning __January 1__ , 19 97 . Such payments shall continue until the entire indebtedness evidenced by this Note is fully paid; provided, however, if not sooner paid, the entire principal amount outstanding and accrued interest thereon, shall be due and payable on __January 1, 1997__ , 19 ////.

2. Borrower shall pay to the Note Holder a late charge of __one__ % of any payment not received by the Note Holder within __ten__ days after the payment is due.

3. Payments received for application to this Note shall be applied first to the payment of late charges, if any, second to the payment of accrued interest specified above, and the balance applied in reduction of the principal amount hereof.

4. If any payment required by this Note is not paid when due, the entire principal amount outstanding and accrued interest thereon shall become due and payable at the option of the Note Holder (Acceleration) twenty days after notice of Acceleration has been given. This time period shall run concurrently with the right to cure, if any, allowed by the Uniform Consumer Credit Code. Such notice of Acceleration shall specify the amount of the nonpayment plus any unpaid late charges and other costs, expenses and fees due under this Note. Until the expiration of said twenty-day period, the Borrower may cure all defaults consisting of a failure to make required payments by tendering the amounts of all unpaid sums due at the time of tender, without Acceleration, as specified by the Note Holder in such notice. Cure restores the Borrower to his rights under this Note as though defaults had not occurred. Any defaults under this Note occurring within twelve months after the Note Holder has once given a notice of Acceleration, entitles Borrower to no right to cure, except as otherwise provided by law. The Note Holder shall be entitled to collect all reasonable costs and expense of collection and/or suit, including, but not limited to reasonable attorneys' fees.

5. Borrower may prepay the principal amount outstanding under this Note, in whole or in part, at any time without penalty. Any partial prepayment shall be applied against the principal amount outstanding and shall not postpone the due date of any subsequent payments or change the amount of such payments.

6. Borrower and all other makers, sureties, guarantors, and endorsers hereby waive presentment, notice of dishonor and protest, and they hereby agree to any extensions of time of payment and partial payments before, at, or after maturity. This Note shall be the joint and several obligation of Borrower and all other makers, sureties, guarantors and endorsers, and their successors and assigns.

7. Any notice to Borrower provided for in this Note shall be in writing and shall be given and be effective upon (1) delivery to Borrower or (2) mailing such notice by first-class U.S. mail, addressed to Borrower at the Borrower's address stated below, or to such other address as Borrower may designate by notice to the Note Holder. Any notice to the Note Holder shall be in writing and shall be given and be effective upon (1) delivery to Note Holder or (2) by mailing such notice by first-class U.S. mail, to the Note Holder at the address stated in the first paragraph of this Note, or to such other address as Note Holder may designate by notice to Borrower.

8. The indebtedness evidenced by this Note is secured by a Deed of Trust dated __August 1__ , 19 __96__ , and until released said Deed of Trust contains additional rights of the Note Holder. Such rights may cause Acceleration of the indebtedness evidenced by this Note. Reference is made to said Deed of Trust for such additional terms. Said Deed of Trust grants rights in the property identified as follows:

```
Unit A, a resubdivision of Lot 66, Block 1, Mountain Valley Subdivision,
Filing No. 1, County of Carbon, State of Colorado
```

Property address: __55-W Coyote Circle, Mountain Valley Subdivision__ ,

_____ , Colorado __80001__ _____

(CAUTION: SIGN ORIGINAL NOTE ONLY/RETAIN COPY)

IF BORROWER IS NATURAL PERSON(S):

__John W. Doe__

_____   doing business as _____

IF BORROWER IS CORPORATION:

ATTEST:

_____
Name of Corporation

_____   by _____
Secretary   President

(SEAL)

IF BORROWER IS PARTNERSHIP:

_____
Name of Partnership

by _____
General Partner

Borrower's address: __55-W Coyote Circle, Mountain Valley Subdivision, Colorado   80001__

KEEP THIS NOTE IN A SAFE PLACE. THE ORIGINAL OF THIS NOTE MUST BE EXHIBITED TO THE PUBLIC TRUSTEE IN ORDER TO RELEASE A DEED OF TRUST SECURING THIS NOTE.

RESPA   If the financing is federally related, compliance with the Real Estate Settlement Procedures Act (RESPA) is required. Financing is *federally related* if it covers any permanent loan secured by a lien on residential real property designed principally for the occupancy of from one to four families and that:

1)   is made by any federally insured lender, or

2)   is made, insured or assisted in any way by an agency of the federal government, or

3)   is intended to be sold to the Federal National Mortgage Association (FannyMae), the Government National Mortgage Association (GinnyMae), the Federal Home Loan Mortgage Corporation (FHA), or a financial institution from which it is to be purchased by the Federal Home Loan Mortgage Corporation, or

4)   is made by a "creditor" as defined in the Consumer Credit Protection Act who makes or invests in residential real estate loans aggregating more than $1,000,000 a year.

If RESPA applies, a ***uniform settlement statement*** must be used in connection with the closing, which form "shall conspicuously and clearly itemize all charges imposed upon the borrower and all charges imposed upon the seller in connection with the settlement." 12 U.S.C. § 2603. The uniform settlement statement form (the *HUD-1 form*) was developed by the Secretary of Housing and Urban Development and is contained in the agency's ***Regulation X***. This regulation also makes requirements with respect to providing good faith estimates of settlement costs, one-day advance inspection of the completed HUD-1 form upon request of the borrower, and other matters relating to the loan and the closing.

Environmental Issues

A relatively new but important issue in the purchase and sale of real estate is whether any environmental hazards are present on the property. Presumably, the real estate contract contains a *due diligence provision* to allow the purchaser to inspect the property and to object to any unacceptable conditions, including environmental hazards that may exist. The purchaser should assure herself that no such hazards are present. The lender likely will require an environmental impact study in connection with commercial properties.

Environmental hazards take a variety of forms. Any area used as a waste disposal site still may have toxic substances present. Gasoline service station sites present risks to any purchaser, including the risk of leaking underground storage tanks. A prospective purchaser may guard against these types of risks by conducting an environmental audit that includes, among other things, soil tests.

The legal risks of owning contaminated property also take a variety of forms. Toxic substances ultimately may find their way into subsurface waters and may pollute neighboring properties and streams. Under the common law doctrine of nuisance, any damage caused by this sort of pollution may become the subject of a claim for damages.

Regulatory agencies may also have jurisdiction to require the remediation (clean-up) of polluted properties, frequently at significant expense to the property owner. In particular, 42 U.S.C. § 9601, et. seq., the Comprehensive Environmental Response, Compensation, and Liability Act (CERCLA) or *Superfund law*, as it has come to be known, imposes liability for clean-up costs on anyone harboring or transporting hazardous substances. While CERCLA ordinarily is applied only to major hazardous waste sites, its provisions are broad and far-reaching.

Delivery of the Deed—The Closing

Once the title search is complete, closing documents are prepared. These documents include a deed and may include a promissory note with either a mortgage or deed of trust. A more complete discussion of deeds and examples of various forms of deeds are discussed more fully in Chapter 8 of this text.

For a deed to be effective in conveying title, it must be delivered to the grantee. Delivery is a matter of intent, rather than a matter of form. What is important is that the grantor unequivocally and unconditionally intends that the deed be actually or constructively in the possession of the grantee for the purpose of conveying title. The physical act of delivery is important only as evidence of the grantor's intent to deliver.

In addition, there is a technical requirement that the grantee accept the deed. The grantee's acceptance is presumed whenever title is beneficial. This technical rule permits a grantee to reject a deed when he does not wish to have title for some reason.

Although possession of the deed by the grantee raises a presumption that title has passed, the presumption can be rebutted by evidence of a contrary intent. Acknowledgment and recording of the deed likewise raise the presumption that title has passed, which is one of the reasons that deeds are recorded. Once recording occurs, the transaction is complete and is not affected by the loss or destruction of the deed.

Delivery can take place even when the deed does not pass into the physical possession of the grantee. For example, when handing the deed to the grantee, the grantor might produce the deed and announce to the grantee, "Now the land is yours." Although the deed was not handed to the grantee, it is clear from the grantor's declaration that title was intended to pass.

It is equally possible that the grantee can come into physical possession of the deed without delivery having occurred. For example, the grantor might hand it to the grantee and announce, "I am handing you this deed for safekeeping; I will tell you if and when I want you to have the property." In this situation, it is apparent that there is no present intent of the grantor that title pass.

Delivery cannot occur without a *present intent* that title pass. Thus, since the expressed intent in the last example is that title will pass in the future, if it passes at all, delivery is not effective. Delivery can be consummated at some time in the future, however. Continuing with the last example, if the grantor later hands a key to the grantee and says, "The house is now yours," delivery is consummated.

From time to time, a person signs a deed with the intent that delivery will take place at the time of that person's death. The person who has signed the deed may deliver it to the prospective grantee and announce, "I want you to have this property when I die." Or he may place the deed in a desk drawer or in some other place of safekeeping, telling the grantee that he has done so. Or the deed simply may be found at the time of the person's death. In none of these examples has delivery occurred. There was no present intent that title pass at the time the deed was signed. There can be no intent after death. In effect, the grantor attempted to devise the property but failed to comply with the requirements of a will.

The general rule is that any delivery is invalid if it is conditional or revocable, such as delivery intended to take effect only upon death. Courts go to great lengths, however, in search of facts to support a finding that the delivery was unconditional. For example, in Ferrell v. Stimson, 233 Iowa 1331, 11 N.W.2d 701 (1943), the decedent had executed a deed before her death and had given it to her housekeeper. She instructed the housekeeper to place it in a box in the decedent's closet and to mail it to the intended grantee upon the decedent's death. She told the intended grantee and others that she had disposed of her property in that fashion. At the decedent's death, the housekeeper mailed the deed as she had been instructed to do; and it was recorded. Relying mainly on the presumption of delivery that arises from recording, the court held that the decedent's heirs had failed to prove the delivery was conditioned upon death and, therefore, ineffective. The general rule remains, however, that when an unrecorded deed is found in a box or other place of safekeeping of the grantor after her death, no presumption of delivery exists. Without any further evidence of intent, the delivery is ineffective.

The Ferrell case also stands for the proposition that delivery to the grantor's agent may be effective if it is combined with declarations of the grantor's intent that title pass at present and not in the future. In effect, the court held that delivery to the housekeeper with instructions was a present delivery, similar to an escrow. Delivery to the grantee's agent caused title to pass on the theory that possession of the deed by the agent was possession by the grantee.

Delivery always is effective when it is made to an agent who is under control of neither party (known as an escrow agent or an escrow holder). Since the grantor has no control over the escrow agent, her delivery of the deed to that agent places the deed beyond her control. She effectively waives the right to recall it. Use of an escrow agent permits a valid conditional delivery, even when it is conditioned on the death of the grantor.

Ordinarily, of course, the escrow is connected to a real estate transaction incorporated into a binding contract for sale. Therefore, not only will the grantor have given up control of the deed, but she also will be legally obligated to convey title. That obligation will be enforceable by specific performance unless a provision states otherwise in the contract for sale.

Whether conveyance of title is done face to face or into escrow, the theory of the real estate contract is that the contractual obligations of the parties—to deliver the deed and to pay the purchase price—are performed simultaneously at a closing.

The real estate closing takes different forms in different parts of the United States. In the eastern, southern, and midwestern parts of the country, the closing more generally occurs in a traditional, face-to-face setting. The parties meet at a bank, title company, or attorney's office to sign documents and to deliver the purchase money.

As one moves toward the West Coast, the closing increasingly is done into *escrow*. When the real estate contract is signed, a copy is delivered to a title company or other escrow agent and an *escrow is opened*. The principals in the transaction then deposit with the escrow agent (according to written instructions to the agent) all of the items to be exchanged between the parties or to be delivered to third parties as required by the contract for sale. Typical instructions would be to record the deposited deed, to update the records following recording, and to deliver the deposited purchase money to the seller only upon issuance of a final policy of title insurance. When these things are done, the *escrow is closed*. In this type of closing, the seller and the purchase never meet during the closing process.

Whatever form the closing takes, its central document is the **settlement statement**. Usually, there are two settlement statements: the seller's settlement statement and the purchaser's settlement statement. A very basic settlement statement for the purchaser might look like this:

Purchaser's Settlement Statement

	Debit	Credit
Purchase price	100,000.00	
Earnest money		1,000.00
Taxes, prorated to closing		500.00
Recording fees	10.00	
Totals	100,010.00	1,500.00
Balance due from purchaser	98,510.00	

A very basic settlement statement for the seller might look like this:

Seller's Settlement Statement

	Debit	Credit
Purchase price		100,000.00
Earnest money	1,000.00	
Title insurance premium	500.00	500.00
Taxes, prorated to closing	500.00	
Totals	2,000.00	100,000.00
Balance owing to seller	98,000.00	

The purchaser receives credit for the earnest money deposited when the real estate contract was signed and for the seller's share of the taxes due after closing (assuming taxes are collected in arrears in that jurisdiction). He owes the balance of the purchase price, together with recording fees. The seller, on the other hand, receives the purchase price minus deductions for the earnest money already paid by the purchaser, for the seller's share of the taxes, and for the cost of title insurance.

Although not shown in the example, the purchaser also receives a credit for any special assessments or other similar charges owing to the local government for special municipal improvements, such as curbs and gutters. This credit is prorated for the year to the date of closing. He may be charged for the prorated share of the premium on any policy of insurance assigned to him, as well as for the prorated share of any condominium assessments paid in advance. If a tenant is in possession, the purchaser receives a credit for his proportionate share of the prepaid rent.

There usually are other charges that may include the closer's fee, appraisal fees, cost of survey, attorney's fee, and so forth. If financing is involved, the loan amount is shown as a credit to the purchaser. If the financing is federally related, a HUD-1 form also is prepared and signed. In many respects, the HUD-1 form repeats the information and calculations of the settlement statements.

FIRPTA   The Foreign Investment in Real Property Tax Act of 1980 (FIRPTA), 26 U.S.C. § 1445, requires that any transferee (grantee) of real property from a foreign person withhold ten percent of the purchase price and pay that amount to the federal Internal Revenue Service unless the transaction is exempt. The transaction is exempt under these circumstances:

1)   if the transferor furnishes to the transferee an affidavit by the transferor stating the transferor's United States taxpayer identification number and stating that the transferor is not a foreign person;

2)   if the transferee obtains from the Internal Revenue Service a "qualifying statement" indicating that the tax has been paid or that arrangements have been made for its payment; or

3)   if the property is being acquired as a residence at a price not exceeding $300,000.

It is essential that one of the listed exemptions apply in order to avoid substantial tax liability.

The closing may include the assumption of an existing debt. If so, one must order a loan assumption statement from the holder of the indebtedness well in advance of the closing. That statement is used to confirm the amount of the outstanding debt, the interest rate, and the terms of repayment. It also provides information concerning the reserve account or escrow account into which money is paid for property insurance and for real estate taxes. Those amounts are shown on the closing statement and are factored into the total amount owed by the purchaser. The amount of the loan assumption fee is stated as well. Loan assumptions are exempt from the requirements of the Real Estate Settlement Procedures Act of 1974 (RESPA). 24 C.F.R. § 3500.5(d)(1990).

Like-Kind Exchange   Rather than the purchaser's assuming an existing debt, the debt often is paid from the proceeds of the new loan. When this is the case, one must obtain from the holder of the existing loan a statement for payoff of the loan, including a statement of the per diem interest rate.

Instead of a cash sale, the parties may elect to exchange one property for another. An exchange may occur simply because the parties want to trade properties. More likely, it will occur as a like-kind exchange under § 1031 of the Internal Revenue Code. Thus, when business or investment property is exchanged for business or investment property, each party postpones the taxation of any gain that is realized from the exchange.

The simplest § 1031 exchange is consummated directly between two parties. However, a three-party exchange is used more often. It is rare that two parties, Alec and Brittany, for example, simultaneously wish to acquire each other's property. A three-party exchange might work this way: The third party, Tina, is a cash purchaser who agrees to buy Brittany's property and, simultaneously, to exchange it for Alec's property. In this way, Tina facilitates the exchange in the process acquiring the property she wants for cash.

A recent amendment to the Internal Revenue Code, I.R.C. § 1031(a)(3), permits a deferred exchange by which a seller escrows the sales price from an old property and later uses that money to buy a new, like-kind property. The like-kind property must be identified within 45 days, and the closing of the purchase of the like-kind property must occur within 180 days (but no later than the due date of that person's tax return).

Finally, a § 1031 exchange can be arranged when someone purchases a new, like-kind property and later sells the old property. When that happens, the new property is owned temporarily by a company formed especially for that purchase. When the old property ultimately is sold, a three-way exchange is arranged, using the specially formed company. The time limits are the same as those described above. Many companies are engaged in the § 1031 exchange business, usually in association with title companies.

Installment Sale Contract

When an *installment sale contract* is used, the purchaser agrees to pay the purchase price over a period of years in amortized installments. The purchaser is not entitled to receive a deed until the entire purchase price is paid. This type of arrangement also is known as a *contract for deed* in some jurisdictions.

An installment sale contract may be used when the purchaser does not qualify for financing; and, at the same time, when the seller does not wish to "take back" a note secured by a mortgage or deed of trust. This may be a matter of economics if the purchaser is able to pay only a small portion of the purchase price as the downpayment. In the event of a default, the seller runs the risk of having to foreclose against the property at a net loss to her. In other words, if a $10,000 downpayment is made and if a foreclosure occurs at a cost of $2,500, the seller nets $7,500 on the transaction. On the other hand, if she receives only

$1,000 as the downpayment and if a foreclosure occurs at a cost of $2,500, the seller loses $1,500 on the transaction.

In theory, the installment sale contract allows the parties to arrange financing without that type of risk to the seller. If the purchaser defaults under the terms of an installment sale contract, the seller merely terminates the agreement and, if necessary, evicts the purchaser.

For that reason, installment sale contracts were used widely to avoid the need for foreclosure upon default. Historically, no right of redemption existed in connection with installment contracts. Today, however, most courts require that installment sale contracts be foreclosed and that some period of redemption be given, usually the same period provided for mortgages or for deeds of trust. As a practical matter, therefore, there may be little difference between an installment sale contract and a mortgage since both require judicial foreclosure. Where a deed of trust may be used, it is preferable to an installment sale contract.

To avoid the risk of the purchaser's inability to obtain the deed upon payment of the full purchase price (because the seller is dead, is under disability, or is otherwise unavailable), an escrow can be created. The seller's deed is deposited at the outset with an escrow agent; payments are made to the escrow agent; and when the purchase price is paid in full, the escrow agent records the deed. A quitclaim deed (signed by the purchaser) also is deposited with the escrow agent so that if the escrow agent is notified of a default, the quitclaim deed may be recorded to restore the seller's title.

The legal assistant should, and usually does, perform an important role in completing the tasks associated with a closing. It is important that the closing documents be well organized, that deadlines be met, that procedural matters be explained to the participants in intelligible language, that every blank line on every document be accounted for (filled in or stricken out), and that every signature be acknowledged properly. The legal assistant often is better suited to these details than is the attorney; and if that is the case, the client benefits from the lower attorney fees connected with the closing.

Chapter 9 Quiz

Fill in each blank with the most correct word or phrase.

1. Evidence of title may be provided in the form of _____, a(n) _____, or a(n) _____.

2. _____ requires that, absent an exemption, any transferee of real property from a "foreign person" withhold a percentage of the purchase price.

3. Under a(n) _____ contract, the purchaser agrees to pay the purchase price over a period of years in amortized payments.

4. State bar associations have adopted _____ to determine whether or not title is marketable.

Circle the most correct answer.

5. True or False. To be enforceable against third parties, a deed or mortgage must be recorded; but liens, contracts, or leases are exempt from this requirement.

6. True or False. Inquiry notice issues arise from constructive knowledge of prior, unrecorded interests.

7. True or False. A contract for sale requires only a description of the parties and the price to be paid, but it may include more.

8. True or False. A purchase contract is a unilateral contract that obligates only the seller to perform, much like an option.

9. True or False. When a purchaser assumes the indebtedness under a mortgage, the seller is released from the indebtedness.

10. True or False. If a timely objection is not made to any unexcepted lien or encumbrance, the objection is waived.

11. True or False. When the seller makes a good faith effort to cure a title defect but is unable to do so, the purchaser ordinarily may terminate the contract; and the seller keeps the earnest deposit.

12. True or False. Compliance with the Real Estate Settlement Procedures Act of 1974 is required in all real estate sales.

13. True or False. A mortgage or deed of trust is the primary evidence of debt, and a promissory note is the primary security interest.

14. True or False. Only a breach in the covenant to make timely payments may result in foreclosure of a deed of trust.

15. True or False. A statutory right of redemption protects the borrower in a foreclosure proceeding.

16. True or False. An acceleration clause in a mortgage gives the mortgagee an opportunity to renegotiate the terms of the loan with the new buyer.

17. True or False. As it relates to RESPA, federally related financing includes financing made by any federally insured lender and requires a HUD-1 settlement statement.

18. True or False. The provisions of CERCLA apply only to major hazardous waste sites, even though its provisions are broad.

19. True or False. Failure to obtain an exemption from FIRPTA may result in substantial tax liability.

20. True or False. The purpose of a like-kind exchange under § 1031 of the Internal Revenue Code is to defer estate tax.

21. True or False. Installment sales contracts avoid the process of foreclosure and the period of redemption in most jurisdictions.

22. True or False. One never should accept a less than perfect title to real property.

23. True or False. Although a quitclaim deed contains no warranties of title, one must own or must believe she owns the property conveyed; or the conveyance is fraudulent.

24. Helenmae and Irvin, brother and sister, owned Blackacre as joint tenants. They became embroiled in a family disagreement and stopped speaking to each other. Irvin was worried that when he died, Helenmae would own Blackacre as the surviving joint tenant. He decided to give his undivided

share of Blackacre to his daughter Lynn. However, since he had no income other than his share of the money derived from crops grown on the farm, he didn't want the conveyance to take effect before he died. He had his lawyer prepare a deed to convey Blackacre to Lynn. He dated and signed it before a notary public, and he placed the deed in his safe deposit box. Lynn found the deed after Irvin's death, and she recorded it. No one recorded Irvin's death certificate. Does Lynn have an interest in Blackacre?

1. Yes. One joint tenant may recover his interest without the consent of the other joint tenant.

2. No. There was no present intent that title pass, and delivery did not occur.

3. Yes. Delivery may take place even though the deed has not passed into the physical possession of the grantee.

4. Yes. The acknowledgment of the deed before a notary public creates a presumption of delivery.

Chapter 10
NATURAL RESOURCES

Natural resources are divided into two groups. They are liquid (water, oil, and gas) and solid (minerals). Liquid resources sometimes are analogized to things *ferae naturae*, which helps to understand the legal rules that relate to them. At common law, things *ferae naturae* (of a wild nature) included animals, birds, and fish. Because they were wild, they belonged to no one in particular or to everyone in general. Only at the point of capture did a wild thing acquire an owner and become the property of that owner.

Water, oil, and gas are similar to things *ferae naturae*. Like wild animals, they have a power of self-transmission. They belong to no one until someone takes exclusive dominion over them. Much of the law of water rights, oil, and gas is devoted to a determination of the point at which those resources move from public domain to private ownership. For purposes of this Review Manual, water is discussed as a separate topic; and oil and gas are discussed with the topic of solid minerals.

Water Rights

There are two distinct approaches to the law of water rights in the United States. The western states, including Texas, Oklahoma, Kansas, Nebraska, the Dakotas, and states to the west of these states, have statutory systems of prior appropriation for water rights. Under this type of statutory system, ownership of water rights is determined by judicial or administrative process, and ownership is assigned a priority based on the purpose for which the water is to be used. This system is dictated by the arid climate in each of these states and the lack of sufficient water for all purposes.

The remaining states follow the common law doctrine of riparian water rights. One who is accustomed to the western system of prior appropriation would describe the riparian doctrine as the absence of any system at all. In the riparian states, as in England, water is plentiful; and little case law has developed. Basically, water is there for all to use on a "first come, first served" basis.

The lawyers of early England gave little, if any, thought to water. Only with the advent of the Industrial Revolution and the use of water in industry did it become necessary to address the issue in England. The issue first was addressed in the United States when the early nineteenth century U. S. Supreme Court borrowed the riparian doctrine from French law. Only later did the doctrine become part of the English common law.

Riparian is a Latin term that means "of or relating to a river." It is different from the term *littoral*, which refers to the shore of an ocean or a lake. The essence of the riparian doctrine is that water—or the right to use it—belongs to the owner of the riverbank by which the water passes. Stated otherwise, a parcel of land is riparian when any part of it is contiguous to a stream and when the balance of it is within the watershed and within a reasonable distance of the stream. Thus, a portion of the land may lose its riparian character if it is severed from that portion of the parcel which is contiguous to the stream.

Unless the water has been captured by being drawn out of a stream or lake or unless the water is part of a lake or pond surrounded entirely by one person's land, the landowner does not own the water itself. Instead, the landowner has only a right to use it, such as by drinking it, swimming in it, fishing in it, or irrigating with it.

The riparian doctrine has two subdoctrines or theories: the natural flow theory and the reasonable use theory. The great majority of American jurisdictions subscribe to the *reasonable use* theory, by which the downstream owner's rights are subordinate to the reasonable use or reasonable exercise of the upstream owner's rights. Under that theory, the downstream owner is not entitled to the full and natural flow of the stream; and natural uses, such as household consumption, are given priority over artificial uses, such as industrial and irrigation uses.

Jurisdictions that subscribe to the *natural flow* theory (England and some American jurisdictions), hold that the downstream owner is entitled to the full or natural flow of the water passing by his property without significant alteration. Some have suggested that the differences between the two theories are differences of water availability and of the development of water law doctrine. In other words, the natural flow theory works fine until landowners compete for the same water supply, necessitating an adjustment of their respective interests. The sensible adjustment of those interests is the reasonable use theory.

Still different rules may apply, depending upon the nature of the water supply. The natural flow theory is applied more easily when *ground water* (water that accumulates underground) or water confined in an *aquifer* (water-bearing rock) is considered. The natural flow theory entitles the surface owner to the unrestricted use of this "captured" water for the benefit of her own land and of the land of others. The only limit on her right is the restriction that she may not maliciously injure her neighbor.

Surface water is water that flows onto one's land outside of a natural channel and presents yet another problem. When water is simply standing on one's land, the natural desire is to get rid of it rather than to use it. Some courts adhere to the *common enemy doctrine,* which gives the landowner an unrestricted right to fend off the water in any way that he can. A variation of that rule is the *reasonable use rule,* which requires the landowner to act only in such a way as not to damage a neighbor's property unnecessarily.

Finally, with respect to surface water, some courts subscribe to the *Roman law rule* of natural drainage. Under that rule, the lower landowner must receive water flowing naturally from higher land and may redirect that flow as reasonably necessary; but the lower landowner cannot obstruct the flow entirely.

In the western states, where the doctrine of prior appropriation is applied, water law has been reduced entirely to statutory rule. To illustrate that doctrine, we review water law in the State of Colorado, the source of much of the water supply in the West.

By Colorado constitutional provision, "the water of every natural stream, not heretofore appropriated," is "declared to be the property of the public, and the same is dedicated to the use of the people of the state, subject to appropriation." By statute, "all water in or tributary to natural surface streams" is subjected to appropriation. Included is all water, whether well water, spring water or surface water hydraulically connected with a surface stream.

Under Colorado statute, *water right* means "a right to use in accordance with its priority a certain portion of the waters of the state by reason of the appropriation of the same." Thus, any person may appropriate water for a beneficial use. *Appropriation* is some act calculated to bring water under control, such as the construction of a dam and a ditch to divert the flow of water from a stream. Water appropriated today, however, will have a very low priority or *junior priority* inasmuch as most flows of water were appropriated and adjudicated in the nineteenth century.

There are two general types of water rights: storage rights and direct flow rights. **Storage rights** permit the storage of water in reservoirs. **Direct flow rights** are rights to divert water for particular uses, including irrigation, industrial uses, agricultural uses, domestic uses, municipal uses, and so forth.

The flow of water is measured in cubic feet per second (cfs). Storage of water is measured in *acre feet*. Thus, a direct flow right might be the right to divert 1.92 cfs from a certain creek. The point of diversion is located by a metes-and-bounds description. A storage right might be the right to store 1,000 acre feet of water in a certain reservoir. The reservoir also is described by metes and bounds.

Before 1969, any court of general jurisdiction in Colorado had authority to adjudicate a water right. Since 1969, seven special water courts have been created, each having jurisdiction over a particular water basin. The judges who sit in those courts are not specially trained. Rather, they are regular district court judges who hear water matters as a part of their regular judicial duties.

A notice of application to the water court is published in the local newspaper and in monthly resumes that are maintained by the water clerk and are mailed to subscribers, (persons having an interest in water rights adjudication, usually by virtue of their ownership of rights). Any person may file a statement of opposition to an application, which places issues into contention. Referees, who have special expertise in the water rights area, are used extensively to determine those issues.

When a water right is adjudicated, it is given two crucial dates. It is given a *date of appropriation*, which is a determination of the date on which the act of appropriation first occurred. That date is established by the testimony of witnesses like any other civil matter. The other date assigned to the water right is the *date of adjudication*. Both dates are important in determining priorities. Earlier adjudications have priority over later ones, even though the later adjudication may carry an earlier date of appropriation. The result is less confusing than one might think since most adjudications occurred in large groups in particular years during the last quarter of the nineteenth century.

The day-to-day administration of water rights priorities is carried out by administrative officials that range from the state engineer at the top to local water commissioners at the bottom of the system. Each of the seven divisions comprising the seven water basins has a division engineer overseeing the local commissioners. Those officials have authority to shut down the diversion of water based upon the priority of the rights involved. Water is not rationed or prorated; it simply is turned off. Theoretically, in an extreme drought, water would be diverted only for the most senior appropriators, and others would go without. The purpose for which the water is diverted is immaterial. If the senior appropriator is entitled to use its water to generate and to sell power, it may do so even when more junior appropriators of water for domestic use are turned off.

Other matters are handled by the water courts. Since most flows of water already have been adjudicated, these other matters take up most of the time of those courts. The major business of the water courts involves the adjudication of changes of use and points of diversion.

Uses of water and points of diversion often are changed as a result of transfers of the rights. For example, a resort area may need additional water to make snow (an industrial use) or to water a golf course (an irrigation use). A mining company fifty miles downstream may have gone out of business and may be willing to sell its senior, industrial use rights to the resort area. Because the water would be used fifty miles upstream, a "change in point of diversion" would be required. Because some of the water would be put to a different use (irrigation versus industrial), a "change in use" also would be required. Such changes are permitted if it is established that the water could be diverted fifty miles upstream and used for a different purpose without causing damage to the owners of rights in between.

Water courts also deal with plans for augmentation. Using the previous example, it might be necessary to protect the intervening owners by providing some storage of water to maintain or to augment stream flows. A plan for augmentation might be devised by the applicant whereby some of the direct flow rights are changed to storage rights to permit the storage of the water. The plan then would require that a certain volume of water be stored so that it can be released when necessary for augmentation purposes.

Water wells are administered separately but are part of the overall appropriation system. Wells are not permitted unless unappropriated water is available to supply them. However, small-capacity "exempt wells" are presumed by statute not to cause injury to senior appropriators and are routinely permitted.

Water rights in Colorado are an interest in real estate appurtenant to the land which they benefit. Since they are an appurtenance, they are conveyed by a deed to the land without express reference to them. They also may be conveyed separately, and they may be abandoned through nonuse. Accordingly, determining ownership of water rights can be difficult when deeds do not describe specifically the rights conveyed or when the rights have not been used. As a matter of practice, ownership of water rights is never warranted. As a practical matter, the records of the State Engineer determine water rights use most reliably by identifying the property benefited by the rights.

Some western states follow the *Colorado Doctrine*, which eliminates the riparian doctrine altogether. In those states, ownership of a water right may be vested in a nonriparian owner. Other states follow the *California Doctrine*, combining a system of prior appropriation with the riparian doctrine. In those states, the rights of appropriators and riparian owners must be reconciled, with the riparian owners likely having priority over those with permits by appropriation.

Whether the riparian doctrine or the prior appropriation doctrine is in effect, water rights also are subject to the rights of the public as well as to federal and other state laws. Navigable waterways (streams and rivers determined to be navigable by the federal government) necessarily are open to public use, including boating, fishing, and other recreational uses. The definition of the term navigable waterways is so broad that it includes nearly all waterways tributary to interstate rivers. Any construction in or about such a waterway may be subject to federal regulation. Finally, both state and federal laws affect stream quality and the liability of persons who pollute those streams.

Mineral Rights

The law of oil and gas is analogous generally to the natural flow theory, discussed above with respect to underground water, which holds that ownership of land carries with it the unrestricted right to use the water captured below the surface. Thus, a majority of those states dealing with oil and gas issues adhere to the *ownership-in-place doctrine*. Under that doctrine, ownership of the oil and gas in place belongs to the surface owner, subject to the possibility of escape.

Part of that doctrine is the *rule of capture*, which entitles the surface owner not only to the oil and gas in place beneath her land, but also to the oil and gas which is drawn from adjoining land through the production process. In other words, when a surface owner drills into and captures the oil and gas contained in an underground formation, that surface owner may draw out all of the oil and gas even though some of it is located below someone else's land. The oil and gas mineral interest comprehended by the natural flow theory is separate and distinct from the surface interest and may be leased or conveyed separately.

Other jurisdictions subscribe to the **exclusive right doctrine**. According to that doctrine, the surface owner is not the literal owner of the oil and gas in place but, rather, has an exclusive right to extract and to take possession of the unproduced oil and gas. Those jurisdictions hold that this right, including the right to go upon the surface and to erect structures to conduct exploration, constitutes a *profit a prendre* that burdens the surface estate.

The law relating to solid minerals might have developed in a similar fashion except that hard rock minerals historically have belonged largely to the government and have not been part of the fee simple interest. In England, for example, all deposits of gold and silver belonged to the monarch as an incident of the right of coinage. However, the monarch also had complete power to dispose of the mineral interest; and in the United States, most of the royal charters in the eastern states expressly included all mines, subject to a twenty percent rent or royalty. In Spain, all mines belonged to the monarch; and this rule remained in force as Mexico succeeded to the Spanish lands of the southwestern United States. Under French law, mines also belonged to the government.

As the United States succeeded to the interests of those various governments, the subsurface mineral interest became a part of the fee interest subject, however, to separate lease or conveyance. The major part of the land ceded by those governments, however, was unoccupied; and the mineral interest as well as the surface interest became the property of the federal government. As gold and silver were discovered in California, in Colorado and later in Nevada, it became necessary to develop rules with respect to production of those minerals on federal lands.

Initially, the rules were a common law of the mining camps. In other words, the miners themselves devised rules with respect to the location of mining claims. Each mining camp established mining courts to determine disputes related to mining claim location. Finally, the Act of May 10, 1872, now 30 U.S.C. § 22, *et seq.*, was adopted by Congress and largely codified the laws of the mining camps. That statute has remained in effect ever since.

The Act of 1872 applies to "gold, silver, cinnabar, lead, tin, copper, or other valuable deposits." Under provisions of the Act, mining claims upon veins or lodes of quartz or other rock bearing those minerals are limited in size to 1,500 feet along the vein or lode and are limited to 300 feet from each side of the vein or lode. Each *lode claim*, therefore, takes the form of a parallelogram along the outcropping of the mineral-bearing rock. 30 U.S.C. § 23. *Placer claims*, which are loose deposits of minerals on the surface, rather than the minerals in place, generally are limited to twenty acres of no particular form. 30 U.S.C. § 35.

Figure 10-1
Lode Claim Map

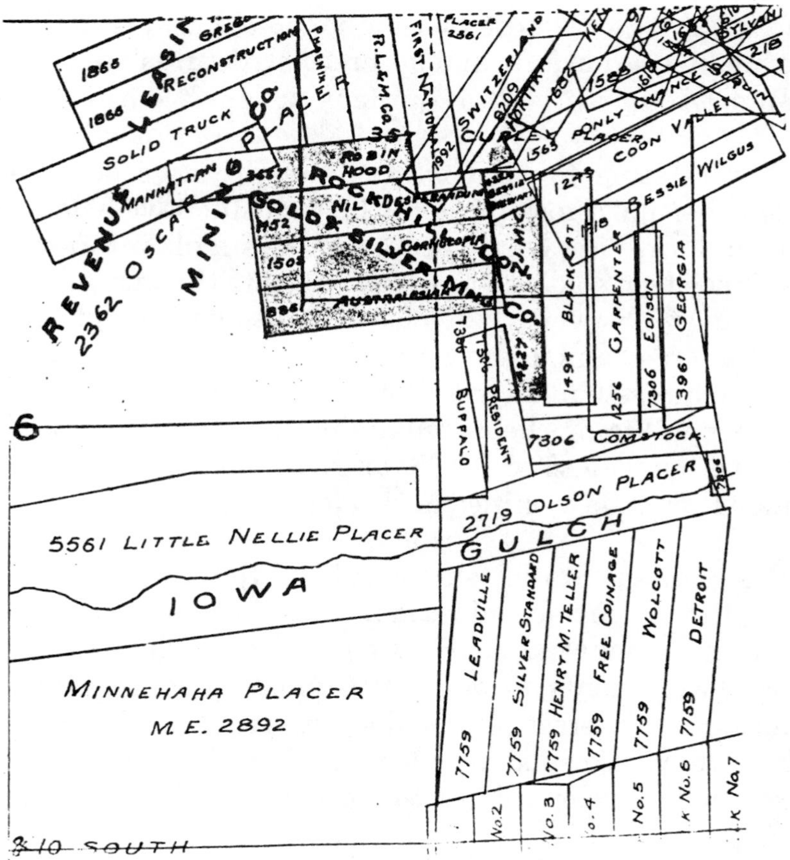

A mining claim is located by filing a location certificate with the office where deeds and other instruments are recorded. The location certificate must contain the names of the locators, the date of the location, and a description of the claim. The corners of the claim, as set through the process of surveying it, must be marked distinctly on the ground. Once the claim is located, annual work having a value of $100 must be performed to maintain possessory rights in the claim. 30 U.S.C. § 28. Once $500 of labor has been performed, the patent to the land, conveying fee simple title, may be applied for and issued. 30 U.S.C. § 29.

Regardless of how the mineral estate is subjected to ownership, it is a separate estate that may be separately conveyed or leased. Once the mineral estate is separately conveyed or is reserved in a conveyance, it is *severed* from the land. Thereafter, it is excepted from the conveyance of the fee estate. Most exploration of minerals is by lease of the severed mineral estate, with the lessor reserving a rental or a royalty of a certain percentage of the minerals produced. In the case of oil and gas, that percentage typically is one-eighth or 12.5%.

Much of the law of mining deals with the relationship of the mineral estate to the surface estate and adjoining property interests. As has been discussed, oil and gas may be drawn from under the surface of adjoining properties in the production process. Similarly, the right to mine a vein or lode also carries with it the right to prospect (follow) the vein or lode beneath adjoining properties. Moreover, the surface estate is subject to a servitude in favor of the mineral estate, permitting discovery and production. The mineral estate, in turn, is obligated to provide subjacent support to the surface estate.

Chapter 10 Quiz

Fill in each blank with the most correct word or phrase.

1. Water, oil and gas have a power of _____ _____ and can be said to be things *ferae naturae.*

2.   The _____ holds that the downstream owner is entitled to the full flow of the water passing by his property without significant interference.

3.   The _____-_____ theory holds that the downstream owner is not entitled to the full and natural flow of the stream, and natural uses are given priority over artificial uses.

4.   An act calculated to bring water under control is a(n) _____.

5.   The two crucial dates in determining the priorities of water rights are the date of _____ and the date of _____.

6.   The doctrine that holds that ownership of the oil and gas in place rests in the surface owner, subject to the possibility of escape is the _____.

7.   Loose deposits of minerals on the surface, as opposed to minerals in place, are _____ claims.

Choose the best answer.

8.   True or False. A portion of a parcel of land severed from the portion of the parcel contiguous to the stream retains its riparian nature.

9.   True or False. Natural resources are divided into liquid resources and solid minerals.

10.   True or False. In locations with an abundance of water, use of it did not become an issue until the Industrial Revolution.

11.   True or False. Water rights are subject to federal and state law, but exempt from the rights of the public.

12.   True or False. The flow of water is measured in acre feet.

13.   True or False. "Riparian" means relating to the shore of an ocean.

14.   True or False. Priority of a water right is always given to the right with the earlier appropriation date.

15.   True or False. Surface water is any water which is not an ocean.

16. True or False. The water in a pond which is completely surrounded by the property of the landowner belongs to the landowner.

17. True or False. Direct flow rights are rights to direct the flow of water into reservoirs.

18. True or False. Irrigation is termed an artificial use of water.

19. True or False. The nature of the water supply may determine which rules apply.

20. True or False. Only water rights may be conveyed separately from real property.

21. True or False. Surface water may be subject to the common enemy doctrine.

22. True or False. Ownership of water rights is never warranted.

23. True or False. Most western states have adopted the riparian doctrine in regulating water rights.

24. True or False. The adjudication of water rights today usually involves change in use and change in points of diversion.

25. True or False. It is possible that during an extreme drought, water in prior appropriation states would be diverted only for the most senior appropriators regardless of the use for which it is intended; and others, even domestic users, would go without.

26. True or False. The California Doctrine of water rights combines a system of prior appropriation with the riparian doctrine.

27. True or False. The Act of May 10, 1872, codified the laws of mining camps but pertains only to gold and silver.

28. True or False. The size and shape of mining claims are determined by federal statute.

29. True or False. The surface estate is subject to a servitude in favor of the mineral estate.

30. True or False. After a mining claim is located, $500 of annual labor must be performed to maintain possessory rights in the claim.

31. True or False. Patent to a mining claim may be applied for but will not be issued until $5,000 of labor has been performed.

32. True or False. Unlike oil and gas, the right to mine a vein or lode does not include the right to follow the vein or lode beneath adjoining properties.

33. A wild thing acquires an owner at the point of:

    1. capture
    2. discovery
    3. filing a claim with the BLM
    4. b and c

34. The two, distinct approaches to the law of water rights in the United States are the:

    1. necessary doctrine and use doctrine
    2. industrial revolution doctrine and *ferae naturae* doctrine
    3. prior appropriation doctrine and riparian doctrine
    4. none of the above

35. Simply stated, the riparian doctrine holds that the:

    1. right to use water belongs to the owner of the riverbank by which the water passes
    2. owner of land contiguous to a stream owns the water
    3. downstream owner is entitled to the full flow of water passing by his property without significant interference
    4. all of the above

36. Two subdoctrines of the riparian doctrine are:

    1. the self-transmission theory and the *ferae naturae* theory
    2. the contiguous land theory and the watershed theory
    3. the placer theory and the minerals-in-place theory
    4. the natural flow theory and the reasonable use theory

37. A parcel of land is deemed riparian when:

    a.   any part of it is contiguous to a stream, with the balance of it within the watershed and within a reasonable distance of the stream

    b.   the downstream owner is entitled to the full flow of the water passing by his property without significant interference

    c.   the downstream owner is not entitled to the full flow of the water passing by his property

    d.   all of the above

38. According to the exclusive right doctrine, the surface owner is not literally the owner of the oil and gas in place but, rather, has an exclusive right to:

    a.   extract and to reduce to her possession the unproduced oil and gas

    b.   reasonable use

    c.   protection under the natural flow theory

    d.   to invoke the Common Enemy doctrine

39. Under the ownership-in-place theory, the surface owner is entitled to:

    a.   only the oil and gas in place beneath his land

    b.   only the oil and gas that is drawn from adjoining land through the production process

    c.   only solid minerals in place beneath his land

    d.   the oil and gas beneath his land and the oil and gas drawn from adjoining land during the production process

Chapter 11
REAL ESTATE LITIGATION

Any discussion of real estate litigation requires an understanding of the difference between the *in rem* jurisdiction and the *in personam* jurisdiction of a court. For purposes of this chapter, jurisdiction is defined as the basis on which a judge exercises her authority in a particular case. Jurisdiction, either in personam or in rem, gives the judge the power to decide a case and to enforce that decision once it is made.

Jurisdiction

Ordinarily, the jurisdiction of a court is ***in personam*** (over the person). Thus, when Patricia files suit against Donald, alleging that Donald struck Patricia and should be required to pay damages to her, the court exercises in personam jurisdiction. The court acts only against the person of Donald. Donald is brought before the court by service of process; the summons, and usually the complaint, must be served on Donald. Otherwise, Donald is under no obligation to appear and file an answer. If the court reaches a decision in favor of Patricia, it enters a judgment against Donald personally, which means that Donald is personally obligated to pay it.

In Rem Jurisdiction   *In rem* jurisdiction, on the other hand, is jurisdiction over a thing. For example, a court has in rem jurisdiction over a marital relationship when it enters a decree of dissolution. In addition and more important for the purposes of this text, a court may exercise in rem jurisdiction over real property. When that happens, the court acquires jurisdiction of the property by service of process on each person who may have an interest in it and by the presence of the property within the geographical area of the court (in rem jurisdiction). In a state court, the court may exercise in rem jurisdiction over property within its state boundary lines, for instance. When the court reaches its decision, the judgment affects the property directly, such as by clearing title to the property.

When in rem jurisdiction is exercised over real property, it is critical that all interests in the property be before the court. If any interest is not before the court, the court's ultimate decision cannot be fully effective. Therefore, it is just as important to obtain current title information before an in rem proceeding is filed as it is to obtain current title information when the property is purchased. Based upon the title information, whether by title commitment or by abstract of title, all persons must be named as plaintiffs (or petitioners) or as defendants (or respondents) in the proceeding.

Service by Publication   When in rem jurisdiction is exercised over real property, service of process generally can be made by publication if personal service cannot be obtained within the state. In other words, the rules of civil procedure of state courts typically provide that service either by mail or by publication is allowed "in cases affecting specific property or status." Upon filing of a verified motion with the court that personal service may not be obtained within the state, either because the defendant is a nonresident or because the defendant cannot be found within the state, the court may order the summons to be published, with copies of the summons to be mailed to the last known address or addresses of the person or persons to be served.

When service by publication is relied upon to acquire jurisdiction, however, the Due Process Clauses of the Fifth and the Fourteenth Amendments come into play. Those clauses provide that no person may be deprived of life, liberty, or property "without due process of law." The United States Supreme Court has held in a series of cases, commencing with Mullane v. Central Bank & Trust Co., 339 U.S. 305 (1950), that *substituted service*, that is, any service other than personal service, must be reasonably calculated to provide actual notice. In Mullane, the court stated that:

> When notice is a person's due process, process which is a mere gesture is not due process. The means employed must be such as one desirous of actually informing the absentee might reasonably adopt to accomplish it. The reasonableness and hence the constitutional validity of any chosen method may be defended on the ground that it is in itself reasonably certain to inform those affected, . . . or, where conditions do not reasonably permit such notice, that

the form chosen is not substantially less likely to bring home notice than the other of the feasible and customary substitutes.

339 U.S. at 314-15. Consequently, whenever in rem jurisdiction is invoked and when service is obtained through publication, two cardinal rules evolve. The first, already discussed, is that all persons must be before the court, either as plaintiff or as defendant. The second rule, which emanates from the <u>Mullane</u> case, is that reasonable efforts must be made to learn the whereabouts of each of those persons; and wherever possible, actual notice must be provided.

Quiet Title Suit

The purpose of the quiet title proceeding is to make title to property marketable. Ordinarily, marketability can be accomplished by obtaining corrective deeds. In some cases, curative statutes provide a period of time after which a particular defect, such as a defective acknowledgment, may be ignored. From time to time, however, title cannot be corrected in those ways; and only a suit to quiet title will suffice to make the title marketable. Such a proceeding is filed under the civil procedure rule for actions concerning real estate, usually Rule 105 of the state rules of civil procedure *(check the specific rule number in your state)*.

The first step in bringing a quiet title suit is an examination of the property's title to determine what defect or defects must be cured and which persons must be named to cure those defects. A conservative approach is followed as a general rule. The theory is that since the proceeding is being filed anyway, one may as well include every conceivable defect, even those cured by statute.

A quiet title suit also may be filed to resolve boundary line issues. When a house encroaches on an adjacent parcel and adverse possession is relied upon to establish ownership of the portion of the parcel encroached upon, a quiet title suit is filed. In that situation, it also is necessary to examine the title of the adjacent parcel (the one adversely possessed). For example, if Patrick's house has encroached for more than the statutory period for adverse possession upon an adjacent parcel owned by Donna, Donna will be a defendant in the quiet title action. Title to Donna's property must be examined as well; and if any defect in that title is discovered, appropriate parties must be added to cure the defect.

The rule is that one must rely upon the strength of one's own title and not on the weakness of the defendant's title. In other words, one must be prepared to prove the marketability of one's own title. It is not sufficient to show that there is a defect in the defendant's title.

Once the parties to the proceeding have been determined, they must be aligned. In other words, one must determine whether they will be plaintiff or defendant. Ordinarily, the plaintiffs will be the persons claiming ownership of the property, and all other persons potentially having an adverse interest will be the defendants. Circumstances may arise, however, that make it necessary to name involuntary plaintiffs. For example, a tenant in common who does not join in the proceeding voluntarily, would have to be named as an involuntary plaintiff.

It may be possible to eliminate parties by excepting certain interests in the property. For example, if the property is subject to a mortgage, it usually would be the practice to except the mortgage rather than to join the mortgagee as a plaintiff. That is accomplished, for instance, by altering a description of lot 1, block 2, to read "lot 1, block 2, EXCEPT mortgage recorded in book 830 at page 29."

Unknown parties usually will be added, particularly when dealing with less than recent title defects. It is possible that some person with a potential adverse interest will have died or will have assigned or conveyed that interest. If that person has died, he will have left heirs or devisees whose identities are unknown. If the person has assigned or conveyed the interest without recording the assignment or conveyance, the identity of the assignee or grantee will be unknown. In theory at least, those persons nevertheless must be before the court. Because they are unknown persons, they are specifically designated as "unknown persons having an interest" in the proceeding.

The complaint or petition will contain allegations that the defendants "claim some right, title, or interest" or words of similar import and will ask that those persons be required to set forth the nature of their claims so that a determination of their validity may be made. The court will be asked to enter a decree determining that the defendants have no right, title, or interest in the property and forever enjoining them from asserting any such interest.

Once the complaint or petition is filed, efforts must be made to locate the defendants. To the extent that they cannot be located (the unknown defendants obviously never can be located), they must be served by publication. This is accomplished by filing a motion with the court, describing the efforts to locate those defendants or stating that the defendants are unknown and requesting an order to permit publication.

Publication of the summons should be straightforward. The summons should describe the property to provide notice to the defendants of what property is involved.

The rule that provides for publication also prescribes publication "for four weeks" or for some other time period. It is important to remember that when publication is required for four weeks, for example, this means that publication must occur once a week for five weeks; if it is published only four times, the time period covered is only three weeks. Studying a calendar makes this principle clear. If the first publication is on the first day of the month, the last publication will be on the 29th day of the month, which is four weeks later. But the notice will have appeared on the first of the month, the eighth of the month, the fifteenth of the month, the 22nd of the month, and the 29th of the month. That is five times. Stated otherwise, there must be a publication of the summons at both the beginning and the end of the four-week publication period.

Publication must be made in an official newspaper that has a general circulation in the area where the court is located. Requirements for an official newspaper may vary but generally include regular publication for a stated period of time and a second-class mailing permit. When the publication is completed, a *proof of publication* is filed with the court. This generally is done by affidavit of the publisher. Publishers of official newspapers routinely provide such affidavits upon request.

When the publication is complete and the necessary time has passed, the plaintiff may go to court to *prove up* her title. The issue may be hotly contested, particularly when adverse possession is an element of proof. More often, the defendants fail to appear in the case, are in default, and a quiet title decree is entered as a matter of course. Recording the quiet title decree makes the title marketable.

As stated earlier, quiet title suits most frequently are used to correct title defects. For example, if the grantor of a deed signed it incorrectly and cannot be located to sign a corrected deed, that person is made a defendant in a lawsuit. This allows her to assert any continuing interest in the property that she may have. If she has none, her potential interest is *quieted*; and the defect can be disregarded.

An action to quiet title may be used to provide record title when title previously was based solely upon adverse possession. Such an action also is used after issuance of a tax deed to eliminate the interests of persons under disability, so as to provide immediately marketable title.

Figure 11-1 is an example of a quiet title complaint in which the plaintiff relies on adverse possession.

Figure 11-1
Quiet Title Complaint

IN THE DISTRICT COURT, COUNTY OF SUPERIOR, STATE OF WHEREVER
Case No. _____

COMPLAINT PURSUANT TO RULE 105

PRISCILLA PARSONS,
          Plaintiff,
vs.

DANIEL DINGLE; AND ALL UNKNOWN PERSONS WHO CLAIM ANY INTEREST IN THE
SUBJECT MATTER OF THIS ACTION,
          Defendants.

COMES NOW the Plaintiff and as a claim pursuant to Rule 105, W.R.C.P., states as follows:

1. Plaintiff is the owner in fee simple and in possession of the following described real property located in the County of Superior and State of Wherever:

> Lot 4, Block 20, Universal Heights, City of Superior, County of Superior, State of Wherever, EXCEPT Deed of Trust recorded October 20, 1995, in book 678 at page 742, ("the real property").

2. The possession of Plaintiff has been actual, open, notorious, hostile, continuous, and uninterrupted for more than eighteen years.

3. Defendants claim or may claim some right, title, estate, or interest in or to the real property adverse to Plaintiff; such claims are without foundation or right.

WHEREFORE, Plaintiff prays as follows:

1. For a complete adjudication of the rights of all parties to this action with respect to the real property.

2. For a decree requiring Defendant and all persons claiming under him to set forth the nature of their claims to the real property.

3. That the decree declare and adjudge that Plaintiff owns in fee simple, and is entitled to quiet and peaceful possession of, the real property and that Defendant and all persons claiming under him have no estate, right, title, lien, or interest in or to the real property or any part thereof.

4. That the decree permanently enjoin Defendant and all persons claiming under him from asserting any adverse claim to Plaintiff's title to the real property.

5. That Plaintiff be awarded her costs.

6. For such other relief as may be proper.

Dated this ___ day of _____, 1996.

PRISCILLA PARSONS, Plaintiff

By_____
Counsel & Counsel
121 Main Street
Superior, WH 98101
(809) 911-0000
Attorneys for Plaintiff

Eminent Domain

Eminent domain proceedings, also known as condemnation proceedings, are instituted when a governmental agency seeks to acquire real property or some interest in property (such as a temporary or permanent easement) for a public purpose.

Ordinarily, the first step in the eminent domain process is negotiation. In fact, an effort to acquire the property voluntarily by negotiation and purchase is a prerequisite to the filing of a petition in eminent domain in many jurisdictions.

Like other proceedings involving real property, obtaining evidence of title is essential to assure that all persons with an interest in the property are joined. In other words, one of the goals of the eminent domain proceeding is to obtain marketable title.

Once the eminent domain petition or complaint is filed, an *immediate possession hearing* generally is held. This allows the condemning governmental authority to proceed with the project for which the property is being taken without waiting for the outcome of the later hearing on fair compensation. At the immediate possession hearing, a prima facie case is presented for the necessity of the public improvement. The government's position concerning the value of the interest being acquired also is presented, usually through the testimony of an appraiser. If the court is satisfied with the proof, it will enter an order for immediate possession conditioned upon the deposit with the court of an amount of money equal to the value of the property as established by the government.

The hearing on compensation may take place before a judge, a commission of landowners, or a jury if request for a jury is made by the owner of the property to be condemned. At that hearing, each side presents the testimony of witnesses, including an appraiser, concerning the value of the property being acquired by the government.

Methods of Appraisal   To understand the condemnation process, one must understand the standard methods of appraisal. In particular, it is necessary to know that interests in real property are valued according to the cost approach, the market approach, the income approach, or some combination thereof.

The *cost approach* is used only for the valuation of improvements to real property, that is, the structures erected upon the property. Most frequently, the *replacement cost approach* is used, although the *reproduction cost approach* also may be used. *Replacement cost* is the cost of replacing the improvement. Theoretically, the appraiser consults with suppliers and contractors and determines what it would cost to replace a building with a building of equal utility, using today's building costs and construction methods. In practice, standard handbooks and computer programs are used to determine instant replacement cost based upon the size of the building, the type of construction, and so forth.

The *reproduction cost approach* is similar and should produce the same result most of the time. An appraiser using this approach determines what it would cost to produce an exact replica, rather than a replacement, of the improvements being appraised. For example, when older buildings are involved that have wide corridors, ornate facades, and similar characteristics, reproduction cost will be much greater than replacement cost. Therefore, the reproduction cost method requires adjustment for depreciation or other obsolescence of the building, which adds a step to the appraisal process. For these reasons, replacement cost is preferred. On the other hand, when unusual or special purpose buildings are involved, the reproduction cost approach may be the only one that is entirely reliable.

The *market approach* is used to determine the value of vacant or unimproved property and of improved properties having characteristics that are similar to other improved properties, such as houses in a large subdivision. In either case, the appraiser selects *comparable sales* of other properties.

Selecting comparable sales of unimproved properties is relatively easy. For example, if one is valuing Alpha Acres, one may discover that Bravo Buttes, located within a few miles of Alpha Acres, had been sold only a few months before. Assume that the sales price of Bravo Buttes was $1,000,000, but that Alpha Acres is twice the size of Bravo Buttes. It is reasonable to assume that Alpha Acres may be worth around $2,000,000 (or twice the Bravo Buttes price).

Selecting comparable sales is more difficult when improved properties are involved. Unless the property is located in a subdivision of identical houses of identical age in identical condition, it will be far more difficult to determine which sales are comparable. The appraiser usually determines the size in square feet of each comparable property and compares square feet, making adjustments for such things as age and condition.

When an improved property is being appraised for which there are no comparable sales, a combination of cost approach and market approach may be employed. The absence of comparable sales may be attributable to the unique character of the building involved or to a slow market. When that happens, the appraiser values the land as if it were unimproved, comparing it with other, unimproved properties. Having arrived at a value of the land, the appraiser adds the land value to the value of the improvements. Recall that the value of improvements is determined by using the cost approach.

Finally, the *income approach* is used to determine the value of income-producing properties. For example, the value of an apartment house may be determined by multiplying the annual income of the property by a *capitalization rate*. Capitalization rates vary according to the type of income-producing property involved, but ten percent is a common rate. If an apartment house has a net annual income of $50,000, the building and land should have a value of $500,000 according to the income approach. It is reasonable to assume that an investor might pay $500,000 for such a property on the theory that, at a net annual income of $50,000, a loan bearing ten percent interest would be paid off in about twenty years.

Using those three approaches to value, the appraiser expresses an opinion about the value of the property being acquired. If a fee simple absolute is being taken by eminent domain, the appraiser simply will testify concerning the value of that estate. If less than the fee is being taken, her task may be more difficult. For example, if only an easement is being acquired, some percentage of the value of the fee must be used, with the percentage determined by the extent of the burden imposed on the land by the easement. Thus, an easement for a road would have the same value as the fee estate, but an easement for underground utilities would have a small percentage of the value of the fee estate because the surface still would be usable for many purposes.

The appraiser is also called upon to make a judgment as to the amount of any damage to the remainder. Assume, for example, that the state condemns the south half of Echo Estates for construction of a highway. The south half of Echo Estates has a certain value. In addition, however, the north half of Echo Estates may have less value because it will abut a highway after the condemnation. Conversely, it may have greater value after the condemnation if its planned use is commercial, rather than residential. In either case, those factors must be taken into consideration.

Once the commission, court, or jury arrives at a value for the property being acquired, an order is entered by the court that vests title to the property in the public entity acquiring it. Such an order, sometimes described as a rule, causes title to vest automatically and without any further act by the property owner.

Partition

Proceedings in partition are instituted to *partition* or sever the interests of tenants in common, joint tenants, or tenants by the entireties. For example, if Amos and Betty are tenants in common and cannot agree on whether their property should be held or sold, either one may file a partition action to have the property split into two parcels: one owned by Amos and the other owned by Betty. Because partition proceedings are fairly rare, their effect sometimes can come as a surprise not only to the parties but also to their attorneys.

As with other proceedings discussed in this chapter, all persons having an interest in the property must be named as parties if the ultimate decree in partition or sale of the property is to be fully effective. A petition or complaint is filed; and after responses or answers are filed, the case is set for hearing.

Partition proceedings are necessary only when the co-owners of the property cannot agree on a voluntary partition. Although there usually is some acrimony involved, the right to partition is statutory and absolute. Therefore, when the matter comes before the court for hearing, the only issue is the appointment of a commissioner or commissioners (sometimes called referees) to proceed with the partition. The commissioners often are professional appraisers. Attorneys whose strategy is to resist the partition altogether soon find that the judge is not interested in that position.

A single commissioner is appointed if the parties can agree on one. That frequently is not the case, and it often is necessary for each party to select one commissioner. Once two commissioners are selected in that fashion, those two commissioners select a third one. If more than two cotenants are involved, the court may be called upon to appoint one, two, or three commissioners of its own choosing.

When unimproved property is involved, the goal of the commissioners is to partition the property *in kind*. Using the prior example of the parcel owned by Amos and Betty, the goal of the commissioners will be to divide their one parcel of real estate into two parcels of equal value. Once they arrive at such a division and arrange for a survey of the two parcels, a report is made to the court. Following a hearing, the court generally adopts the recommendation and enters a decree of partition. The decree vests the title automatically, with no further action on the part of Amos or Betty.

However, if the court determines that no partition can be made as recommended by the commissioners or if the commissioners themselves recommend that partition of the property is impossible or impractical, the court will order the property to be sold. If the property is improved, it most often will be sold. When proceedings in partition are used in connection with such properties as single family dwellings, condominium units, and similar properties, partition in kind is impossible. Alternatively, if the improvements are not of great value, the payment of *owelty* will be ordered to effect an equal division. For example, if there is a cabin worth $1,000 on the land, one owner might receive the cabin but be ordered to pay $500 to the other owner.

When the property cannot be partitioned in kind and is ordered to be sold instead, the practical effect is that the property is auctioned; and the co-owners usually are the only bidders. Once the highest bid is accepted by the commissioner or commissioners, the court approves the sale procedure and authorizes the commissioner or commissioners to convey the property to the highest bidder. The proceeds of the sale are ordered paid to the co-owners, causing the highest bidder to receive one-half of his money back.

Figure 11-2 illustrates a complaint that might be filed in a partition proceeding.

Figure 11-2
Complaint in Partition

IN THE DISTRICT COURT, COUNTY OF SUPERIOR, STATE OF WHEREVER
Case No. _____

COMPLAINT IN PARTITION

TINA TENNANT,
                    Plaintiff,
vs.

TERRELL TENNANT,
                    Defendant.

COMES NOW the Plaintiff and as a claim for relief states as follows:

1. Plaintiff and Defendant are the owners, as tenants in common, of the following described real property located in the County of Superior and State of Wherever:

Lot 16, Block 2, Alabaster Estates, County of Superior, State of Wherever ("the property").

2. Plaintiff and Defendant each has an undivided one-half interest in and to the property.

3. There are no liens and encumbrances of record affecting the property, and Plaintiff has no knowledge of any parties who may claim an interest in the property or who will be affected by this action.

4. Plaintiff is entitled to a decree for partition of the property by virtue of § 19-44-1, W.R.S.

5. The prosecution of this action is for the mutual benefit of the parties hereto, and Plaintiff has incurred and will continue to incur attorney's fees and costs of this proceeding including the cost of title examination, commissioners' fees and publication costs, which costs should be divided between the parties.

WHEREFORE, Plaintiff prays as follows:

1. That the Court enter a decree for partition of the property according to the respective rights and interests of the parties hereto.

2. That a commissioner or commissioners be appointed to make their report to the Court as to the manner in which partition should be effected.

3. That, if it be determined by such commissioner or commissioners that the property cannot be partitioned in kind, the sale of the property be ordered, with the proceeds therefrom to be divided between the parties according to their respective rights and interests.

4. For costs of partition, including reasonable attorney's fees incurred herein.

5. For such other relief as may be deemed proper.

Dated the 5th day of November, 1996.

TINA TENNANT, Plaintiff.

By:_____ .
Carla Counsel
121 Main Street
Superior, WH 98101
(809) 911-0000

Judicial Foreclosure

The simplest and earliest form of mortgage was a deed from the borrower to the lender containing the condition subsequent that if the borrower repaid the loan on time, the deed was void. If the borrower did not repay, the deed was valid; and it conveyed the property to the lender. Often, however, the land was worth more than was owed, which provided the lender with a windfall. To prevent such an injustice, equity routinely permitted late payment (redemption) by the borrower.

The possibility of redemption created uncertainty for the lender who then resorted to the courts to *foreclose* or to terminate the *equity of redemption*. Initially, the foreclosure proceeding amounted to setting a date by which the borrower was foreclosed if he did not pay. In other words, he no longer could redeem his equity in the property.

Ultimately, courts of equity required that the property be sold at a foreclosure sale and that the proceeds be applied to discharge the debt. If more than the amount of the debt was realized from the sale, the surplus was paid to the borrower. If less than the amount of the debt was realized from the sale, a deficiency remained, which was reduced to a judgment against the borrower. The lender then could attempt to collect the judgment by the conventional means of garnishment and execution if the borrower did not pay it voluntarily.

When we speak of a foreclosure today, we speak of a judicial or administrative proceeding where it is determined that a debt exists; and a foreclosure sale is provided to discharge that debt. Judicial foreclosure proceedings are used not only in connection with mortgages but also in connection with mechanics' liens and other, statutory liens such as tax liens. Whether the foreclosure is judicial or administrative, *redemption* generally means a statutory right to recover the property after the sale by paying the amount owed, together with the costs of the sale.

To initiate a judicial foreclosure, a complaint or petition is filed with the court that names all interested parties and requests that the property be sold to satisfy the underlying debt. If the allegation of the indebtedness is denied, a hearing is held to determine whether or not the debt exists.

Once the amount of the debt is determined, the sheriff or some other official is ordered to conduct a public sale. Notice of the sale is given by publication. At the sale the amount of the debt is *bid in* by the holder of the debt. In other words, the holder of the debt is not obligated to make a cash bid but, instead, may bid all or some part of the amount owed. Others may bid additional amounts, but they must bid in cash. The property then is *struck off* to the highest bidder.

Frequently, other persons do not bid; and the only bidder is the holder of the debt. In that case, particularly in jurisdictions that permit a deficiency bid, the amount of the bid must be determined with care. If it is more than the market value of the property, the debt will be discharged; and the holder of the debt will be left owning property valued at less than the amount owed against it.

> Barry borrowed $100,000 from Silver Buckle Savings and gave Silver Buckle a mortgage on his home, which was worth $100,000 at the time of the loan. The home declined in value and was worth only $75,000. Barry defaulted, and Silver Buckle filed for foreclosure. At the foreclosure sale, Silver Buckle bid in the entire $100,000 owed to it. After the foreclosure sale, Silver Buckle owned the home; but its $100,000 loan had been replaced by a $75,000 asset. Barry no longer owed Silver Buckle any part of the debt because the entire amount of the debt was bid in.

On the other hand, if the amount bid is only a small percentage of the value of the property, the court could find the bid to have been in bad faith, causing the sale to be set aside. Alternatively, the debtor may redeem the property from sale and sell it free of the mortgage.

> Using the same example, Silver Buckle might decide to bid in only $25,000 of what is owed, leaving a deficiency on the loan of $75,000. Barry could object to the sale, claiming the bid was not in good faith. If the court agreed, the sale would be set aside and a new sale ordered. Or Barry could redeem the property from foreclosure for $25,000. If he did that, he would have the house back free of the mortgage and would be able to sell it for the $75,000 it is worth. He still would owe Silver Buckle the $75,000 balance on the loan, but Silver Buckle would have lost its security.

The holders of subsequent liens, including second mortgages, judgments, and other encumbrances, must be made parties to the foreclosure proceeding and must be given notice of the sale if their rights are to be affected. By statute in many jurisdictions, both the owner of the property and subordinate or subsequent lienors have a *right of redemption*. This is a statutory right to purchase the property from the person to whom the property is sold at the foreclosure sale. The owner's period of redemption may be a comparatively long one, whereas the period of redemption of subordinate lienors may be shorter. If the owner or subordinate lienors fail to redeem the property, their liens will be extinguished.

Once all periods of redemption have expired, a deed is issued by the official who conducted the sale. Although subsequent liens are extinguished by that deed, title defects and prior liens remain in place.

A borrower may be able to avoid the foreclosure process by delivering a deed in lieu of foreclosure. When this occurs, the mortgagor conveys her legal title to the mortgagee, causing a merger of the two interests. Ordinarily, the debt is fully discharged by such a deed. Deeds in lieu of foreclosure cannot be used when there are subsequent lienors; in that case, only a formal foreclosure will extinguish those subsequent interests.

Figure 11-3 shows a complaint to foreclose a mortgage against property that is encumbered by a second mortgage and by a mechanic's lien.

Figure 11-3
Mortgage Foreclosure Complaint

IN THE DISTRICT COURT, COUNTY OF SUPERIOR, STATE OF WHEREVER
Case No. _____

COMPLAINT IN FORECLOSURE

PAULA PEABODY,
      Plaintiff,
vs.

DENNIS DINWIDDIE; SILVER BUCKLE SAVINGS AND
LOAN ASSOCIATION; and INDEPENDENT LUMBER COMPANY,
      Defendants.

COMES NOW the Plaintiff and as her claim for relief states as follows:

1. On or about the 10th day of March, 1992, the Defendant, Dennis Dinwiddie ("Dinwiddie") made and delivered to Plaintiff his promissory note date March 10, 1992, in the principal amount of

$110,000.00, together with accrued interest thereon at the rate of 12% per annum, to become due and payable on March 10, 1995.

2. As security for the payment of the promissory note aforesaid, Dinwiddie executed and delivered to Plaintiff, whereby Dinwiddie granted, bargained and mortgaged to Plaintiff the following described real property located in the County of Superior and State of Wherever:

Lot 8, Block 63, Excellent Estates, City of Superior, County of Superior and State of Wherever ("the property").

3. The aforesaid mortgage was recorded April 1, 1992, in book 892 at page 53, Superior County records.

4. Dinwiddie is in default pursuant to the promissory note aforesaid in that he failed to pay the principal amount thereof, together with accrued interest, when the same came due.

5. Plaintiff, on February 28, 1996, paid the real estate taxes assessed against the property, in the amount of $1,463.

6. There is now due and owing to Plaintiff the sum of $101,463, together with interest on the principal amount of the promissory note from March 10, 1992.

7. The promissory note provides that, in the event the same is placed for collection, the holder shall be entitled to recover her costs of collection including reasonable attorney's fees.

8. Plaintiff is now the holder of the promissory note.

9. Defendants, other than Dinwiddie, have or claim to have some interest in, or a lien upon, the property or some part thereof, which interest or lien, if any, is subsequent and subordinate to the mortgage given to the Plaintiff.

WHEREFORE, Plaintiff prays for judgment as follows:

1. That Plaintiff be awarded judgment against Dinwiddie in the amount of $101,463, together with interest at the rate of 12% per annum from March 10, 1992, and Plaintiff's costs of collection, including reasonable attorney's fees.

2. That the Defendants and every person whose interest in the property is acquired subsequent to the recording of a notice of the pendency of this action be forever barred and foreclosed of all right, claim, lien and equity of redemption in the property.

3. That a decree enter that the property be sold according to law.

4. That the proceeds of such sale be brought into court and applied in satisfaction, whether partial or full, of the judgment entered in favor of Plaintiff.

5. That the Sheriff of this county be authorized to execute a sheriff's deed conveying the property to the purchaser of the property.

6. For such other relief as the court may deem proper.

DATED the 1st day of April, 1996.

PAULA PEABODY, Plaintiff

By_____
Carla Counsel
Counsel & Counsel
121 East Main Street
Superior WH 89101
809-911-0000

Notice of Lis Pendens

At common law, the purchaser of real estate was considered to have constructive knowledge of any litigation pending with respect to that real estate. To avoid the harshness of that doctrine, the concept of the notice of lis pendens was incorporated into the rules of civil procedure of all states. Most states also have statutes governing the notice of lis pendens; and in some jurisdictions, statutes now have supplanted the civil rules.

The *notice of lis pendens* is a document recorded in the registrar's office. In it, the litigant's attorney states that a proceeding has been commenced which affects the property described in the notice and further states that certain relief is sought in the proceeding which could affect title to the property described in the notice. Recording the notice has the effect of encumbering the property, generally causing it to be unmarketable. The notice ordinarily remains of record until the proceeding is concluded.

Figure 11-4 illustrates a typical notice of lis pendens.

Figure 11-4
Notice of Lis Pendens

IN THE DISTRICT COURT, COUNTY OF SUPERIOR, STATE OF WHEREVER
Case No. _____

NOTICE OF LIS PENDENS

PAULA PEABODY,
                 Plaintiff,

vs.

DENNIS DINWIDDIE,
                 Defendant.

    NOTICE IS HEREBY GIVEN that the above-named Plaintiff has filed an action in the District Court for the County of Superior wherein she seeks to foreclose a mortgage recorded April 1, 1992, in book 892 at page 53, Superior County Records, encumbering the following described real property located in the County of Superior and State of Wherever:

        Lot 8, Block 63, Excellent Estates, City of Superior,
        County of Superior and State of Wherever.

    DATED the 1st day of April, 1996.

                              _____
                              Carla Counsel
                              Counsel & Counsel
                              121 East Main Street
                              Superior WH 89101
                              809-911-0000

    As a general rule, a notice of lis pendens should be filed any time litigation is commenced that affects real estate. Examples include foreclosures of mortgages and mechanics' liens, quiet title proceedings, and partition suits.

    In addition to understanding the theory of real estate litigation, a legal assistant should become familiar with the procedures and requirements for commencing and processing the real estate actions in his or her local court systems. Acquiring this type of familiarity makes the legal assistant most effective in working with the real estate practitioner.

Chapter 11 Quiz

Fill in each blank with the most correct word or phrase.

1. Types of litigation involving real property include _____, _____, _____, and _____.

2. Recording a(n) _____ generally causes real property to be unmarketable.

3. _____ is a judicial proceeding wherein it is determined that an indebtedness exists and a sale of real property is ordered to discharge that indebtedness.

4. A proceeding in _____ is instituted to sever the interests of co-tenants.

5. Interests in real property are valued according to the _____ approach, the _____ approach, the _____ approach or a combination of these.

6. Hearing on compensation to the landowner in an eminent domain proceeding may be held before a(n) _____, a(n) _____ or a(n) _____.

7. One of the goals in an eminent domain proceeding is to obtain _____ title.

8. The purpose of a(n) _____ proceeding is to cause title to property to be marketable when it otherwise is not.

9. _____ jurisdiction is jurisdiction "over a thing."

10. When service of process is made by publication the _____ and the _____ Amendments to the Constitution of the United States are implicated.

Circle the most correct answer.

11. True or False. Curative statutes may allow some defects in title to be ignored.

12.   True or False. The right of co-owners to partition is statutory and absolute.

13.   True or False. In litigation involving title to real property one may rely on the weaknesses of the defendant's title to "prove up" the marketability of the plaintiff's title.

14.   True or False. The government must make an effort to acquire property voluntarily through negotiation and purchase before it can file an eminent domain proceeding.

15.   True or False. The reproduction cost approach is the only reliable method for appraising new buildings.

16.   True or False. Appraisers use comparable sales in determining value under the market approach.

17.   True or False. The value of an income-producing property may be determined by multiplying the purchase price by a capitalization rate.

18.   True or False. Even when parties agree on a voluntary partition, a proceeding in partition must be filed and a decree entered to allow title to be marketable.

19.   True or False. To partition in kind is to divide the real property into two parcels of equal size.

20.   True or False. A payment in owelty is an equalization charge.

21.   True or False. In quiet title actions, some plaintiffs may be designated as unknown persons having an interest.

22.   True or False. A rule providing for publication of a summons for four weeks means the summons must be published four times in an official newspaper.

23.   True or False. An immediate possession hearing allows the condemning authority to take the property without waiting for the outcome of the later hearing on fair compensation.

24. True or False. The governmental entity acquiring title by eminent domain is required to compensate the owner only for the property actually taken and is not responsible for any damage to the remainder.

25. True or False. The right of redemption in foreclosure sales is reserved only to owners of the property.

26. True or False. Only the holder of the indebtedness being foreclosed may bid in the amount owed; all other bids must be cash bids.

27. True or False. It always is advantageous for the holder of the indebtedness to bid in the full amount of the indebtedness.

28. True or False. A deed given as a result of a foreclosure sale conveys the property free and clear of defects in title and prior encumbrances.

29. True or False. If he is the only bidder, it always is good strategy for the holder of the indebtedness to bid in only a small percentage of the value of the property.

30. True or False. A deed in lieu of foreclosure may be used in any circumstances agreed to by the mortgagee.

31. True or False. A notice of lis pendens must set out in detail the basis for the plaintiff's claim to the real property.

32. Virginia granted a mortgage to First Mortgage Company to finance the purchase of a home which needed repair. Before she occupied the house, she hired DunnRite Construction to repair the roof. After she moved in, she discovered the roof leaked and withheld final payment to DunnRite, advising them she would pay when they fixed the roof. DunnRite recorded a mechanic's lien and filed a proceeding in foreclosure. Is DunnRite entitled to proceed in this fashion?

    1. Yes, subject to First Mortgage Company's mortgage.
    2. No. Only mortgages, deeds of trust and tax liens may be foreclosed. DunnRite must file a complaint for damages.
    3. No. DunnRite cannot foreclose because the mortgage held by First Mortgage Company, having been recorded first, is superior to DunnRite's lien. DunnRite has only a right of redemption if First Mortgage Company forecloses its lien.
    4. None of the above.

33.   When service of process is made by publication, the principal rules which must be followed are:

    1.   The summons must contain a description of the real property and set out the defendant's rights under the Fifth and Fourteenth Amendments to the Constitution of the United States.

    2.   Reasonable efforts must be made to learn the whereabouts of each defendant; and where possible, actual notice must be provided.

    3.   The summons must give the defendant's last-known address, refer to the defendant's rights under the Fifth and Fourteenth Amendments to the Constitution of the United States, and contain a description of the real property

    4.   Reasonable efforts must be made to learn the whereabouts of each defendant; where possible, actual notice must be provided; and all parties in interest must be before the court.

ANSWER KEY for CHAPTER QUIZZES

Chapter 1

1. Title to real property always is vested in someone
2. Freehold estates
3. Fee simple absolute
4. Fee simple subject to condition subsequent
5. Damages, injunction
6. Ownership and possession
7. Nonfreehold
8. False
9. True
10. False
11. True
12. False
13. False
14. True
15. d
16. b
17. d
18. Yes, subject to right of entry for condition broken. The deed creates a power of termination and not an automatic reversion.
19. David Doe, as John Doe's only heir. Power of termination for condition broken. A suit for ejectment and a quiet title action.
20. The devise of the real property contained in Tita's will is void because a life estate is not an estate of inheritance.

Chapter 2

1. Present, possession
2. Reversion
3. Vested, contingent
4. Reversion
5. Right of re-entry
6. Possibility of reverter
7. Remainderman
8. Right of re-entry
9. Remainder
10. Trusts
11. True
12. True
13. False
14. True
15. True
16. True
17. True
18. True
19. True
20. True
21. False
22. True
23. True
24. False
25. True
26. a
27. (i)   c
     (ii)   b
     (iii) a
     (iv) d

Chapter 3

1.
   a.   Time
   b.   Interest
   c.   Possession
   d.   Title
2.   Ameliorative
3.   Passive
4.   Tenancy by the entireties
5.   Dower, curtesy
6.   True
7.   True
8.   False
9.   False
10.   False
11.   False
12.   False
13.   True
14.   True
15.   False
16.   True
17.   True
18.   False
19.   False
20.   False
21.   False
22.   d
23.   b
24.   d
25.   As a tenant in common, Chris has an undivided interest in the entire premises. Each tenant in common is entitled to exercise all rights of ownership as if he or she were the sole owner. Therefore, Chris may lease the premises to Charles for any time period without the permission of the other co-owners. Chris has a duty to account to Grace and Helen for the profits of the leasehold, however, and may be entitled to offset any expense incurred in deriving the profit. Charles is entitled to the premises during the period of his lease. Helen and Grace have the same undivided interest in the entire premises as Chris, and they are not limited to using only part of the premises or limited to a specific time.

Chapter 4

1.   cooperatives
2.   shareholders
3.   airspace, common elements
4.   condominium declaration
5.   right of first refusal
6.   planned community
7.   protective covenants
8.   True
9.   True
10.   False
11.   True
12.   True
13.   False
14.   False
15.   False
16.   True
17.   True
18.   True
19.   True
20.   True
21.   True
22.   True
23.   True
24.   True
25.   True
26.   True

27. Yes. Sections 5.4 and 9.05(b) allow such an assessment.
28. Section 5.8. The bill is incorrect: only one late charge can be made for each month.
29. Provision 6.9 of the Condominium Declaration allows the association to take such action.
30. None.
31. It governs the composition of the board of directors of the association.
32. 75%. (Section 10.02)

Chapter 5

1. possession, ownership
2. tenancy for years, periodic tenancy, tenancy at will, tenancy at sufferance
3. tenancy for years
4. tenancy for years
5. tenancy at will
6. tenancy at sufferance
7. periodic tenancy
8. constructive eviction
9. True
10. False
11. False
12. True
13. False
14. True
15. True
16. True
17. False
18. True
19. True
20. True
21. False
22. True

23. True
24. True
25. True
26. True
27. True
28. True
29. True
30. False
31. True
32. True
33. True
34. False
35. True
36. b. Statute of Frauds requires the lease to be written. Since it is not, a tenancy at will is created.
37. I. Lessor can claim Jane did not use due precaution against freezing of waste pipes and is, therefore, liable. Jane can assert she used due precaution, the extremely low temperatures could not have been foreseen, and she is not liable.
38. E, H, K. (1) Damage is structural and is excepted from repair by Lessee. (2) Damage was caused by reasonable use and wear; thus, it is excepted from repair by Lessee. (3) Lease requires Lessee to repair damage caused by pets; the horses were not pets.
39. The first payment of rent and the partial security deposit must be paid before the date of the lease (January 1, 1996).
40. Insurance

Chapter 6

1. profits, easement, license
2. equitable servitudes
3. use, possession
4. appurtenant
5. grant (express), implication, necessity, prescription
6. dominant
7. injunction, damages, specific performance
8. temporary, personal, may not
9. physically, economically
10. False
11. True
12. True
13. False
14. True
15. True
16. True
17. False
18. True
19. False
20. True
21. True
22. False
23. False
24. True
25. False
26. True
27. True
28. True
29. True
30. True
31. d
32. True

Chapter 7

1. use, area
2. the master plan
3. contract
4. subdivision
5. a certificate of occupancy
6. True
7. True
8. False
9. True
10. False
11. True
12. True
13. True
14. False
15. False
16. False
17. False
18. False
19. False
20. True
21. False
22. False
23. f
24. a
25. a
26. b
27. c
28. f
29. b
30. the subdivider; paragraph 11

Chapter 8

1. prescription, adverse possession
2. (1) open
3. (2) hostile
4. (3) notorious
5. (4) under claim of right
6. (5) continuous
7. (6) uninterrupted
8. (7) exclusive
9. tacking

10. quiet title
11. the state or federal government
12. pure race, pure notice, race notice
13. witness
14. distances, directions or courses
15. accretion, reliction
16. True
17. True
18. False
19. True
20. True
21. False
22. False
23. True
24. True
25. False
26. False
27. False
28. True
29. False
30. True
31. False
32. True
33. True
34. True
35. True
36. False
37. a
38. d
39. a
40. d
41. d

Chapter 9

1. an abstract of title, a title insurance commitment, a Torrens certificate

2. FIRPTA (Foreign Investments in Real Property Tax Act of 1980)
3. installment sale
4. title standards
5. False
6. True
7. False
8. False
9. False
10. True
11. False
12. False
13. False
14. False
15. True
16. True
17. True
18. False
19. True
20. False
21. False
22. False
23. False
24. b

Chapter 10

1. self-transmission
2. natural flow theory
3. reasonable use
4. appropriation
5. appropriation, adjudication
6. ownership-in-place doctrine
7. placer
8. False
9. False
10. True
11. False
12. False
13. False

14.	False	11.	True
15.	False	12.	True
16.	True	13.	False
17.	False	14.	False
18.	True	15.	False
19.	True	16.	True
20.	False	17.	False
21.	True	18.	False
22.	True	19.	False
23.	False	20.	True
24.	True	21.	False
25.	True	22.	False
26.	True	23.	True
27.	False	24.	False
28.	True	25.	False
29.	True	26.	True
30.	False	27.	False
31.	False	28.	False
32.	False	29.	False
33.	a	30.	False
34.	c	31.	False
35.	a	32.	a
36.	d	33.	d
37.	a		
38.	a		
39.	d		

Chapter 11

1. quiet title, eminent domain, partition, foreclosure
2. notice of lis pendens
3. foreclosure
4. partition
5. cost, market, income
6. judge, panel of commissioners, jury
7. marketable
8. quiet title
9. in rem
10. Fifty and Fourteenth

BIBLIOGRAPHY

Bernhardt, <u>Property</u> (Black Letter Series), West Publishing Company.

Bernhardt, <u>Real Property</u> (Nutshell), 2nd Ed., West Publishing Company.

Flynn, <u>Introduction to Real Estate Law</u>, West Publishing Company.

Hinkel, <u>Essentials of Practical Real Estate Law</u>, West Publishing Company.

Hinkel, <u>Practical Real Estate Law</u>, West Publishing Company.

Jefferson, <u>The Compact Guide to Property Law: A Civilized Approach to the Law</u>, West Publishing Company.

Koerselman, <u>CLA® Review Manual</u>, West Publishing Company.

Patton, <u>On Titles</u>, West Publishing Company.

Powell, <u>On Real Property</u>, Matthew Bender Publishing Company, New York.

Siedel, <u>Real Estate Law</u>, 3rd Ed., West Publishing Company.

INDEX

A

Abstract of title 197, 202
Acceleration clause 215
Accretion 169
Acknowledgment 172, 204
Act of 1872 238
Adverse possession 108, 151, 153-156, 159,
        247, 249
Affirmative covenant 112
After-acquired title 173
Airspace 118
Americans With Disabilities Act 146
Appraisal 191, 192, 224
      cost approach 252
      income approach 253
      market approach 252
      replacement cost 252
      reproduction cost approach 252
Appurtenances 170
Area variances 133
Assignment 50, 84-88, 90, 97, 204, 248
      of rents 215
Assumption 188
Attest 171
Attornment 88
Avigation easement 119
Avulsion 169

B

bargain and sale deed 19, 20, 169
Building Codes 77, 79, 96, 145, 146, 148

C

California Doctrine 236, 241
CERCLA 220, 229
Cestui que vie 9
Chain of title 203
Closing 187-198, 204, 219-227
Colorado Doctrine 236
Commendation 1
Common enemy doctrine 233, 241, 243
COMMON INTEREST OWNERSHIP 41-67
CONCURRENT OWNERSHIP 31-39
Condemnation 76, 254

Conditional use 131
Condominium 16, 21, 24, 41-50, 115, 137,
      140, 161, 179, 224, 255
      declaration 43-45, 48, 115
      map 46
      plat 45
Constructive eviction 75
Constructive notice 158
Contingent remainder 17, 28, 29
Contract zoning 136
Contract for Sale 13, 170, 172, 187-191, 193,
      197, 222, 223
Cooperative 21, 42, 47
Coupled with an interest 110
Courts of Chancery 4, 15, 19, 20
Covenant to stand seized 20
Covenants of title 172
Curtesy 36, 39

D

Dedication 101
Deed
      conservator's 176
      contract for 226
      corrective 168
      delivery of 176,222
      grant 175
      personal representative's 176
      poll 176
      quitclaim 175-176, 179, 204, 227
      sheriff's 176, 180, 261
      special warranty 175-176, 178
      tax 151-152, 249
      warranty 169, 171-172, 175-178, 185
Deed of trust 44, 52, 144, 172, 188, 197, 200,
      204-210, 214-216, 220, 226,
      250
Design review regulations 145
Direct flow rights 234-235, 241
Doctrine of Worthier Title 22
Domesday Book 2
Dominant estate 101, 111
Dower 20, 36, 39, 173, 268
Down-zoning 136

Due diligence period 190
Due diligence provision 219
Due-on-sale 188, 215

E

Easement 99-113, 120, 139, 144, 158, 251, 253
    affirmative 104
    appurtenant 111
    by implication 106
    by prescription 107
    by reservation 106
    in gross 102, 104, 111
    negative 104
Ejectment 3, 82, 153, 182
Eminent domain 60, 76, 88, 101, 108, 119, 251, 253
Environmental hazards 133, 219-220
Equitable servitude 99, 113
Escalator clause 78
Escheat 2-4, 19
Escrow 142, 188, 222-227
Estoppel certificate 88-89
Euclidean zoning 126, 137
Evidence of title 189, 197, 228, 251
Exactions 138
Exclusive right doctrine 237, 243
Executory interest 18, 29

F

Fealty 2, 3
Fee Simple 4-8, 16-19, 21, 36, 42, 73, 102, 170, 189, 200, 205, 237, 250, 253
    defeasible 6-8
    determinable 6-8, 11-13, 16, 26, 185
    subject to condition subsequent 8, 11, 13, 26, 267
Fee tail 5, 8-11, 13, 16, 22, 73
Feoffment to uses 19
Ferae naturae 231, 239, 242
Feudalism 1, 2, 22
FIRPTA 225, 229, 271
Foreclosure 88, 176, 180, 209, 214-216, 226, 227, 257-259
FREEHOLD ESTATES 5, 11, 16, 73, 99, 267
Free tenure 4
Future covenants 174
FUTURE INTERESTS 15, 16, 23, 26

G

Gap coverage 198
Ground lease 73
Ground water 233

H

Habendum 170
Habitability 79
Hereditaments 170
Homage 1-3
Homestead 176
HUD-1 Form 219, 224

I

Impact fees 139
Indenture 176
Inquiry notice 159
Installment sale contract 20, 187, 226-227
Intestate succession 9
Inverse condemnation 119
Invitees 77
In rem 245-247, 272
Issue 8

J

Joint tenancy 31-35, 38-39

L

Land patent 151, 156
LANDLORD AND TENANT 73-97
Lateral support 118
Lease, leasehold 42, 49, 73-94, 158-159, 190, 237
License 99, 100, 106, 110-111
Life estate 15-18, 22, 36, 73
Like-kind exchange 225, 229
Liquidated damages 188
Lis pendens 261, 262
Littoral 232
Lode claim 238

M

Marketable title 189
Marketable title acts 204
Master plan 125
Merger 109
Mesne lord 2, 4
Metes and bounds 111, 161-165, 183, 234
Mineral rights 188, 236
Mining courts 237
Mortgage 21, 42, 76, 88, 172, 187-188, 197-198, 200-206, 214-216, 219-

220, 226-229, 248, 257-260,
262, 265
    lien theory 214
    partial release provision 216
    release of 209
    title theory 214
Mortgage foreclosure complaint 259

N

Natural flow theory 232, 236, 242
Nonconforming use 132, 134
Nonfreehold estates 5, 73, 95
Notice to quit 82
Notice to Quit 82, 97
Nuisance 56, 116-119, 220

O

Option 188
Owelty 255
Owners association 43
Ownership-in-place 236, 243, 271

P

Partition 21, 33, 35, 254-257, 262, 264, 272
    complaint for 256
Party wall 48
Party wall agreement 49, 64
Periodic tenancy 16, 73-75, 83-84
Plan for augmentation 235
Planned community 47
Planned unit development (PUD) 47, 137
Possibility of reverter 7, 8, 15-17, 23
Power of termination 7, 16
Praecipe in capite 3
Prescriptive title 153
Present covenants 174
Primogeniture 8, 22
Prior appropriation 188, 231-233, 236
Privity 112
Profit a prendre 237
Profits 3, 19, 99, 100, 170, 177, 178, 191
Promissory note 144, 188-189, 197, 204, 216-
    217, 220, 229, 259-260
Proof of publication 249
Protective covenant 114

Q

Quiet title 11, 156, 204, 247, 249-250, 262
    complaint 250

R

Real covenant 112-114
Reasonable use rule 233

Reasonable use theory 232, 233, 242
Receivership clause 215
Recording acts 157, 159, 170
    pure notice statute 160
    pure race statute 160
    race notice statute 160
Reformation 168
Regulation X 219
Reliction 169
Remainder 9
RESPA 205, 219, 225, 229
Restitution, writ of 82-83
Restrictive covenant 112
Reversion 9
Right of redemption 214, 258
Right of entry 7, 8, 16, 23, 105
Right of way 102, 120, 201
Riparian 188, 201, 232, 236, 240-243
Roman law rule of natural drainage 233
Royal courts 3, 23
Rule against Perpetuities 22-25
Rule in Shelley's Case 22
Rule of capture 237
Runs with the land 104, 113-114, 121, 123

S

SALE & FINANCING OF LAND 187-239
Seisin 5, 19, 20, 73, 169, 172-174
Self-help 82
Service
    by publication 246
    substituted 246
Servient estate 101, 111
SERVITUDES 99-124, 173
Settlement statement 219, 223-224, 229
Spot zoning 136
Standard exceptions 198
Statute of Frauds 73, 74, 100, 157, 171, 187
Statute of Uses 18, 20, 21, 23, 169
Statute Quia Emptores 6, 21, 100
Statutory deed forms 175
Storage rights 234, 235
Subdivision improvements agreement 140
Subdivision regulations 140
Subinfeudation 2, 4
Subjacent support 118, 239
Sublease 84, 86, 88
Superfund Law *see CERCLA this Index*
Surface water 233, 240, 241
Survey monument 168

T

Tacking 156

Tenancy
       at sufferance 73-75
       at will 73-75, 83
       by the entireties 31, 32, 35
       for Years 73-75, 84
       in Common 31, 33-35
Tenant in capite 2
Tenant in demesne 2
Tenure 2, 4, 22
Testimonium clause 171
Time of the essence provision. 191
Time share estate 50
Title commitment 197, 202
Title opinion 197
Title search 197
Title insurance 153, 189, 197-201, 223, 224
Torrens System 204
Touch and concern 114
Township 102, 162-164, 166
Triple net lease 87
Trust deed *see deed of trust this Index*

U
Uniform Common Interest Ownership Act
       41-48, 161
Uniform Residential Landlord and Tenant
       Act 81, 90
Unities of ownership 32

V
Variances 132
Vested remainder 17
Virgin title 151

W
Wardship and marriage 3
Warranties of title 172
Waste
       active 77
       ameliorative10
       passive 77
       permissive 10
       voluntary 10
Water courts 234, 235
Water Rights 188, 231-236
Words of limitation 6, 11-12
Words of purchase 6, 185
Writ 3, 82-83

Z
ZONING 125-146, 202